**Ninth Edition**

# Sportsmanlike Driving

Coordinating  Author:   Dr. Francis C. Kenel
                        Staff Director of Traffic Safety
                        American Automobile Association, Falls Church, VA

Consulting  Authors:    Dr. Ronald W. Hales
                        Professor of Safety Education
                        Central Safety Center
                        Central Washington University, Ellensburg, WA

                        Dr. John W. Palmer
                        Associate Professor
                        St. Cloud State University, St. Cloud, MN

                        Dr. Maurice E. Dennis
                        Coordinator and Professor
                        Safety Education Program
                        College of Education
                        Texas A & M University, College Station, TX

**Ninth Edition**

# Sportsmanlike Driving

**AMERICAN
AUTOMOBILE
ASSOCIATION**

Falls Church, Virginia

## *GLENCOE*

Macmillan/McGraw-Hill

Lake Forest, Illinois   Columbus, Ohio   Mission Hills, California   Peoria, Illinois

# CREDITS

Editor-in-Chief: Martha O'Neill

Editor: Alexa Ripley Barre

Coordinating Editor: Rita Tomkins

Design Supervisor: James Darby

Production Manager: Salvador Gonzales

Managing Photo Editor: Suzanne V. Skloot

Photo Editor: Nancy E. Grimes

Design: Donald R. Long Design

Cover: Gary Gladstone/The Image Bank

This book was set in 11 point New Century Schoolbook by Typographic Sales.

## Library of Congress Cataloging-in-Publication Data

Send all inquiries to:
GLENCOE DIVISION
Macmillan/McGraw-Hill
936 Eastwind Drive
Westerville, Ohio 43081

ISBN 0-07-001338-1 (pupil's ed.)
ISBN 0-07-001339-X (pupil's ed. : soft)
ISBN 0-07-001337-3 (teacher's ed.)

8 9 10 11 12 13 14 15   A-HAW   00 99 98 97 96 95 94 93 92

# CONSULTANTS

Carol Ankele
Arlington, Texas

Kathy Bacino
Garland, Texas

James P. Barnes
Philadelphia, Pennsylvania

Fred M. Bates
San Diego, California

Ellsworth Buck
Lewisburg, West Virginia

Gerald M. Christensen
Topeka, Kansas

Phil Lewis
Joplin, Missouri

Grant Martin
Salt Lake City, Utah

Philip F. McGirt, Jr.
Fayetteville, North Carolina

Gerrie Mitchell
Birdville, Texas

Lucious Leon Newhouse
Dallas, Texas

John C. Oman
Prairie Village, Kansas

Spencer Sartorius
Helena, Montana

Doug Scott
Dallas, Texas

Dale Simons
Salt Lake City, Utah

H.L. Sorrell, Jr.
Itarnett County, North Carolina

Alvin Reese Sutton
Killeen, Texas

Victor M. Takeuchi
Fresno, California

Robert W. Wier, Jr.
San Antonio, Texas

# CONTENTS

# PREFACE

The ninth edition of *Sportsmanlike Driving* presents in a well-illustrated, easy-to-read format the information you need to become a safe, efficient driver. Your driver education course will teach you to apply the concepts presented in this book as you get behind the wheel and learn to become a good driver. This includes important information about basic driving maneuvers. There is also information you can use to help you control the potential for high-hazard situations and manage situations that could lead to collisions.

Ideally, the course you are enrolled in should be scheduled so that your experiences in the car and in the classroom support each other. Lessons should be planned so that the knowledge you gain in class can be applied when you get in the car. Then, the experiences you have in the car can be discussed the next time you attend class. In other cases, you can practice driving procedures, such as time-space gap evaluation, as a pedestrian or as a passenger.

In addition to the projects suggested in the text, other parts of the *Sportsmanlike Driving* program are designed to bridge the gap between your class lessons, simulated driving, and in-car experiences. These aids include the Tests, the Workbook, and the Behind-the-Wheel Checklist, which has step-by-step instructions for performing various driving maneuvers. This information can be found in your textbook, but it is also printed on reproducible sheets. These can be used by your in-car instructor, and by the adult who rides with you when you practice driving outside of school, to help you perfect your basic driving maneuvers and to monitor your progress. Another aid is the AAA Driver Improvement Program, which is now available on a series of video cassettes entitled "Helping Your New Driver."

When you have finished your driver education course, you will have the basic information and skills necessary to become a competent driver. However, to best develop these skills, you will need continued guidance from an experienced, licensed driver while you gain experience behind the wheel yourself.

When your parents give you the keys to the family car, they are demonstrating their trust in you. It is up to you to become the kind of driver who deserves that trust.

# You and the Highway System

## Chapter Objectives

In this chapter you will learn how to:

- become a courteous, cooperative driver.
- name the parts and understand the workings of the highway transportation system.
- understand the purpose of driver education.
- understand the administrative laws that apply to drivers and vehicles.
- accept your responsibilities if you are involved in an accident.

## Sportsmanlike Driving

The United States has a large, complex network of streets, roads, and highways. This network can be used safely and efficiently only if all drivers cooperate with each other and exercise a sense of courtesy and fair play. Safe driving requires team effort and sportsmanship. In fact, driving and sports are alike in several ways. Highway users have to cooperate with each other, just as members of a winning team must cooperate. "Winning" on a highway means the safe movement of people and goods from place to place. Both driving and sports take place on regulated facilities. Both highway users and athletes must play by the rules. In the highway transportation system, traffic laws regulate the actions of drivers, bicyclists, and pedestrians. The facilities are the roadways, sidewalks, and parking areas regulated by signs, signals, and markings. In sports, equipment must meet certain design and construction standards. The same is true of cars and other vehicles. In organized sports, players who do not do well are dropped from the team. Drivers are not as thoroughly tested before they are given a license as athletes are before they can play professionally, but a driver who does not follow the rules and regulations of the road will lose the privilege to drive.

However, there are also some important differences between driving and sports. The immediate goal of an athletic team is to win a game. Highway users, on the other hand, have many immediate goals. These goals differ and often come into conflict. Each day, millions of drivers, bicyclists, and pedestrians try to get to and from many different points. Often, their paths cross and their goals are in conflict.

Another difference between driving and sports is that, whereas players' performances are constantly evaluated in organized sports, drivers are not *carefully* evaluated through all the years that they drive. Some drivers are simply not as skilled or as careful as others. This is important to remember as you begin to drive.

The differences between sports and driving cause problems that make it most important for each operator of a motor vehicle to drive in a sportsmanlike manner. Emphasis must be put on cooperation, not on competition. This means that, as a driver, you must make every effort to drive safely. It means that you must know and obey the laws that regulate driving. In addition, you must learn to look for and adjust to the faults of other highway users. In short, sportsmanship in driving means that you help every other driver to become a winner.

**Roadway safety is based on cooperation, patience, and courtesy among people who use the highway system.**

# Why Driver Education?

Why take driver education? What will you learn? Your driver education course and your textbook bring together the most advanced information available on driving maneuvers and decisions, traffic laws, and vehicle control. This information will help you to make good driving decisions. Your course will focus on factors relating to vehicles, drivers, and the highway—parts of the system with which you must learn to interact. One of the primary purposes of driver education is to help you become more aware of the elements around you as you drive. These elements should influence your selection of speed and position in traffic. Another, broader purpose is to help you develop the knowledge and skills to become a safe, effective user of the highway transportation system. You will need this knowledge and these skills not only as a driver of a motor vehicle but also as a pedestrian, a passenger, or a bicyclist.

The importance of knowing where to find your car's controls and how to use them is obvious. Less obvious is the importance of proper seat and mirror adjustment and of safety-belt use. If your seat is improperly adjusted—too high or too low, too far forward or too far back—your ability to control your car is reduced. Failure to properly adjust both the inside and outside mirrors reduces the area you can see and often leads to dangerous actions. Failure to fasten your safety belt reduces your ability to control your car in an emergency situation and increases your chances of being injured.

One of the major marks of a good driver is the ability to identify in advance cues that show a problem may be developing. To control the risks

**Driver education supplies you with the latest information available and helps you to develop the skills necessary for the complex task of operating a motor vehicle.**

involved in driving, you must know what to look for, where to look, and how to look. You must learn how and where to search for information. You must learn to evaluate the information available to you so that you can better predict the possible behavior of other highway users.

To make such evaluations, you will have to know and understand the purpose of traffic laws, signs, signals, and markings. You will have to be aware of the performance and handling characteristics of your car. You will also have to identify cues concerning other cars, trucks, buses, motorcycles, pedestrians, and bicyclists—cues that can alert you to possible problems.

In addition, you will have to evaluate the influence that roadway conditions, weather, and time of day may have on your ability to control your car. These factors can also influence your ability to identify and respond to traffic situations. So you must develop your perception, judgment, and driving skills, as well as decision-making ability. Then you can learn to evaluate and predict driving situations and to make the best selection of speed and position.

Development of these abilities, however, does not guarantee that you will be a safe, efficient driver. Safe driving requires more than knowledge, the ability to control your car, and the ability to judge time and space needs. It also requires an awareness and consideration of factors that can have a negative effect on your ability to drive. These factors can be either temporary or permanent. Temporary factors include things like your emotional state, the effects of an illness, or stress. Alcohol and drugs can also greatly impair your ability to make good judgments and decisions. More permanent factors might include your attitude regarding rules and regulations, your values, or physical impairments, such as a heart condition.

The facts you learn and the skills you develop in driver education will add to the pleasure that comes with being a good driver. But only you can determine how you are going to drive. You will have to make that decision every time you get behind the wheel of a motor vehicle.

# The Highway Transportation System

The highway transportation system is made up of vehicles, highways, and people. Each plays an important part in reaching the same goal: the safe and efficient movement of people and goods throughout this country. When any part of the system fails, the highway transportation system fails.

**Motor Vehicles in the System**
The highway transportation system is designed and operated for the use of **vehicles,** machines that have wheels and are designed to carry people and goods. Over 168 million registered vehicles, including cars, trucks, buses, motorcycles, and

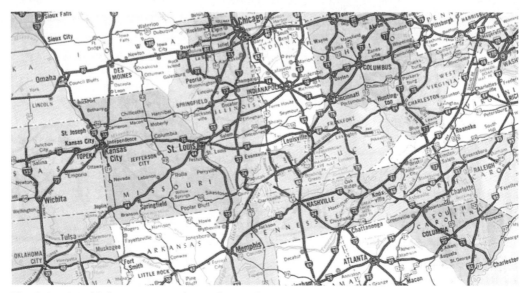

**The interstate highway system is made up of a network of modern roadways linking together most of the large cities in the United States.**

mopeds, move within the system. In addition, there are over 75 million special vehicles, such as bicycles and snowmobiles. When these vehicles are made, they are required to meet minimum safety standards.

However, they do not all "handle" the same way. In other words, each type of vehicle has its own performance capability. The vehicles accelerate, brake, and steer in different ways. For example, a large truck cannot pick up speed as fast as a small car. Vehicles differ also in how well they protect passengers in case of an accident. If there is a crash, a motorcycle does not protect as well as a large station wagon.

The **maintenance** (upkeep) of vehicles is the responsibility of each owner or operator. Some people take better care of their cars than others do, so the quality of maintenance

runs from nearly perfect to dangerously bad. Before you drive any car or buy a used car, you should be sure to check its condition. It is up to you, the driver, to keep the car you drive in the best possible shape.

**Highways in the System**  A vast network of roads—more than 3.9 million miles—reaches into the smallest communities in this country. Without this network, the United States would be an entirely different place in which to live. Highways permit us to travel to and from school, work, shops, and vacations. They make it possible for supplies to be moved easily from one part of the country to another. In times of natural disasters, such as floods, highways are used to carry those who are threatened to safety. Clearly, highways are important to the health and welfare of our nation.

The improvement of the system of roads in the United States since World War II has been dramatic. This has been especially true since the Federal Highway Act of 1956 was passed. This act provided funds for over 40,000 miles of the interstate system. Today, this system links nearly all cities that have 50,000 or more people. Highways in the interstate system must meet minimum design and construction standards. They must have 12-foot-wide lanes, wide, firm shoulder areas, and guardrails where appropriate. In addition, they are **limited access** roads, meaning that only certain vehicles may use them (for example, no bicycles or mopeds) and there are limited points of entry and exit. But even with these standards, some hazards still exist on the interstate system.

The federal government also gives the states money to build and improve state and local highways. Still, these roads often have far more hazards than do the interstate highways. For example, the lanes are not as wide, and there are many more entrances and exits. A highway's design or condition may cause accidents or make a driver's errors worse. Drivers must adjust to meet these conditions.

To help drivers, there are signs, signals, and markings that give information about driving rules and potential hazards. Some state the speed limit or forbid U-turns, for instance. Others warn drivers about environmental factors, such as curves in the road, bumps or breaks in the pavement, or other conditions that will limit a car's traction or a driver's visibility.

New highways in the interstate system must meet certain minimum standards in design and construction. These standards were established to promote safety and ease of use.

Drivers should keep in mind that vehicles of different sizes and shapes must share the roadway. These different types of vehicles accelerate, brake, and steer differently.

**People in the System**   Nearly all of the more than 240 million people in this land can be counted as pedestrians. Many of them also ride the more than 70 million bicycles now in use. Also, over 152 million people are licensed to drive a motor vehicle. The people who use the highway transportation system are the single greatest cause of system breakdowns. Such breakdowns occur for many reasons. Sometimes people do not have enough knowledge on which to base good decisions. For example, a 2-year-old child who tries to cross the street is not able to judge the hazards. A driver who sees the child may panic and "freeze" on the brake pedal, not aware that steering control is lost when the brakes are locked.

Often drivers think that they will be all right as long as they do not break the law. They do not anticipate the actions of other users, or they fail to look for clues that can tell them a problem is arising. They have not thought of ways to solve the problem. As a result, they do not know how to act in case of an emergency.

## The Federal Government's Role

For a long time, motor vehicle and traffic regulation were primarily a state responsibility. This is still true to a large extent. In your driver education class, you will study your own state's driver handbook as you prepare to take the written test and later the road test. On some subjects, including parking, one-way streets, and certain pedestrian regulations, states share the power to regulate traffic with counties, cities, and towns.

In 1966, after a careful study of the statistics on traffic accidents throughout the country, Congress recognized that federal action was necessary to establish uniform standards for vehicles, drivers, laws, and other factors which determine the safety of our streets and highways. In that year, the following two laws were passed:

- **The National Traffic and Motor Vehicle Safety Act** requires that motor vehicles be constructed with certain safety features and provides for correction by automobile manufacturers of any vehicle defects which may be recognized after car models are sold. Fines may be levied for failure to comply with the requirements. Today these federal standards include provision for safety features like safety belts, collapsible steering columns, shatterproof windows, and bumpers that will better absorb the impact of a collision.

- **The Highway Safety Act** establishes standards which are specific requirements for state highway safety programs. The state programs must include acceptable provisions for state and/or local action in regard to a number of areas, including motor vehicle registration and inspection, motorcycle safety, driver education and driver licensing, traffic laws and traffic courts, emergency medical ser-

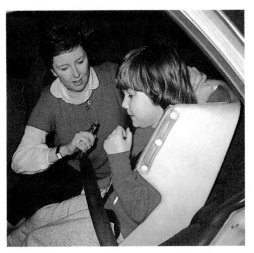

States, too, have safety legislation. The mandatory child safety restraint laws in all the states have saved many young lives.

vices, traffic control devices, pedestrian safety, as well as highway design, construction, and maintenance.

Since that time, another important federal law was passed. In 1974, a speed limit of 55 **miles per hour (mph)** was established to conserve gasoline supplies. (The faster a vehicle is driven, the more fuel it uses.) The new speed limit does more than save fuel; it also saves lives. High speed contributes to accidents. Also, as speed increases, damage and injuries resulting from accidents become more severe.

## Administrative Laws

Each state has laws that regulate the licensing of drivers and the registering of motor vehicles. There are also laws that set standards of finan-

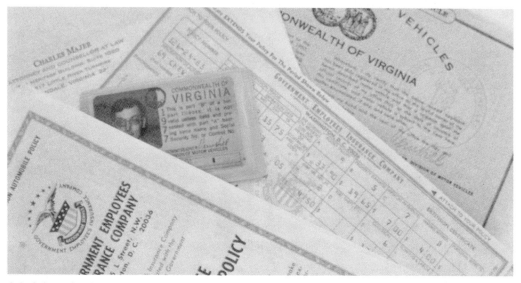

Administrative laws set minimum standards with which motor vehicles and drivers must comply. These laws are carried out at the state level.

cial responsibility for drivers and owners. Other laws regulate the minimum equipment and care a vehicle must have. These are called **administrative laws.** They are designed to keep track of who owns a vehicle, who has a license, and the violations of traffic laws that drivers commit.

In their laws, the states try to follow the standards for rules of the road and motor vehicle equipment that are suggested in the Uniform Vehicle Code. This way, the laws in all parts of the United States are as similar as possible.

**Driver's License** Before you can get a license, you must take some tests. These tests find out if you meet minimum standards of vision, hearing, and physical condition. You will also be tested to see if you know the basic rules of the road. Then you will

take a driving test that measures how well you can perform basic driving maneuvers. If you pass each of these tests, you will qualify for a driver's license.

**The Point System** To keep your license after you get it, you must meet certain standards. Otherwise, your license may be revoked or suspended. To **revoke** a license means to take it away permanently. To **suspend** a license means to take it away temporarily. Each state has its own rules and procedures for revoking or suspending a driver's license.

Most states use a point system. Where such a system is used, each violation of a traffic regulation has a number of points assigned to it, depending on how serious it is. When a driver is found guilty of violating a law, a report is sent to the State Department of Motor Vehicles, which assigns that number of points to the driver's record.

For example, a driver who gets more than 4 or 5 points within a period of time (usually 2 years) may be sent a warning letter. One who gets 6 or 7 points may have to go for an interview at the Department of Motor Vehicles. A driver with 8 to 11 points may be called in for a hearing. This could lead to a suspension of the driver's license. After the suspension period is over, if the driver is convicted of further violations and gets more points, the driver's license generally will be revoked. Some regulations are so important that you will lose your license automatically if you are found guilty of violating them. Examples of such violations include driving under the influence of alcohol or other drugs, leaving the scene of an accident in which there has been an injury, and using a motor vehicle in a crime.

Rules about revoking and suspending licenses vary from state to state. The system is designed to make people drive carefully. The right to drive can be taken away from those who do not obey the law.

## National Driver Register Service

In 1960, the United States Congress established the National Driver Register Service. The register stores the

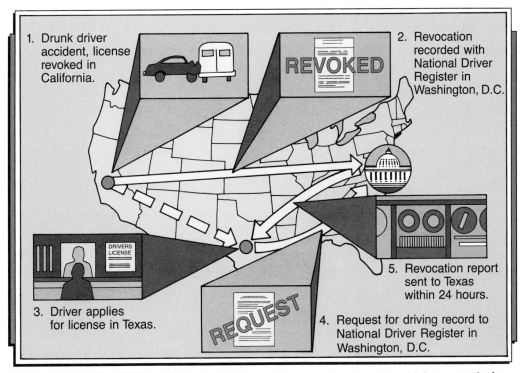

1. Drunk driver accident, license revoked in California.

REVOKED

2. Revocation recorded with National Driver Register in Washington, D.C.

3. Driver applies for license in Texas.

REQUEST

4. Request for driving record to National Driver Register in Washington, D.C.

5. Revocation report sent to Texas within 24 hours.

**Through the National Driver Register Service, states can check on the driving record of a person who applies for a driver's license.**

names of drivers whose licenses have been suspended or revoked. The motor vehicle department of a state may ask the service about the driving record of a person who applies for a license. States can find out, for instance, if an applicant has had a license revoked in another state or if the applicant could not get a license for health reasons.

**Certificate of Title** Almost every state issues a certificate of title when you buy a car. It identifies the make, style, serial and engine numbers, and owner. Before a vehicle can be sold, the seller must prove ownership by producing the certificate of title.

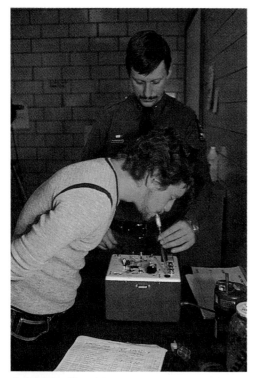

A driver with a blood-alcohol concentration of .10 percent can be charged with driving while intoxicated.

You may buy a car without having a license to drive it.

## Vehicle Registration and License Plates

The states also register motor vehicles and issue license plates. You must own a vehicle before you can register it. When it is registered, the Department of Motor Vehicles gives the owner a certificate of registration and license plates. The certificate identifies both the car and the owner. It must be in the vehicle any time the vehicle is in use. The license plates allow the police and others to identify a car. Some police departments now have computer systems in their patrol cars to check on stolen or abandoned vehicles instantly.

**Driving while Intoxicated** A court of law must determine whether a driver is guilty of **driving while intoxicated (DWI)**. An officer who suspects a driver is **intoxicated** (drunk) must first make an arrest. To convict the driver in court, the officer has to show evidence that the driver was intoxicated. This evidence includes the officer's notes about the way the person was driving, the time, the date, and the place. Usually, the results of a chemical test that show the amount of alcohol or drugs in the driver's blood must be presented to the court. Some states permit the use of a test for alcohol before an arrest has been made. But in most states, tests for **blood-alcohol concentration (BAC)**—the amount of alcohol found in the

**If you are in an accident, no matter how minor, you have certain legal responsibilities which are important for the physical and financial protection of everyone involved.**

blood—can be given only after an arrest.

Most states also have a lesser offense called **driving while impaired.** A driver may be charged with this offense when the BAC at the time of arrest falls between 0.05 percent and 0.10 percent. (See Chapter 15 for a fuller explanation of these numbers.)

Under the **implied consent law,** any driver arrested for being drunk must agree to take a chemical test for the presence of alcohol. If a driver will not take the test, the state Department of Motor Vehicles usually has the right to take away the driver's license. In most states, a suspension under the implied consent law is for 3 to 6 months.

Chemical tests for the presence of alcohol or other drugs can consist of an examination of breath, blood, or urine samples. The breath test is the one most often used to find the BAC.

## Responsibilities when Involved in an Accident

If you are in an accident, there are certain things you must do right away. If you fail to meet these obligations, you could be in serious trouble. After an accident, you should:

- Stop immediately, as close to the scene as you safely can.

- Be extremely careful, but do what you can to warn oncoming traffic of the accident. Turn on your hazard flashers if possible.

- Give help and get medical aid. Call an ambulance, if needed. (See *First Aid* feature on pages 314 and 315.)

- Call the police if there has been an injury or death. (In most states, you must call the police if there is property damage over a certain amount.)

- Exchange names, addresses, driver's license information, and vehicle identification with other persons involved. Do not discuss who is at fault.
- Get the names and addresses of witnesses.
- Stay at the scene of an accident until your help is no longer needed.
- Make accident reports promptly to the police and the Department of Motor Vehicles, as required. Also, inform your insurance company.

**Legal Results**  If you break a traffic law at the time of the accident, you may be penalized in several ways. You may be fined and have to pay court costs. Your license could be suspended or revoked. You could even be sent to jail. Remember also that severe penalties are given in all states to drivers who **hit and run** (flee from the scene of an accident that they were involved in).

You are not required to give an opinion concerning the cause of an accident. You have the legal right to consult a lawyer before giving any statement.

You may be sued for damages if there are injuries or property damages. Damages awarded by courts in injury or death cases may come to hundreds of thousands of dollars. If the sums are more than your insurance covers, you have to pay the rest yourself. People have lost their cars, homes, and other possessions as the result of such cases. Others have had part of their wages taken for years.

**Since failures in vehicle systems can cause accidents, some states require yearly inspection of all motor vehicles.**

## Arriving at the Scene of an Accident

You have a moral responsibility to stop if you come upon an accident shortly after it happens and you can see that help is needed. Be certain that you stop in a safe place. If the police have taken charge, do not stop unless you are asked to do so. You do not want to get in the way and create an additional hazard.

**Accident Investigation** When the police investigate an accident, they must gather all evidence available. They note the final position and direction of travel of the vehicles involved. They check the condition of the drivers, road, and vehicles. They will usually measure the skid marks, and they will ask witnesses what they saw. Often, some **violation** has been committed (law has been broken) when an accident takes place. If so, one or more of the drivers may get a **citation** (ticket) for a violation.

**Motor Vehicle Inspection** Vehicle failure can cause accidents. Because of this, all states have laws that say you must keep your car in good working condition. A number of states have inspection laws to make sure that vehicles meet minimum standards. Some states require inspections at set times of the year. In other states, inspections are done by police spot-checks.

Where laws require inspection, states may choose to check vehicles at state inspection centers or at private garages approved by the state. These inspections usually include tests of the brakes, lights, horn, exhaust systems, steering and suspension, directional signals, tires, and **emission-control** (antipollution) devices. If any part is not working properly, it must be repaired in a given period of time. The owner must show proof of the repairs before the car can be certified as having passed the inspection. Your car should be checked regularly.

## Projects

1. In a brief report, explain the purpose of the highway transportation system. List the main parts of the system and make a display that shows how the system has changed the way of life in this country. Use drawings, photos, and magazine clippings as a part of your report.

2. Interview people who drive and who do not. Ask them what is more important for a driver: driving skill or attitude toward driving. Ask them to describe what they think the ideal driver's attitude should be. Can you draw any conclusions from the answers they give?

## Words to Know

maintenance  
The National Traffic and  
  Motor Vehicle Safety  
  Act  
The Highway Safety Act  

administrative  
  laws  
revoke  
suspend  
implied consent law  

hit-and-run  
violation  
citation  
emission-control  

## Stop and Review

1. List and explain some of the advantages of having a driver's license.
2. Explain how the word *sportsmanship* can be applied to driving.
3. Why must you cooperate with other highway users (drivers, bicyclists, and pedestrians) when you drive?
4. What responsibilities do you have as an operator of a motor vehicle? What are the duties of others who use the highway system, such as pedestrians and bicyclists?
5. What is the purpose of the highway transportation system?
6. How can vehicle maintenance affect the way you drive?
7. List 3 design and construction standards for highways in the interstate system.
8. Explain why people are the major contributors to the breakdown of the highway transportation system.
9. What are some of the reasons for failures in the highway transportation system?
10. In your opinion, what part of the highway transportation system needs to be improved? Explain your answer.
11. What is the purpose of the National Traffic and Motor Vehicle Safety Act?
12. Name the law that sets requirements for state highway safety programs.
13. Why does the United States have national standards for motor vehicle and traffic laws?
14. Explain how a person gets a driver's license.
15. What are some reasons why a person's license might be suspended or revoked?
16. Define the aim of the National Driver Register Service.
17. Why are vehicle registration and insurance needed?
18. What do police look for when they investigate an accident?
19. Why might a driver get a citation as the result of a traffic accident?
20. What is the purpose of motor vehicle inspections?

You have stopped at the intersection shown above and are signaling a right turn. The red traffic light should turn green in a few seconds. A car to your left on the cross street is speeding toward the intersection. Look for other cues, and identify as many potential hazards as you can.

1. What other highway users must you watch for? What might they do? What should you do?

As you complete your turn, a parked car pulls out and hits the side of your car.

2. What things must you do? Could you have helped avoid the accident?

# CHAPTER 1 TEST

Complete the sentences by filling in the blanks with the correct terms.

| | |
|---|---|
| people | lives |
| Federal Highway | National Driver |
| Act of 1956 | Register |
| inspection laws | vehicles |
| certificate of title | |

| | |
|---|---|
| certificate of | maintenance |
| registration | interstate |
| Highway | fuel |
| Safety Act | highways |

1. The highway transportation system is made up of _____ , _____ , and _____ .

2. Vehicle owners are responsible for the _____ of their vehicles.

3. The _____ provided funds for the interstate system of roads.

4. Requirements for state highway safety programs were established by the _____ .

5. Highways in the _____ system must meet minimum design and construction standards.

6. In 1974, a federal law was passed setting the maximum speed limit at 55 mph in order to save _____ . This law has also been saving _____ .

7. The names of drivers whose licenses have been suspended or revoked are stored in the _____ .

8. The _____ lists the owner, style, make, and serial number of a car.

9. The _____ identifies the car and owner, and must be in the car when it is in use.

10. A number of states have _____ to make sure that vehicles meet minimum standards.

---

Decide whether each of the following sentences is true or false.

11. Traffic laws regulate the actions of pedestrians.

12. Performance capability differs depending on the type of vehicle.

13. State highways must have 12-foot-wide lanes.

14. The Uniform Vehicle Code sets forth standards for rules of the road and motor vehicle equipment.

15. If your license is revoked, it has been taken away permanently.

# Preparing to Drive

## Chapter Objectives:

In this chapter you will learn how to:

- identify and use the protective system in your car.
- identify and use the comfort system in your car.
- identify and use the control system in your car.
- identify and use the vehicle-check system in your car.
- identify and use the visibility system in your car.
- identify and use the communications system in your car.
- identify and use the antitheft system in your car.
- execute predriving checks and procedures.
- enter and leave the car safely.

You are probably familiar with the various vehicle systems that you have seen drivers use. Some allow you to control the motion of the car, check on its condition, and communicate your path of travel to other high-way users. Other systems provide for the safety and comfort of the passengers and some protect against theft of the vehicle.

You should learn where the instrument switches and control devices are and what they do. When you drive, you will have to steer and maintain speed without taking your eyes from the road. You will also have to find and adjust a number of controls and switches while you pay attention to the traffic around you.

# Protective System

A car's protective devices help guard you from possible injury if there is a collision or sudden emergency maneuver. There are some **passive** parts of the protective system that the driver and passengers do not have to adjust, such as air bags, passive restraint belts, impact-resistant bumpers, side-bar door beams, and padding. But other devices, such as lap-shoulder belts and adjustable head restraints, do require action on the part of the user.

**Safety Belts** Lap belts should be strapped snugly across the hips. They help keep you behind the steering wheel and in control of the car if you have to brake hard or swerve sharply and they prevent your passengers from being thrown around inside the car or thrown out of it. Shoulder safety belts are used with lap belts to provide added protection. These belts are strapped across the shoulder and the chest. They lessen the chance that you or your passenger will be thrown against the dashboard, through the windshield, or out a door which has sprung open as the result of a collision. A shoulder belt should not be adjusted too tightly.

You should be able to put your fist between the belt and your chest. These combination lap-shoulder safety belts became standard equipment in new cars in 1968. Most new safety belts operate on an **inertia reel** system, which allows the belt to unreel freely (for greater comfort) unless there is a sudden deceleration.

All cars manufactured since January 1, 1972, have a safety-belt warning light and buzzer that remind drivers to buckle up. A number of states now have laws that require the driver and the front seat passengers to wear their safety belts. Hopefully, in the next few years, even more states will adopt such laws. All of the 50 states have passed laws requiring that safety-tested and approved child restraints be used by young children.

If you are wearing a lap-shoulder belt at the time of an accident, your chances of being killed are reduced by about 50 percent.

## Air Bags and Passive Safety Belts

A few new cars are now equipped with **air bags** in the steering column. Airbags are passive safety restraints which have been shown to be very effective in reducing injuries, especially when the car is involved in a frontal collision. They inflate to protect in any collision over 12 mph, then deflate again, in a fraction of a second. A **passive safety belt** is a shoulder restraint that connects from the center of the seat to the

20

upper rear corner of the door. Unlike regular safety belts, neither passive safety belts nor air bags have to be fastened by the driver or passengers. However, the driver and passengers must use a regular lap belt with a passive belt, or a combination lap-shoulder belt with an air bag, in order to have the best protection in side collisions and rollovers.

**Head Restraints** Head restraints help to prevent **whiplash** (neck injury). These safety devices are standard equipment on front seats and optional on the rear seats of some new cars. They are either fixed or adjustable. When you are riding in a car with an adjustable head restraint, make sure it is high enough

to make contact with the back of your head, not with the base of your skull. Otherwise, in a collision, serious injury could result.

**Door Locks** Doors should be locked while you are driving your car. A locked door is less likely to open in the event of a collision or a rollover, and it cannot be opened accidentally while the car is in motion. Also, locked doors help keep uninvited people out of your car.

## Comfort System

Comfort-system devices help you drive more efficiently by making driving more comfortable and less

**Head restraints prevent neck injury when properly adjusted. Safety belts prevent you from being thrown out of the car. Adjust your safety belt so that it fits comfortably.**

**Controls for comfort-system devices are located in a convenient place on the dashboard. Shown here are the heater and the air conditioner.**

tiring. These systems are of two types. The first type includes devices that reduce muscle strain, such as the seat adjustments and cruise control. The second type are climate-control devices, such as the air conditioner, heater, and air vents.

**Seat Adjustments** The driver's seat can be moved forward or back by pulling a lever under the seat and pushing on the seat at the same time. With your seat adjusted properly, you should be able to reach all the car's controls and switches. Adjust your seat so that you can look over the steering wheel and hood and see the road 12 feet in front of your car. Your right foot should rest comfortably on the accelerator, and the

brake pedal should be within easy reach. If you are driving a car with a manual shift, you must be able to push the clutch pedal all the way to the floor with your left foot. Even with a full-range power seat or an adjustable steering wheel, you may still need pedal extensions or seat cushions to sit and drive properly. If you need cushions or pedal extensions in a driver-education car or a driving simulator, you are likely to need them in the car that you drive at home.

**Cruise, or Speed, Control** **Cruise control** lets you keep driving at a given speed without keeping your foot on the accelerator. This device was designed for highway driving. When you have reached the speed you want to maintain, you press a control button that is usually on the steering wheel or at the end of the turn-indicator arm. This causes the speed-control system to operate. In order to control the speed of the car manually again, you either touch the button or tap the brake pedal, but it takes practice to learn how to use it properly. There is a danger that a driver may become less alert when using speed control. Drivers sometimes fail to adjust the speed and drive into situations that need a quick response. Cruise control should not be used in situations when speed must be monitored closely and braking could be dangerous, such as when the road is slick with rain or ice.

**Air Conditioner** The air conditioner helps to keep the driver alert by lowering the temperature and humidity in the car.

Nearly all air conditioners have a *normal* and a *maximum* setting for cooling the car. The *normal* air-conditioning setting cools air that is drawn in from the outside. The *maximum* air-conditioning setting provides faster cooling. It recirculates air that is in the car along with a small amount of fresh air that is drawn in from the outside. Some cars also have a *bilevel* setting. This setting provides conditioned air through the heater and the air-conditioner vents. In addition, it provides air through the defroster. This setting is very useful in rainy weather

when fog appears on the windshield and side window glass.

**Heater** This device provides comfort and safety in cold weather. The heater should be adjusted to keep a moderate temperature. If the temperature inside the car is too warm, it can make the driver drowsy.

**Air Vents** These vents are usually located on the dashboard or in the front-seat section of the car at the left and right sides. They let outside air flow into the vehicle to increase passenger comfort. You can select how much air you want to come in by adjusting the air-vent controls.

## Control System

Control-system devices are used to start the car, to control its speed and direction, and to bring it to a stop.

**Ignition Switch** Usually an ignition switch has five positions. They are *on, start, off, lock,* and *accessory (acc.)*. *On* turns on the electrical system, the ignition system, and the information gauges. You can read the gauges without starting the engine. When you turn the ignition key to *start,* you engage a motor that starts the engine. In the *off* position, the engine stops, but you cannot remove the key from the switch. *Lock* locks the steering wheel, the ignition switch, and the automatic transmission. It also makes it possible to remove the key. *Accessory* lets you turn on electrical equipment, such as the radio, without starting the engine.

**Cars with a manual transmission have a gearshift instead of a selector lever. The gearshift can have 3, 4, or 5 speeds.**

## Selector Lever and Gear-Indicator Quadrant

Cars with an automatic transmission have a **selector lever** and **gear-indicator quadrant**. The lever lets you choose the gear in which you want to drive, and the quadrant tells you which gear the car is in. A pointer on the quadrant moves as you move the lever. These are the symbols on a standard quadrant:

P *(park)* — No gears are engaged. The drive wheels are locked when the car is in *park* and the ignition key is removed. The engine should be started with the gear selector at *park*.

R *(reverse)* — *Reverse* gear is used for backing up. If the selector lever is on the steering column, you have to pull the lever toward you slightly, with your palm up, and then move it down toward the floor to shift into *reverse*.

N *(neutral)* — In this position, the gears are not engaged, and all the wheels are free to roll. So, the car may roll downhill if left in *neutral* with the parking brake not set.

D *(drive)* — *Drive* is the basic forward gear. If the engine is set at a **fast idle**, the car may start to move as soon as you shift into *drive* even if you do not press your foot on the accelerator. Keep your foot on the brake pedal as you shift gears.

**2 and 1 or L** These are lower drive gears. They allow the engine to deliver more power to the wheels at low speeds. You may choose these gears when you drive in mud or sand. They can also be used to climb steep grades, to hold a car back when driving down a long, steep hill, or to pull a trailer on a hill.

**Steering Wheel** You control the direction of your car with the steering wheel. When you drive, your hands should grasp the steering wheel at approximately the 9 o'clock and 3 o'clock positions. If the seat is properly adjusted and your hands are on the wheel in this way, your upper arms should rest against your ribs. This reduces arm and shoulder strain and permits the best handling for steady, straight steering and for moderate turning. This position will also enable you to respond quickly in emergency situations when you have to make hard, fast reversals of the steering wheel.

**Accelerator, or Gas Pedal** The speed of the car is controlled by the amount of fuel that flows into the engine. You control the flow of fuel by the amount of pressure you apply to the **accelerator** (gas pedal). Gradual acceleration is achieved by applying even, gentle pressure until your car is moving at the desired speed. Then you hold the pedal at the level necessary to maintain the speed. For most driving, this is the safest method. Accelerating this way also uses up less fuel than is needed for quick starts.

**Brake Pedal** By stepping on the brake pedal, you can slow or stop the car. How fast the car stops depends on how hard you push down on the pedal. The amount of movement that takes place before the desired action begins to occur is called "play." There is normally some play in the foot pedal. If you press the pedal gently as the car moves, you will find that the pedal moves about an inch or so before the car begins to slow down.

Power-assisted brakes make it easier to slow or stop the car. They increase the pressure beyond that exerted by your foot. However, power-assisted brakes do not shorten the distance it takes to stop. As you use either regular or power brakes, you will adapt to the feel of them and learn how much foot pressure to apply. When you change to a car with the other type of brakes, you will have to adjust the amount of pedal pressure you use.

A technique used by some experienced drivers when they are approaching a situation in which they might have to brake is to **cover** the brake with the left foot. This means that the foot is in a ready position, but not actually applying pressure on the brake.

**Parking Brake** This brake is also known as the **hand brake** or **emergency brake**. The parking brake is used to keep a parked car from rolling, but it can also be used to stop a moving car in an emergency. The parking brake holds the two rear wheels; it is separate from the foot brake, which works on all four wheels. The control lever is either a small pedal located at the left of the foot brake, a lever that is located below the dash and is worked by hand, or a lever mounted on the floor between the driver and the front-seat passenger.

**This person is applying the brakes. The right foot is centered on the brake pedal and the left foot is on the floor.**

## Vehicle-Check System

In this system, also called the instrument panel, lights and gauges on the dashboard allow the driver to check certain conditions of the car while it is running.

**Speedometer and Odometer** The **speedometer** shows, in miles per hour and kilometers per hour, how fast the car is moving. As you drive, glance at the speedometer from time to time to check how fast you are going. The **odometer** shows the total number of miles (or kilometers) the car has been driven.

**Alternator Gauge** This device, which is also called an **ammeter**, tells you if the alternator is making enough electricity. If it is not, the engine will have to use stored electricity from the battery. The gauge is a scale that goes from *Discharge* (*D*

or −) to *Charge* (*C* or +). Check it occasionally as you drive. If the needle on the gauge points to *Discharge,* or if a red warning light comes on, it means that the battery is being drained. Turn off any unnecessary electrical devices, such as the radio, and have a mechanic check the battery and electrical system as soon as possible.

### Temperature Gauge or Warning Light

This device, too, comes as a gauge or a light. Either one shows whether the engine is running at the right temperature. A hot engine may be either the cause or the result of fluid leaking from the cooling system. Overheating can lead to serious engine damage.

### Oil-Pressure Gauge or Warning Light

Either device shows the pressure at which the oil is being pumped to the moving parts of the engine. The gauge or light does not show how much oil there is in the engine, but rather the operating pressure. When the light is on, the pressure is low. If the oil-pressure light comes on or the gauge drops, stop the car as quickly as you can.

**Fuel Gauge** This gauge shows the approximate amount of gasoline in the fuel tank. The markings usually read: *E* (empty), ¼, ½, ¾, and *F* (full).

**Parking-Brake Light** This light flashes if the engine is turned on while the parking brake is set. This is to remind the driver to release the brake before trying to move the car. Late-model cars also have a light that shows when the fluid in the brake system is low.

**High-Beam Indicator Light** Usually, this light is located near the center of the speedometer. It goes on when you turn on the car's **high-beam** (bright) headlights.

Instrument panel: (1) tachometer (indicates engine speed) (2) speedometer (3) odometer (4) fuel gauge (5) temperature gauge (6) alternator light (7) oil pressure light (8) high-beam indicator (9) turn-signal indicators (10) parking brake/brake failure warning light (11) safety belt light (12) cruise control indicator (13) low-fuel indicator

**Use high-beam headlights with care. Do *not* use them when the car in front of you is close, when a car is passing you, or when a car is approaching from the opposite direction.**

## Visibility System

These are devices that help the driver see as much as possible, no matter what the weather or time of day. It is essential that you see the road ahead and the area bordering the path you wish to travel.

**Headlights** Drivers must use headlights to help them see at night, during bad weather, and at any other time when visibility is poor. Headlights also help other drivers and pedestrians to see you. Usually, headlight beams can be changed from *low* to *high* or *high* to *low* by pulling the turn-indicator lever toward you. In some older vehicles, the switch is on the floor, to the left of the foot controls. High-beam headlights should be used with caution. They should not be used when the car in front of you is close, when a car is passing you, or when a car is approaching you from the opposite direction.

When you turn on your headlights, the dashboard also lights up. This lets you see the selector quadrant, the speedometer, and the other dials and gauges. These lights can be made bright or dim by turning a knob which is usually located on the headlight switch. The dashboard lights should be kept dim most of the time so that they do not make it difficult to see outside the car.

Controls for some devices are found on stalks coming from the steering column: (1) directional-signal lever (2) cruise control (3) windshield wipers (4) windshield spray

## Rear-View and Side-View Mirrors

Up to a point, these mirrors allow you to see cars that are to the side and to the rear of your car. When they are set correctly, the two mirrors can do away with most, but not all, **blind spots** (areas that you cannot see). Be sure the mirrors are mounted either above or below eye level. Many rear-view mirrors can also be adjusted to reduce the glare from headlights of cars behind you when you drive at night.

## Wiper-Washer

Most cars have windshield spray nozzles and two- or three-speed windshield wipers. Water from the spray nozzles (mixed with an antifreeze solution) helps the wipers clean the dirt from the windshield.

## Sun Visors

The sun visors can be moved to keep most of the sun's glare from your eyes. They should not be set so that they block your view. For instance, they should not keep you from seeing overhead traffic lights. Also, do not use them to store things that may fall and distract you.

## Defroster

The defroster clears the moisture or frost from the inside of the front and rear windows and keeps it from collecting on the inside of the glass. It also melts any ice or frost that may gather on the outside of the glass.

## Interior Dome Light

In most cars, the interior dome light goes on whenever either of the front doors is opened. It can also be turned on and off by an inside switch. This light should not be on when you drive at night. Any light in the car makes it more difficult to see outside.

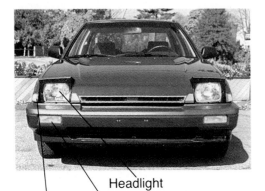

Headlight

Directional signal

Parking light

**Front view**

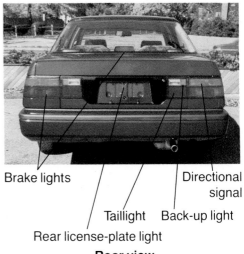

Brake lights

Directional signal

Taillight     Back-up light

Rear license-plate light

**Rear view**

# Communications System

These devices let other drivers know where you are and what immediate direction you intend to take.

**Parking Lights** The parking lights should be used only when your car is stopped; for example, if you pull to the curb to wait for a passenger. They make your car more visible to other drivers. They are not designed to light the road in front of your car.

**Horn** A horn is a warning device. It should be used to tell others on the road that there may be danger. A gentle honk will usually be enough to get the attention of animals, pedestrians, or other drivers. If you use it this way rather than sound a blast, the horn is less likely to startle people or animals into some dangerous move. Unnecessary use of the horn is against the law in many places.

The horn is usually operated by pressing against the center of the steering wheel, though in some cases there are smaller buttons closer to where your hands rest that operate the horn.

## Directional or Lane-Change Signals

**Directional** (turn) signals tell other drivers that you plan to turn or move to the right or left. The signal control makes a light blink at both the front and rear of the car on the right or left side. To use these turn lights, move the turn signal lever up for right and down for left. The lights should go off automatically when the wheel straightens out after a turn. In most cars, you can hear the click of a turn signal. If the lights continue to flash after you have made your move, turn them off by hand by moving the lever back to the middle point.

To signal a lane change, instead of switching the signal on, you can lightly press and hold the switch in

**Hand signals are better than turn-signal lights in some situations. These are the hand signals for a right turn, a left turn, and for stopping or slowing down.**

the desired direction. By not locking the signal in position, you eliminate the chance of leaving it on. The signal will go off after you release the switch.

In bright weather, the sun may shine on these lights and make them hard for others to see. If this happens, use hand signals. To signal by hand, you must put your left arm out the window. Hold your arm straight out the window to signal a left turn. Bend your arm up from the elbow to signal a right turn. Bend your arm down from the elbow to signal slowing down or stopping. (You will have to use hand signals if your electric turn signals are not working or in a traffic situation, such as a close line of cars, where a hand signal will be more visible to other drivers.)

**Hazard Flashers** The **hazard** or **four-way emergency** flashers tell other drivers that a vehicle on or off the road ahead either has stopped or is moving very slowly. These flashers are usually worked by a switch on the steering column. This switch makes all four turn-signal lights flash at the same time. The turn-signal light on most cars will not work when the four-way emergency flashers are turned on.

**Taillight Assembly** This unit contains several lights: **red brake lights** that go on when you press the brake pedal, **red taillights** that go on when you turn on your parking lights or headlights, and **white back-up lights** that go on when you shift to reverse.

Standard equipment on cars manufactured in 1986 and later is a third red brake light mounted in the rear window.

**Rear License-Plate Light** This light goes on when you turn on your parking lights or headlights. This light aids in identifying vehicles, and under the law, all vehicles must have a rear license-plate light.

**Side-Marker Lights** These lights also go on with the headlights. They help drivers to see your car when you are **intersecting** (crossing) streets.

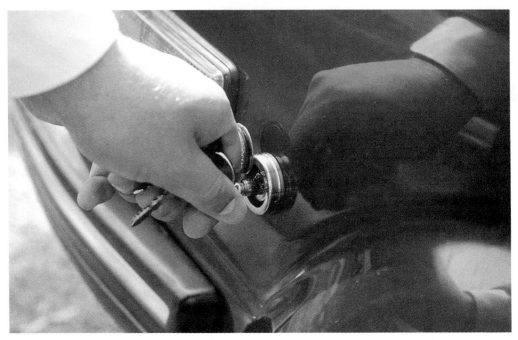

**Always remember to close your windows and lock your doors when you park your car. Use an alarm to frighten away thieves.**

## Antitheft System

The devices in the antitheft system make it harder for anyone to break into or steal your car.

**Ignition Buzzer** The buzzer is designed to remind you to take your keys when you leave the car. When the key is left in the ignition switch and the driver's door is opened, the buzzer sounds. This buzzer has two purposes: to stop you from locking yourself out if you leave your keys in the car, and to remind you to take the keys from the ignition to reduce the chance of theft.

**Steering-Column Lock** When you turn the ignition key to the *lock* position, the steering wheel locks in

place. When this lock is on in a car with an automatic transmission, the steering wheel and gear-selector lever will not move. In a car with a manual transmission, you usually can move the gear-shift lever, but you cannot turn the steering wheel.

**Door Locks** Door locks help to keep people out. They also are a safety device because locked doors are less likely to open if there is a collision.

**Trunk, Hood, Gas-Tank Locks** To prevent tampering with your car from the outside, trunks have locks that can be opened with a key. Usually there is also a lever within reach of the driver's seat to release the trunk lock from inside. The engine hood can usually only be opened by releasing an inside lever. Gas tanks on new cars must be unlocked from the outside with a key or by pulling a lever near the driver's seat.

# Predriving Checks and Procedures

People who just get in a car and drive away show a lack of concern both for themselves and the car. They also show a lack of concern for the welfare of other people.

**Outside Checks**  When you go to your car, look for small children who may be playing near it—approximately 200 children under 6 years of age are killed each year while playing in the family driveway.

Note which way the front wheels are turned. If the front wheels do not point straight ahead, the car will move left or right as soon as you start to drive. If you do not anticipate this kind of move to the side, you could have an accident.

If you plan to drive far, take time to check under the hood before you start. Be sure to look at the water in the battery, the windshield-wiper fluid, the coolant in the radiator, and the engine oil level.

1. Make sure there are no people, animals, or objects that may interfere with moving the car.

2. Check to see if there is any damage to the body of the car. (Notice the missing side-view mirror in the diagram below.)

3. Look at the ground under the car to make sure there is no fluid that may have leaked from the engine. (Notice the locations of different leaks in the diagram on the following page.)

4. Check that the headlights, the taillights, the windows, and the side-view mirror are all clean and undamaged.

5. See that the tires appear to be properly inflated, and notice in which direction the front wheels are turned.

**Before you get into you car and drive off, look for nearby people or objects, check for leaks or damage to the car, and check the position of the tires.**

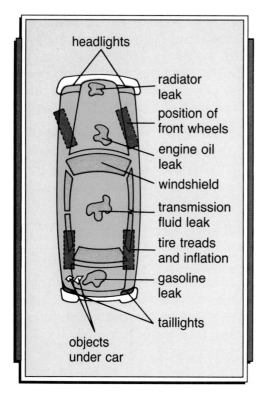

headlights

radiator leak

position of front wheels

engine oil leak

windshield

transmission fluid leak

tire treads and inflation

gasoline leak

taillights

objects under car

**After you have adjusted your seat and your head restraint, adjust your side-view and rear-view mirrors.**

**If your side-view and rear-view mirrors are adjusted properly, you can use them without turning your head.**

## Entering the Car Safely

1. Load packages and have passengers enter from the curb side of the car whenever you can.

2. Look carefully for approaching traffic before stepping off the curb. Walk around the front of the car, always facing oncoming traffic as you unlock the door. Before you open the door, make sure there is a break in traffic long enough for you to enter the car.

3. Open the car door only enough to allow you to enter safely.

4. Enter the car quickly, and close and lock your door.

**Inside Checks** Once you are in the car, you should follow a prestart routine. Your owner's manual may suggest that you do things in a way slightly different from what is here. The important thing is to set up a good routine and follow it. You should be able to complete the following 9 steps within 1 minute:

1. See that the key fits easily into the ignition switch.

2. Make sure all doors are locked.

3. Adjust the seat so that you can

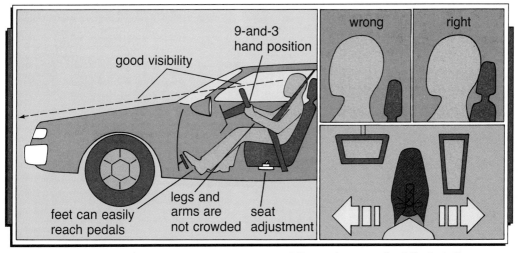

good visibility

9-and-3
hand position

wrong

right

legs and
arms are
not crowded

feet can easily
reach pedals

seat
adjustment

**As part of your prestart routine, adjust your seat while resting your foot first on the accelerator and then on the brake pedal. The head restraint should be high enough to make contact with the back of your head and not the base of your skull.**

see over the steering wheel while resting your right foot first on the accelerator and then on the brake pedal. Make sure your hands are comfortable in approximately a 9 o'clock and 3 o'clock position on the steering wheel and your arms have enough room to turn the wheel fully in both directions.

4. Adjust the head restraint to the level of the back of your head. Make sure you are able to check your blind spots.

5. Adjust the rear-view and side-view mirrors so you can use them without moving your head. (With your back pressed firmly against the back of your seat, turn your head only to check that you can see the line of your fenders and any cars approaching from the rear in your side-view mirror. Facing forward, move your eyes only to check if you can see the rear window and slightly to the right of the car in the rear-view mirror.)

6. Check the insides of the windows to see if they need to be cleaned or defrosted.

7. Make sure there are no articles inside the car that block your view or will fly around if you have to stop quickly.

8. Locate the controls for any devices you may need to use (headlights, turn signal, windshield wipers, parking brake).

9. Fasten your safety belt, and see that passengers do the same. With adjustable safety belts the lap belt should fit snugly across the hips and the shoulder belt should be slack enough for your fist to fit between it and the middle of your chest.

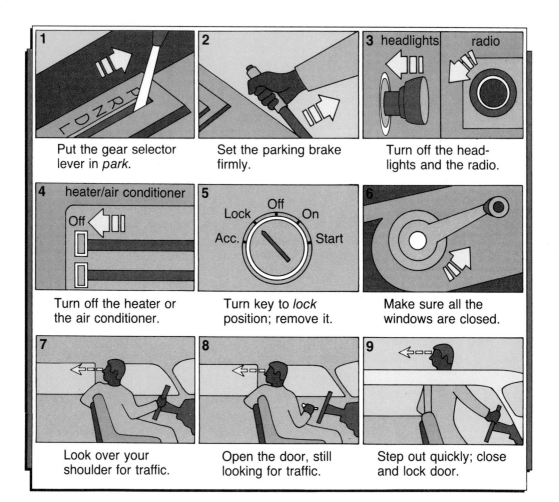

**1** Put the gear selector lever in *park.*

**2** Set the parking brake firmly.

**3** Turn off the headlights and the radio.

**4** Turn off the heater or the air conditioner.

**5** Turn key to *lock* position; remove it.

**6** Make sure all the windows are closed.

**7** Look over your shoulder for traffic.

**8** Open the door, still looking for traffic.

**9** Step out quickly; close and lock door.

## Leaving the Car Safely

1. With your foot firmly on the brake pedal, put the gear-selector lever in the proper gear (*park* for a car with an automatic transmission, *reverse* for a manual-shift car).

2. Set the parking brake firmly.

3. Turn off all accessories (headlights, radio, heater or air conditioner). Turn the key to the *lock* position and remove it from the ignition switch.

4. Close all the windows. (Do this before taking the key from the ignition if you have power windows.)

5. Use both mirrors, then look over your shoulder for any traffic coming on your side of the road.

6. When safe to do so, open the door just far enough to get out. Keep checking traffic at the same time.

7. Step out and close and lock the door as quickly as possible, always keeping an eye on the traffic, and move toward the rear of the vehicle.

If you are getting out of the car on the curb side, you must still be alert and look around. Pedestrians, bicyclists, or other obstructions may be too close for you to open the door safely. Far too often, drivers swing the door open, step out of the car, and then look to see if anything is coming. Remember to follow the steps listed on the preceding page when you get out of a car parked in a parking lot as well.

**Study your car's owner's manual. It will help you become familiar with your vehicle and tell you how to take care of it.**

## *Projects*

1. Make a list of vehicle safety devices found in the visibility, communications, and protective systems of a new car that a 10-year-old car may not have.
   (Note: You can get this information from school and public libraries, car magazines, consumer magazines, car dealers, service stations, family members, insurance agents, and police officers.)

2. If your state does not already have a law requiring the use of safety belts, write to your state representative and tell him or her why you think your state should pass such a law. Use statistics to support your argument. These could be obtained from your local library, police department, or AAA office, if there is one in your area.

# Words to Know

accelerator      high-beam      selector lever

alternator gauge      odometer      hazard or 4-way

blind spots      gear-selector quadrant      emergency flashers

fast idle      speedometer

# Stop and Review

1. Name the 7 driving systems that will help you to operate a car properly, safely, and comfortably.
2. Give two reasons for wearing safety belts. Explain how to properly adjust the shoulder strap.
3. Describe the various parts of the comfort system. How will using them properly help you to drive better?
4. What are the functions of the control-system devices?
5. Describe the correct positioning of your hands on the steering wheel. Why use that position?
6. How can you make your vehicle reach and maintain a desired speed?
7. Name the gears in an automatic transmission. Give the function of each.
8. List the 5 positions on the ignition switch.
9. What information about the car is revealed by the lights and gauges in the vehicle-check system (instrument panel)?
10. How can each part of the visibility system help you to see more of the roadway?
11. List 3 situations in which you should *not* use your high-beam headlights.
12. How can a driver use different parts of the communication system to warn other drivers of possible danger?
13. Describe the parts of the tail-light assembly.
14. List 3 antitheft devices and tell how they protect your car.
15. What predriving checks should you make before you enter your parked car?
16. What predriving checks should you make once you are inside the car?
17. What is the purpose of the head restraints? How should they be adjusted?
18. Describe the seating position that gives a driver the best control.
19. What steps should you take to secure your car when you leave it?
20. Describe the procedure for leaving the car safely.

## What if...

You plan to drive 3 friends to a football game in a town 20 miles away. Your older brother, Bob, has agreed to lend you his car for the trip. He has told you in no uncertain terms that you would have to pay for any damage. You have ridden in Bob's car before, but you have not driven it.

1. What things should you do before you start out to drive Bob's car?
2. What should you have your friends do as they get into the car?
3. What should you do when you park in the stadium parking lot?
4. Suppose you have to drive home at night. What special predriving checks should you make?

Complete the sentences by filling in the blanks with the correct terms.

cruise control    whiplash    quadrant
play    odometer    injuries
*accessory*    *park*    accelerator
*neutral*

1. The flow of fuel is controlled by the _____ .

2. When the car is in _____ , no gears are engaged.

3. _____ lets you listen to the car radio without starting the engine.

4. The total number of miles the car has been driven is shown on the _____ .

5. The main purpose of the car's protective system is to prevent _____ .

6. Head restraints help to prevent _____ .

7. _____ lets you drive at a given speed without keeping your foot on the accelerator.

8. The amount of movement that takes place before the desired action begins is called _____ .

9. A glance at the _____ tells you which gear the car is in.

10. The drive wheels are locked when the car is in _____ .

Decide whether each of the following sentences is true or false.

11. Cars with power-assisted brakes use less distance to stop than cars without power-assisted brakes.

12. You can eliminate all blind spots by correctly adjusting your mirrors.

13. Bending your arm up from the elbow signals a left turn.

14. In *neutral*, the wheels of your car are free to roll.

15. Parking lights can help you see the road ahead better.

SIGNAL AHEAD

DEPT OF TRAFFIC

# The Rules of the Road

## Chapter Objectives:

In this chapter you will learn how to:

- identify the 8 rules of the road.
- observe right-of-way rules.
- state the basic speed rule.
- define regulatory signs and give examples.
- describe warning signs and list three dangers they warn drivers about.
- state the purpose of information signs.
- describe traffic-control signals and state their purpose.
- describe pavement markings and state their purpose.

Traffic laws are rules for drivers. They allow travel with the least possible risk and help you to predict what other drivers will do. For example, you expect drivers to signal lane changes, and you expect that drivers on cross streets will not drive through red lights.

Unfortunately, you cannot depend on other highway users' obeying the law all the time. People make mistakes. So you must be sure that *you* know the traffic laws, obey them at all times, and stay alert. Be ready to compensate for the possible faults of other drivers.

Signs, signals, and markings tell drivers about rules or laws and warn them of hazards. Drivers need good information to make the right decisions. Traffic signs have standard shapes and colors that have special meanings. If drivers know these meanings, they can recognize and understand signs from far away. This gives a driver more time to react to hazards ahead. Study the signs, signals, and markings in this chapter. Learn them well so you will know them at a glance.

## Rules of the Road

Some rules of the road apply in all parts of the United States. They lead to a safer and more orderly flow of traffic. Memorize the rules listed here:

- Drive to the right of the center of the road except to pass vehicles moving in your direction.
- Pass to the right of vehicles coming toward you.
- Pass other vehicles on the left, unless you are on a road with more than one lane going in the same direction.
- Pass vehicles going in the same direction as you are only when it is safe to do so.
- Allow vehicles that are gaining on you to pass.
- If you drive slowly, keep to the right-hand lane when there is more than one lane.
- Signal when you intend to reduce speed, stop, turn, change lanes, or pass.
- Always drive at a speed that fits the existing conditions.

Directions from a police officer, a sign, a signal, or a marking on the roadway take priority over these general rules of the road. There is one more rule that you must never forget: It is always against the law to drive under the influence of alcohol or other drugs.

# Right-of-Way

Who has the right-of-way where the paths of motor vehicles, pedestrians, and bicyclists cross?

**Right-of-way** rules require one person to **yield**—that is, to let another go first. It is very important to know and obey the right-of-way laws in your state. Not knowing these laws or disobeying them can lead to accidents.

The Uniform Vehicle Code, on which most state laws are based, recommends several basic right-of-way rules that all drivers must obey. Some of these are:

- If two vehicles, at the same time, come to or enter an intersection not controlled by a traffic sign or signal light, the driver on the left shall yield to the driver on his or her right.

- Drivers approaching an intersection must yield to vehicles already in the intersection.

- Drivers shall yield to pedestrians crossing legally at intersections or at marked crosswalks between intersections and to blind pedestrians no matter where they cross.

- A driver who intends to turn left shall yield the right-of-way to vehicles coming the other way if they

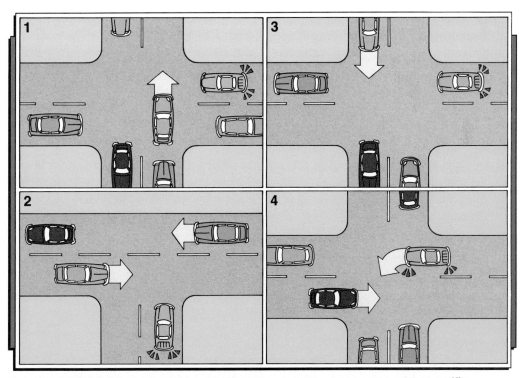

**You must yield right-of-way: (1) to vehicles already in the intersection, (2) to traffic on the main thoroughfare, (3) to vehicles on your right, (4) before turning.**

are so close that they are an immediate hazard.

- A vehicle coming out of a driveway or an alley shall yield the right-of-way to vehicles on the street and to pedestrians.

- When moving to the left or right into a lane being used by other drivers, a driver must yield to any vehicle that is passing or is so close that it presents a hazard.

- Drivers traveling in either direction on a non-divided highway with a school bus must stop when the school bus stops, with its red lights flashing, to pick up or drop off children.

- Drivers must pull to the right and come to a stop or otherwise provide a clear path of travel when being followed by an emergency vehicle that has its lights flashing or its siren on.

## Speed Limits

Some states have fixed (or absolute) speed limits to guide drivers. Other states have flexible limits. Since speed-limit signs cannot be changed easily when there are changes in the road, the traffic, or the weather, think of posted speed limits as the maximum speed in the best of conditions.

**Fixed Speed Limits** Fixed limits set the maximum or "absolute" speed. You may not exceed a posted speed limit for any reason, or you may be arrested and made to pay a penalty. You could also be penalized for driving so far below the posted

You must yield the right-of-way to emergency vehicles. When you see flashing red lights or hear a siren, move to the far right of the road, stopping if necessary to make way.

**Maximum/minimum speed-limit signs are used on high-speed roads. They serve to keep the flow of traffic moving smoothly.**

speed limit that you cause traffic congestion or back-up. Under bad road conditions, though, you may drive below the fixed speed limit for the sake of safety.

States that use fixed speed limits usually do so for these reasons:

- The limits can be set by traffic engineers, using scientific research on vehicle cornering abilities and varied weather conditions, to best fit road, visibility, and traffic conditions in that area.

- It is easier to enforce fixed limits.

**Flexible Speed Limits** Flexible (or *prima facie*) speed limits are based on the idea that no one speed is best under all conditions. The posted speed is the speed that is recommended under ideal conditions. A reasonable maximum speed depends on the type and condition of the road and on such things as the traffic, weather, and light. Drivers who are charged with driving over the posted

limit can use the defense that their speed was not too fast for existing conditions. The court must then decide if the driver is right. Of course, no driver may legally exceed 55 mph, which the federal government has established as the highest allowable speed limit.

A driver can be arrested for speeding even if he or she is driving slower than the posted limit. The officer who makes the arrest must show the court that the driver was driving too fast for the existing conditions. For example, the road may have been icy or traffic may have been heavy.

With a flexible speed limit, you can also be arrested for driving too slowly. In this case, the officer must show that the speed was so slow as to cause danger to other drivers.

**The Basic Speed Rule** Nearly all states have put some version of the basic speed rule in their traffic laws. This rule states: "Always drive at a speed that is reasonable and proper

## Facts About Speed

Many people think that too much speed is the greatest cause of accidents. While others may disagree, there are some facts about speed that cannot be argued.

- The higher the speed, the less time the driver has to spot hazards and take action.
- The higher the speed, the greater the time and distance it takes to stop a vehicle.
- The higher the speed, the greater the chance the car will skid or roll over on a turn.
- The higher the speed, the greater the danger if there is a blowout in one of the tires.
- The higher the speed, the greater the force of impact will be in a collision.
- The higher the speed, the greater the personal injuries and property damage in a collision.

for existing conditions." So no matter what the posted speed limit, you must select a speed that is safe. The right speed at any time is determined more by the situation than by the posted limit—fixed or flexible.

In a collision, the faster the car is moving, the greater the injury to the driver and passengers.

**Day and Night Speed Limits** Because it is hard to see in the dark, some states post different speed limits for the day and for the night. Driving at a lower speed at night gives drivers more time to search for visual clues and to spot hazards.

**Minimum Speed** Minimum speed limits are posted on most interstate highways and on some heavily traveled state and local roads. The minimum speed limit is designed to keep traffic moving and to reduce the

**When weather or visibility conditions are bad, you should always reduce your speed, regardless of the posted speed limit.**

chance of collisions between vehicles going at different speeds. But, when driving conditions are poor, you may drive slower than the minimum posted speed limit.

**Speed Zoning**  One speed limit cannot meet the conditions found on all sections of a road. So **speed zoning** is used. Surveys are made by traffic engineers, who decide what speed is best for the road under normal conditions, and signs are posted to tell drivers the speed limit in each zone. Whole sections of a highway may be zoned at one speed. Lower speed limits may be set for curves, intersections, bridges, school zones, business and residential districts, or other special areas.

## Regulatory Signs

Regulatory **signs** tell drivers what they may and may not do. They are usually a rectangular shape. Exceptions are stop signs, yield signs, and railroad crossbucks.

**Stop Sign**  The **stop** sign is always a red **octagon** (eight-sided figure) with white lettering and is found at intersections. It tells drivers to come to a **full** (complete) stop.

Stop at a stop sign before any part of your car is in the intersection or crosswalk. After your car has come to a full stop, you may go when it is safe to do so. Usually, stop signs are placed so that drivers can see them well in advance. By slowing down before you reach the stop sign, you alert cross traffic and drivers behind you that you intend to stop. This gives the drivers behind you a chance to respond gradually, and allows drivers on the cross street to pay more attention to other conflicts they may face.

At an intersection where all the streets are controlled by stop signs, the first vehicle to reach the intersection should be given the right-of-way. All of the other drivers should then take their turns.

**Yield Sign**  The yield sign is a triangle with red letters on a white background. It requires a driver to be prepared to give the right-of-way (stopping if necessary). Yield signs can be found at points where streets cross or merge.

Slowing down may give a yielding driver enough time to complete a move safely. Whatever move is made, it should not break the flow of traffic in the lanes being crossed or entered. If traffic is heavy the driver must come to a full stop and wait until the move can be made without breaking through cross traffic.

**Railroad Crossings**  Railroad crossings have a number of warning devices. One is a round, yellow **warning** sign with a black RR and black X

on it. It is found several hundred feet before the railroad crossing. Another sign is a large, white X called a **crossbuck**. This is placed a few feet from the railroad tracks. A small rectangular sign just below the crossbuck shows how many tracks there are at the crossing.

Railroad crossings that get heavy train traffic may have a gate or barrier that is lowered across the road to stop cars when a train nears the crossing. A pair of red lights mounted on a post with the crossbuck will flash when the train is approaching.

Approach railroad crossings with great caution even if the lights are not flashing and the gates are not down. (The lights and gates could be broken.) If there are no lights or gates at a railroad crossing, approach it with still more caution. Look and listen for signs of an approaching train.

**Other Regulatory Signs**  There are many other kinds of regulatory signs. These include speed-limit signs, parking signs, "Wrong Way" signs, "One Way" signs, and "Do Not Enter" signs. There are also warnings against littering, unnecessary noise, and making unlawful driving maneuvers. The size and color of some signs will vary from one city or state to another. Watch carefully for signs when you drive in unfamiliar places. Not recognizing regulatory signs or failing to notice them is no excuse. You are always expected to obey them.

# International Traffic Signs

**International traffic** signs are being seen more frequently. These signs have pictures and symbols instead of words. They can be easily understood in any country.

International traffic signs use easily understandable symbols or drawings in place of words. What does this sign warn you about?

# Warning Signs

A **warning sign** is yellow and is either diamond-shaped or round, with black letters or symbols. Drivers should prepare to change their

**Parking Signs**

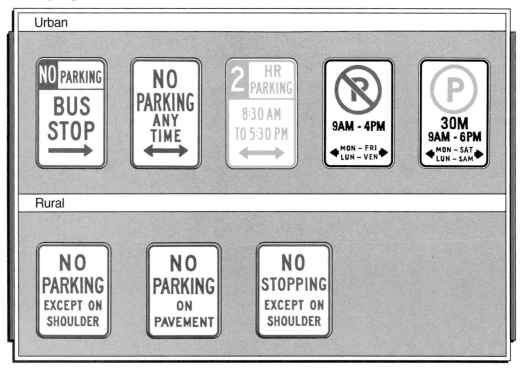

## Pedestrian-Crossing Signs

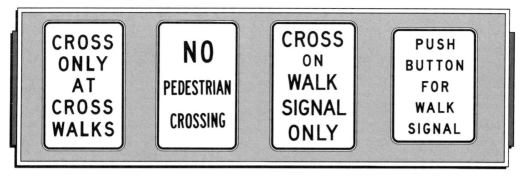

## International Traffic Signs

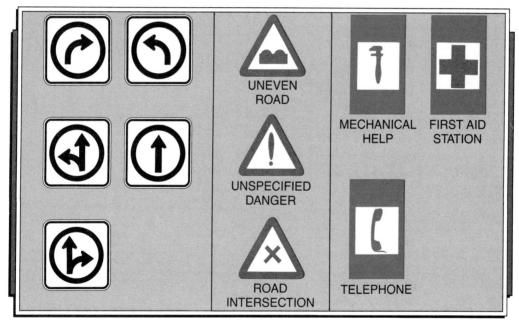

## Traffic-Control Signs

speed or position when they see a warning sign.

Some of the dangers that these signs warn drivers about are hills, curves, school or railroad crossings, intersections, merging traffic, and bad road surfaces.

**Construction** and **maintenance signs** are also considered to be warning signs. They are diamond-shaped, too, but they are orange instead of yellow. They warn drivers that road crews are working on or near the road.

**Construction Signs**

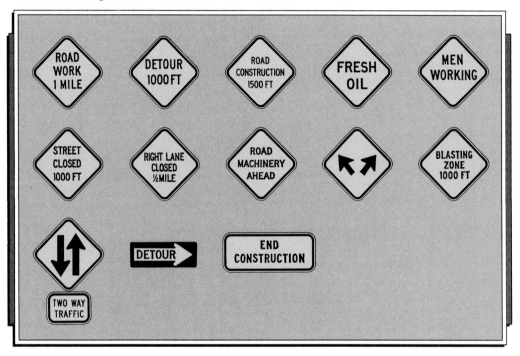

**Railroad-Crossing Signs**

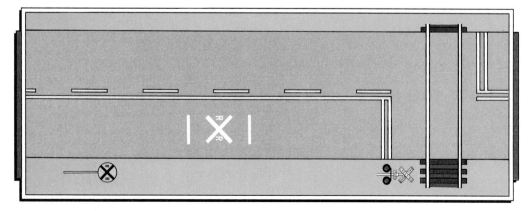

## Warning Signs

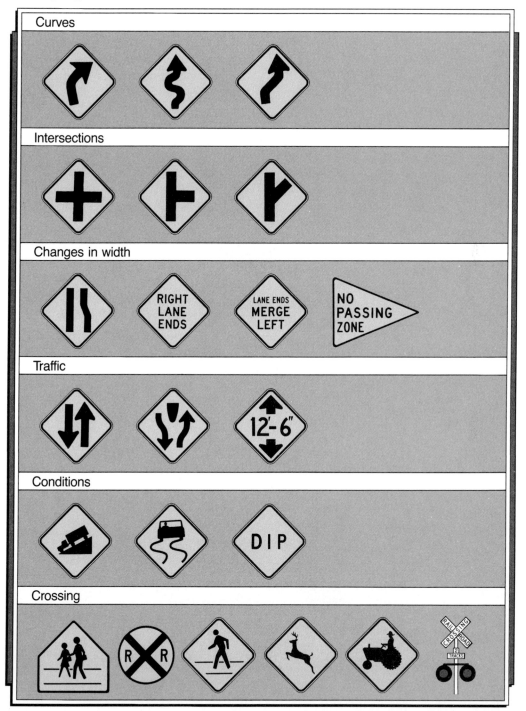

**Curves**

**Intersections**

**Changes in width**

RIGHT LANE ENDS

LANE ENDS MERGE LEFT

NO PASSING ZONE

**Traffic**

12'-6"

**Conditions**

DIP

**Crossing**

RAIL ROAD CROSSING
2 TRACKS

# Information Signs

Information signs serve as guides and direct drivers to service areas. They all have symbols that can be easily recognized. **Guide signs** include route markers and destination signs showing directions and distances. They may also show points of interest or recreation, such as scenic areas and campgrounds. **Service signs** tell drivers where to find food, gas, and rest areas.

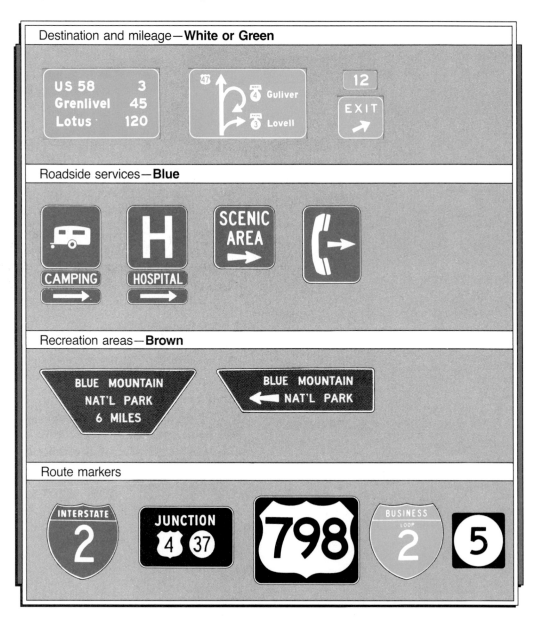

| Regulatory signs | | |
|---|---|---|
| | Triangle **Red** | Yield sign |
| | Pennant **Yellow** | No passing zone |
| | Horizontal rectangle **Black** | One way |
| | Square **Red** | Do not enter |
| | Square **White** | General regulatory signs |
| | Horizontal rectangle **Red** | Wrong way |
| | Square and horizontal rectangle **White** | General regulatory signs |
| | Vertical rectangle **White** | Speed limit |
| | Vertical rectangle **White** | General regulatory signs |
| | Octagon **Red** | Stop sign |
| | Vertical rectangle **Yellow** | Reduced speed limit |

| Warning signs | | |
|---|---|---|
| | Crossbuck **White** | Railroad crossing |
| | Horizontal rectangle **Orange** | Construction warning signs |
| | Pentagon **Yellow** | School crossing |
| | Round **Yellow** | Railroad crossing |
| | Diamond and Horizontal Rectangle **Yellow** | General warnings |
| | Diamond **Orange** | Construction warnings |

| Information signs | | |
|---|---|---|
| | Horizontal rectangle **Green** | Mileage information signs |
| | Trapezoid **Brown** | Recreation and park signs |
| | Square and horizontal rectangle **Blue** | Service signs |
| | Vertical rectangle **Blue** | Service signs |
| | Medallion **Red, white and blue** | Interstate route marker |
| | Square with two horizontal rectangles **Black and white** | Guide signs |
| | Horizontal rectangle **Green** | Guide signs |
| | Horizontal rectangle **Brown** | Recreation information |

# Traffic-Control Signals

## Red, Yellow, and Green Traffic Lights

The most common traffic signal is the three-lens red, yellow, and green light. These lights may be on posts at the corners of intersections or hung over the roadway. For quick recognition, signals have standardized positions. Vertically, the red light is on the top, the yellow in the middle, and the green at the bottom. When the signals are placed horizontally, the red is on the left, the yellow in the middle, and the green on the right. These fixed positions help color-blind drivers and pedestrians tell which light is on.

When the red lens is lit, you must stop your car. There may be a line that shows where to stop. If not, stop before the intersection. Do not go beyond the crosswalk.

When the yellow lens is lit, the red will follow very shortly, so you should proceed with caution and prepare to stop if possible. When you come to a traffic signal, think about the time and distance you need to stop. Also, keep in mind the traffic in front and in back of you. Entering an intersection on a yellow light is extremely hazardous because cross traffic may be preparing to move. But it may be safer to continue through the intersection if you cannot safely stop so that you are out of the path of cross traffic. Will you be able to brake to a stop before you reach the intersection? If you stop,

Some traffic lights have arrows as well as full round lenses. These allow cars in certain lanes to move in specific directions, which speeds the flow of traffic.

will the driver behind you crash into you? Will you be able to speed up to get through the intersection if necessary to avoid being hit? Don't wait until after the light turns yellow to make a decision whether to stop or proceed. You could find yourself entering the intersection on a red light, still trying to decide.

When the green lens is lit, you may go through the intersection if it is clear. If the light has just turned green, yield to any cross traffic or pedestrians already in the intersection. As you near a green light, note how long it has been green. If the green light has been on for some time, it is called a **stale** green light. There is a good chance the light will soon turn yellow.

**Right and Left Turn on Red**  In most places, right turns are permitted when the traffic light is red. Some areas permit a right turn on red only if a sign is posted.

Many areas also permit left turns on red lights, but generally only if the driver is turning from a one-way street onto another one-way street. (Check your state driver's guide for the rules in your state.)

When turning either left or right on a red light, drivers must first make a full stop. They must make sure that the path of travel is clear of both pedestrians and cars.

**Walk/Don't Walk Signs**  Walk/ Don't Walk signs are traffic lights for pedestrians. Pedestrians may not walk against a steady "Don't Walk" signal. They may start across the street only on a "Walk" signal. A flashing "Don't Walk" light means that there is not enough time to cross the street safely. It can also alert drivers that the green traffic-signal light is stale. At some pedestrian crosswalks, there is a button that can be pressed to change the light from red to green.

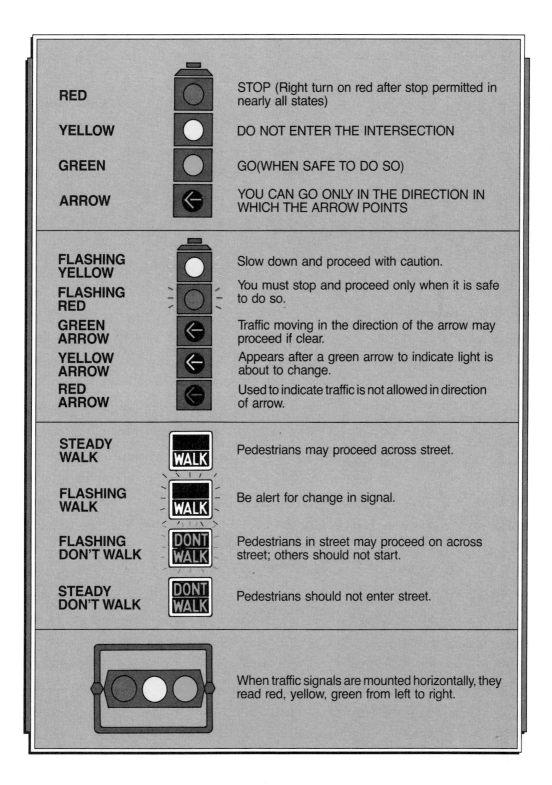

| RED | STOP (Right turn on red after stop permitted in nearly all states) |
| YELLOW | DO NOT ENTER THE INTERSECTION |
| GREEN | GO(WHEN SAFE TO DO SO) |
| ARROW | YOU CAN GO ONLY IN THE DIRECTION IN WHICH THE ARROW POINTS |

| FLASHING YELLOW | Slow down and proceed with caution. |
| FLASHING RED | You must stop and proceed only when it is safe to do so. |
| GREEN ARROW | Traffic moving in the direction of the arrow may proceed if clear. |
| YELLOW ARROW | Appears after a green arrow to indicate light is about to change. |
| RED ARROW | Used to indicate traffic is not allowed in direction of arrow. |

| STEADY WALK | Pedestrians may proceed across street. |
| FLASHING WALK | Be alert for change in signal. |
| FLASHING DON'T WALK | Pedestrians in street may proceed on across street; others should not start. |
| STEADY DON'T WALK | Pedestrians should not enter street. |

When traffic signals are mounted horizontally, they read red, yellow, green from left to right.

## Green, Yellow, and Red Arrows

Besides red, yellow, and green lights, a traffic signal may have red, yellow, and/or green arrows. A **round green lens** tells the driver to go in any direction, but a **green arrow** permits movement only in the direction shown by the arrow. A **yellow arrow** means that movement in that direction is about to end. A **red arrow prohibits** (forbids by law) movement *only* in the direction of the arrow. (Traffic in a turning lane, for example, may not turn.)

## Flashing Red Lights

A **flashing red light** means that you must come to a full stop before proceeding. It is found at hazardous intersections where there is not enough cross-street traffic to warrant a red-yellow-green traffic light.

## Flashing Yellow Lights

A **flashing yellow light** signals a possible hazard. It means slow down, check traffic, and proceed with caution (prepare to stop). The flashing yellow light may be used in many places, such as intersections, fire houses, and school zones. Determine the purpose of the light as you approach it.

## Special Lane-Control Lights

Sometimes, there are changes in the direction of traffic flow. For instance, some lanes may be used by traffic going one way in the morning and

**Lane-Use Lights**

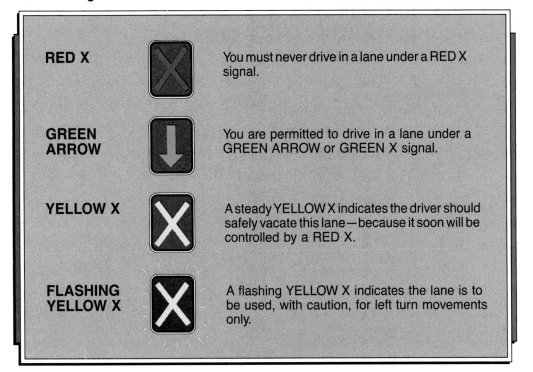

| | | |
|---|---|---|
| **RED X** | | You must never drive in a lane under a RED X signal. |
| **GREEN ARROW** | | You are permitted to drive in a lane under a GREEN ARROW or GREEN X signal. |
| **YELLOW X** | | A steady YELLOW X indicates the driver should safely vacate this lane—because it soon will be controlled by a RED X. |
| **FLASHING YELLOW X** | | A flashing YELLOW X indicates the lane is to be used, with caution, for left turn movements only. |

**Special lane-control lights may look confusing at first. You must learn to recognize their meanings at a glance.**

the other way in the evening. To help avoid the hazard of head-on collisions, signal lights may be hung over the lanes. If the signal is a **green arrow** or a **green X,** the lane is open to traffic facing the signal. If the signal is a **yellow X,** traffic flowing in the direction of the signal is about to end. If there is a **flashing yellow X,** then that lane is for left-turning vehicles only. The lane is closed to those vehicles facing a **red X** signal.

# Pavement Markings

Markings on the pavement are used alone or with signs and signals in places where a driver might not see the signs or signals.

### Lane and Center-Line Markings
The most common roadway markings are lane lines and center lines. These lines may be either yellow or white. A **solid** or **broken yellow line** divides traffic traveling in *opposite* directions. A **solid** or **broken white** line separates traffic going in the *same* direction.

A **solid white** line is used where extra caution must be taken. If a **solid yellow line** is used, you cannot legally cross it. If the line is broken, you may cross it to pass another vehicle, to change lanes, or to turn.

Double yellow broken lines indicate reversible lanes. You may cross these lines only at certain times. Special pavement markings and signs will tell you when it is not safe to pass.

**No-Passing Zone** On two-way roads, the center of the road generally is marked with a broken yellow line. However, on the approach to the crest of a hill or on a curve, a solid line usually will appear on one side of the broken yellow center line. When the solid line is on your side of the center line, you may not cross it. The line shows that the car is coming to a potentially hazardous spot or that the field of vision is limited. Drivers whose cars are traveling with the broken line on the side near them

## Special Pavement Markings

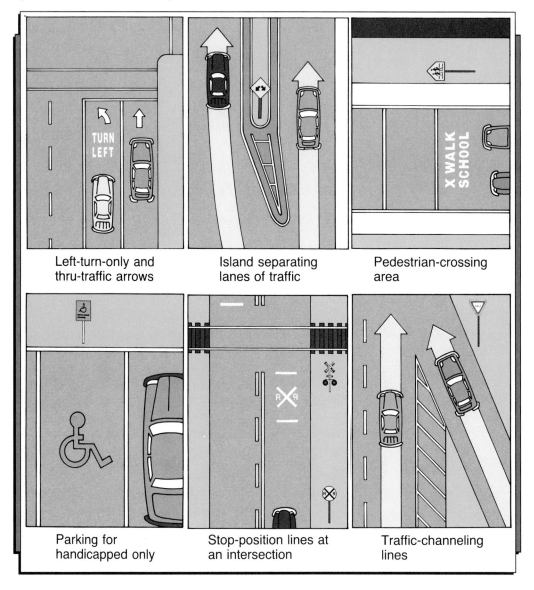

Left-turn-only and thru-traffic arrows

Island separating lanes of traffic

Pedestrian-crossing area

Parking for handicapped only

Stop-position lines at an intersection

Traffic-channeling lines

may pass with caution. If there is a double solid yellow line, passing is not allowed in either direction.

Many highways have solid white **edge lines.** These are used to mark the outside edge of the outermost lanes. Edge lines help drivers stay in position in the lane, particularly when visibility is poor.

### Special Pavement Markings
Traffic regulations are sometimes painted on the surface of the road. Examples are: "Left Turn Only,"

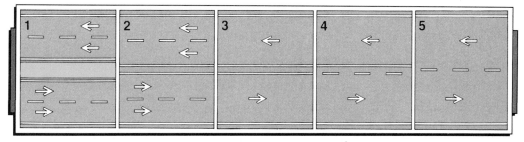

(1) Divided highway with median (2) Four-lane highway, no median (3) No passing in either direction (4) Only driver on right may pass (5) Traffic traveling in opposite directions

"Right Turn Only," and "Thru Traffic." With these words, there may also be painted arrows, signs, or signals. The letters RR painted on the surface of a road are often used along with other signs and signals to warn drivers of a railroad crossing.

Heavy white lines are used with stop signs or traffic lights to show where vehicles should stop. They also mark pedestrian crosswalks, which sometimes have perpendicular or diagonal lines painted on them to make them easier to see.

Diagonal lines, or "zebra" lines, are often used to mark fixed obstructions, such as traffic islands and lane barriers. Once in a while, they are used to mark no-passing zones. Do not drive or park in places marked with diagonal lines.

Sometimes drivers moving in either direction must use the same lane for left turns. Never enter a **shared left turn lane** too soon, be sure to watch for other cars turning into this lane, and do not use it for anything but turns.

## *Projects*

1. Interview a police officer. Ask what methods he or she uses to enforce speed laws. Is enforcement stricter in some places than in others? If so, why? What are the main problems the officer must face in enforcing speed limits? Report your findings to the class, and add some conclusions of your own.

2. Watch traffic at an intersection that has a traffic light. How many drivers go through the intersection when the light is yellow? How often do waiting drivers "jump" the light by moving into the intersection before the light turns from red to green? What hazards do these drivers cause for others? Tell your class what you find.

## Words to Know

construction signs
crossbuck
do-not-enter signs
guide signs
information signs
international traffic
  signs

maintenance
  signs
octagon
one-way sign
prohibits
regulatory signs

service signs
stop signs
walk/don't walk signs
warning signs
wrong-way signs
yield signs

## Stop and Review

1. List the 8 basic rules of the road. Why must these basic rules be the same throughout the United States?
2. List 8 basic right-of-way rules.
3. Describe 3 situations involving right-of-way conflicts. How should each of the conflicts be resolved?
4. List 2 reasons for using fixed speed limits.
5. When could a driver be stopped for speeding even when driving at or below the posted speed limit? What hazards can such a driver cause for other highway users?
6. What is the basic speed rule?
7. Why is excessive speed a factor in many traffic accidents?
8. What does a reasonable maximum speed depend on? Why do some states use fixed and flexible speed limits?
9. What is the purpose of minimum speed limits?
10. Explain how traffic signs, sig-nals, and roadway markings are useful to both drivers and pedestrians.
11. What is the purpose of regulatory signs?
12. What are the shapes and colors of stop and yield signs? How must drivers respond to each?
13. Who has the right-of-way at an intersection where all the streets have stop signs?
14. What is the main advantage of international traffic signs?
15. What do warning signs look like? Give 3 examples of dangers they warn drivers about.
16. What is the purpose of information signs?
17. Describe the most common traffic signal.
18. Describe the purpose of red, green, and yellow arrows.
19. What are the most common roadway markings?
20. What are some clues that warn you of a no-passing zone on a two-way road?

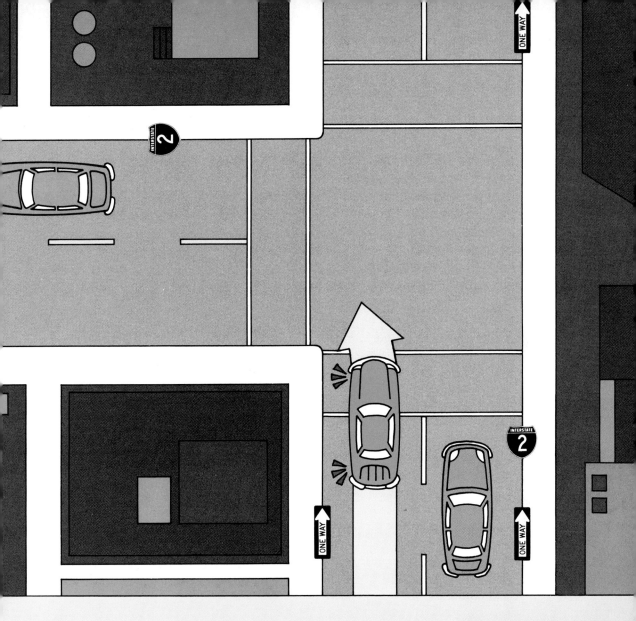

You missed the highway bypass and are on the business route going into a town. Ahead is an intersection with a flashing red light. No cars are close on the cross street.

1. What will you do? Why?

Business-route traffic has been turning through a series of one-way streets. You have moved into the left lane to make a left turn, following route signs. The street onto which you are turning has a broken yellow line down the middle.

2. What will you do? Why?

# CHAPTER 3 TEST

Complete the sentences by filling in the blanks with the correct terms.

stale    warning sign   yield   regulatory    yellow
55 mph   guide        red    X        crosswalks

1. Right-of-way rules require that one person _____ .

2. The federal government has established _____ as the highest allowable speed limit.

3. _____ signs tell drivers what they may and may not do.

4. A _____ is yellow and alerts drivers that they should be prepared to change speed or position.

5. Route markers and destination signs are examples of _____ signs.

6. One sign that warns you of a railroad crossing is a large, white _____ called a crossbuck.

7. A light that has been green for a while is called a _____ green light.

8. You cannot legally cross a solid _____ line.

9. Flashing _____ lights are a signal to come to a full stop before proceeding.

10. Heavy white lines show where vehicles should stop and also mark pedestrian _____ .

---

Select the one best answer to each of the following questions.

11. Which of the following take priority over rules of the road?
(a) a signal   (b) a sign   (c) a marking on the road   (d) all of these

12. Which is *not* a rule of the road?
(a) Signal when you intend to turn.   (b) Pass to the right of vehicles coming toward you.   (c) *Prima facie* speed limits are to be observed at all times.   (d) Allow vehicles that are gaining on you to pass.

13. Which of the following is true?
(a) You must always drive at a speed that is reasonable and proper for existing conditions. (b) All states have 2 speed limits, one for day and one for night.
(c) It is impossible to drive too slowly.   (d) Some states have posted speed limits higher than 55 miles per hour.

14. A yield sign:
(a) requires that drivers come to a full stop.   (b) has white letters on a red background.   (c) requires that drivers be prepared to give the right-of-way.   (d) is usually found at the beginning of a dead-end street.

15. A steady yellow light means:
(a) you should proceed with caution and be ready to stop if necessary and possible.   (b) you must stop your car.   (c) you may make a left turn.   (d) it is a signal for pedestrians to proceed.

# Basic Vehicle Control

## Chapter Objectives:

In this chapter you will learn how to:

■ start your car.

■ execute driving procedures required for the safe operation of your car.

■ drive a car with a manual-shift transmission.

## Starting the Engine

When you have done all the pre-driving checks both outside and inside your car, and you are ready to start the engine and prepare to move, it is again important to get in the habit of following a set way of doing things.

In a car with an automatic transmission, follow these steps:

1. Make sure the gear selector lever is in the *park* position.

2. Make sure the parking brake is set.

3. In general, if the engine is cold, set the automatic choke by

pressing the accelerator to the floor and then releasing it. (Check owner's manual for correct procedure in your car.)

4. Turn the key to the *on* position and check the gauges.

5. Place your right foot on the ac-

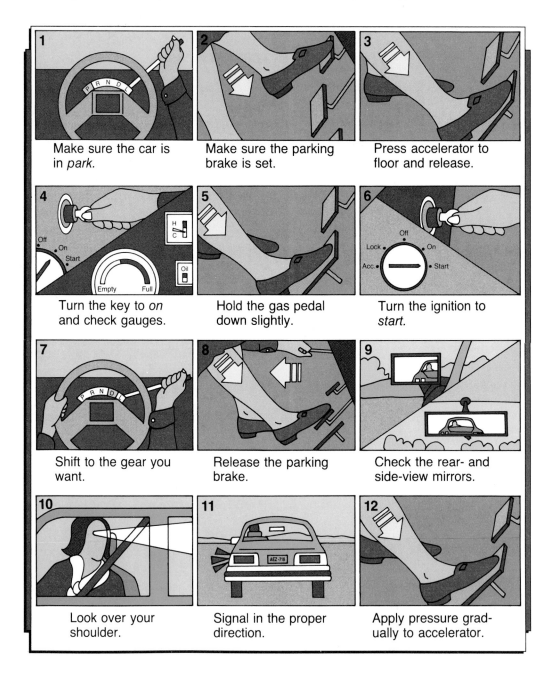

1. Make sure the car is in *park*.

2. Make sure the parking brake is set.

3. Press accelerator to floor and release.

4. Turn the key to *on* and check gauges.

5. Hold the gas pedal down slightly.

6. Turn the ignition to *start*.

7. Shift to the gear you want.

8. Release the parking brake.

9. Check the rear- and side-view mirrors.

10. Look over your shoulder.

11. Signal in the proper direction.

12. Apply pressure gradually to accelerator.

celerator and hold it down slightly.

6. Turn ignition switch to *start,* let go of the key when the engine starts, and let up on the gas pedal. Let the engine **idle** (run in *park* gear) for a few seconds.

7. With your left hand, grasp the steering wheel. Decide which way you will move. With your right hand, shift the gear selector lever to *drive* or *reverse.*

8. Take your right foot off the accelerator and press down on the brake pedal, then release the parking brake fully.

9. Check your rear-view and side-view mirrors.

10. Look over your shoulders to check your blind spots.

11. When the way clears, signal the direction you will be moving.

12. Move your foot from the brake to the accelerator. Apply pressure gradually.

Note: See page 76 for Starting a Car with a Manual Shift.

# Acceleration

**Acceleration,** or pickup, is an increase in speed. The time it takes to accelerate from a stop or from one speed to another is called the **rate of acceleration.** Acceleration depends on engine power, transmission and differential gear ratios, friction between the drive wheels and the road surface, and the weight the engine is pulling.

The ability of cars to maintain a given speed varies. An underpowered subcompact car may not be able to hold its speed on a hill because of its small engine. Large passenger cars, especially those that have high-horsepower six- or eight-cylinder engines, or turbo-charged small engines, generally have good acceleration and can hold their speed. Other large vehicles, however, do not. Tractor-trailer rigs and interstate buses have huge engines, but they accelerate very slowly.

For the best control of the accelerator, place the sole of your right foot on the pedal, with the back of your heel on the floor at the base of the pedal. (If you sometimes wear high-heeled shoes, keep a pair of low-heeled shoes in the car to wear when you drive.) To increase speed, press the pedal gently with the sole of your foot.

Generally, it is best to accelerate gradually. Beginning drivers, especially, sometimes make errors when they increase speed quickly.

**Acceleration Rate Varies** The rate of acceleration varies with speed. As the speed of a vehicle increases, the rate of acceleration decreases, so it generally takes more time to accelerate from 45 to 55 mph than from 20 to 30 mph.

**Monitoring Your Speed** It is especially difficult for new drivers to estimate speed accurately. Learn to

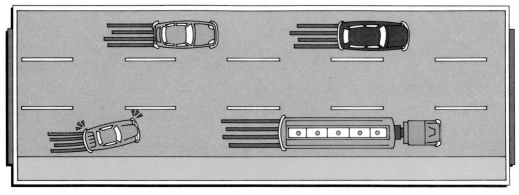

**Different types of vehicles accelerate at different rates. Tractor-trailer trucks accelerate very slowly, in spite of their huge engines.**

check your speedometer. With experience, you should become more aware of your speed without looking at the speedometer. For instance, as speed varies, you will notice a difference in the car's vibrations and in the level of sound from the tires, the wind, and the engine.

It is more difficult to estimate your speed after a large change in speed. If you have been driving at 20 to 30 mph and suddenly accelerate to 45 mph, you will feel as if you are mov-

**Monitor your speed by checking your speedometer. With experience, you will have to look at it less often.**

ing much faster. On the other hand, if you have been traveling at highway speeds and suddenly enter a 25 mph zone, you are likely to slow down less than you should because you are used to higher speeds. The only way to prevent yourself from speeding in this case is to check your speedometer.

## Braking

For smooth braking, you need a sense of timing and the right amount of pressure on the brake pedal. The amount of brake pressure needed to stop depends on the size of the vehicle, its speed, the space it has in which to move, the type of brakes it has, and the road surface. With practice, you will learn to use just the right amount of pressure.

Watch the way experienced drivers brake to a stop. You can learn when to break and how to stop more smoothly by watching what they do. For instance, at what point does the driver take his or her foot off the gas pedal and start to press on the brake? If the driver applies pressure gradually, the pressure stays constant until the car slows down almost to a stop. At this point, the driver eases up slightly on the brake pedal and then uses pressure as needed to avoid a jerky stop.

1. Check mirrors for any cars that may be following.

2. Apply smooth, constant, firm pressure to the brake pedal, easing up slightly as you come to a stop.

3. When stopping behind another car, leave enough room for you to see that car's rear tires.

4. At intersections, stop behind the crosswalk or the stop line. If there are no lines, come to a full stop when your front bumper is even with the stop sign.

5. Come to a full stop at stop signs and blinking red lights. Make sure you stop long enough to check for traffic from the left, straight ahead, and right.

The braking procedures used to stop on ice or under other emergency conditions are somewhat different. Even under such conditions, however, timing and application of controlled brake pressure remain the most critical factors.

## Tracking

**Tracking** means keeping the car moving on the path of travel you have chosen. This is done by making

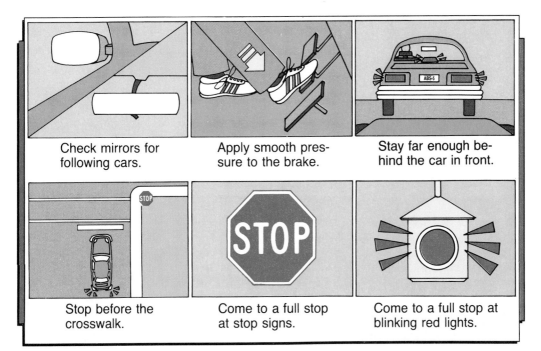

Check mirrors for following cars.

Apply smooth pressure to the brake.

Stay far enough behind the car in front.

Stop before the crosswalk.

Come to a full stop at stop signs.

Come to a full stop at blinking red lights.

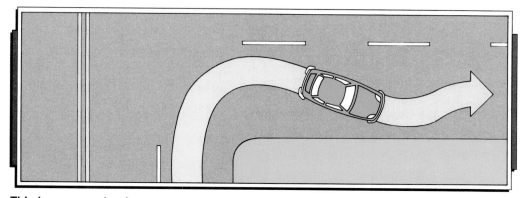

This is an example of poor recovery. The driver began to come out of the turn too late and went past the straight-ahead position.

those steering changes needed to keep on the path. New drivers often fail to see slight or gradual changes in the position of the car. They do not correct their steering in time and the car moves down the street in a series of jerks, left and right. To track smoothly, you will have to learn to steer to points well ahead on the road. Choose these points on the basis of traffic conditions and where you want to go.

**Tracking in a Straight Line** The steering adjustments you will have to make on a straight road are small but critical. If you are not aware of gradual changes in the car's position, you may let it "wander" in its lane. When you try to correct this position, you may turn the steering wheel too much. This will cause the car to move too far in the opposite direction. To track smoothly, steer to a point in the center of your path. Look well ahead as you drive. Usually, only a slight turn of the steering wheel is needed to keep you on track.

To better understand how to steer smoothly, watch and question drivers when you are riding. See how much steering-wheel movement is needed to correct or maintain a car's position in a lane. You might ask the driver such questions as: Where in the path ahead are you looking? Why did you choose this lane?

1. Remember to keep your hands in approximately the 9 o'clock and 3 o'clock position on the steering wheel.

2. Look far enough ahead in the lane in which you are driving to be able to identify steering mistakes early and correct them gradually. Steer to a point in the center of your path.

3. Check both mirrors quickly before changing speed. To check the rear-view mirror, move only your eyes. To check the side-view mirror, move your head only slightly. Do not look at either mirror for longer than 2 seconds at a time.

**Tracking on Turns** Tracking smoothly through a turn requires much more steering-wheel movement than does lane positioning. Turning a corner smoothly requires the right timing and looking in the right places.

When you steer through a turn, consider several things. First, the rear wheels do not follow the same path as the front wheels. They have a smaller turning radius, so you must allow extra space on the side of the car in the direction you are turning. You need this extra space so that your rear wheels do not hit the curb or other objects. Second, a different steering technique is required. To turn a corner, you should use **hand-over-hand steering**. This method of steering gives you the most steering control while you turn. Third, you have to recover on the turn, that is, steer back to the straight-ahead position.

1. Look beyond the turn to the point you want to reach. Identify this point before you turn.

2. Check both mirrors before turning and after you have completed your turn. It is best to check your mirrors when the wheels are straight.

3. On a sharp curve, slow down enough to maintain steering control as you enter the turn, then accelerate gently halfway through to pull the car out of it.

4. Allow enough space on the side of the car in the direction you are turning so that the rear wheels do not hit the curb.

5. Use hand-over-hand steering.

6. When the car is about halfway through the turn, keep your eyes on the point you want to reach and start to steer back to the straight-ahead position. You can do this by reversing the hand-over-hand procedure or by using the controlled slipping method.

7. Accelerate as you leave the curve.

**Hand-Over-Hand Steering** These steps describe making a right turn. To make a left turn, reverse the method.

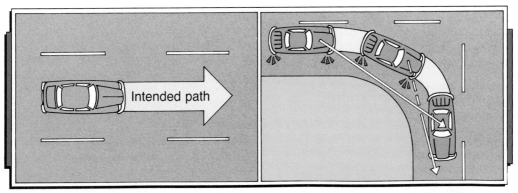

Look well ahead when you track in a straight line. Steer to a point in the center of your path.

Look beyond the turn to the point you want to reach. Use hand-over-hand steering for a smooth turn.

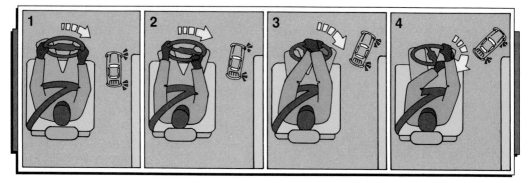

**Hand-over-hand steering for a right turn: (1)** Signal. Move your car into the correct position for turning. **(2)** With your left hand, push the steering wheel up, around, and down. Release your right hand when it reaches the bottom. **(3)** The left hand continues turning while the right hand crosses over it to the other side of the wheel. **(4)** The right hand then resumes turning as the left hand nears the bottom. Repeat as often as needed.

1. Whenever you are making a turn (not just going around a curve in the road), use your directional signal. Slow down enough to make the turn safely. Check your mirrors and ahead for pedestrians and traffic.

2. Grasp the steering wheel firmly with your left hand and push it up, around, and down to the right. Release your right hand as it reaches the bottom.

3. As you are turning with your left hand, reach across with your right hand to the other side of the wheel.

4. Continue turning the wheel with your right hand as your left hand reaches the bottom. Move your left hand back to its original 9 o'clock position and repeat these movements as often and as fast as needed to bring the car where you want it to be. Correct your steering when necessary. If you have

turned too far right, turn back to the left a little, then right again.

You can recover from a turn by reversing the hand-over-hand procedure or by using the **controlled slipping** method. To do this, let the steering wheel slip back through your hands, then tighten your hold on the wheel when the car is pointed in the direction you want to go. Controlled slipping may be difficult to learn, especially in a car with power steering or when you are moving at a very slow speed. You may want to use the hand-over-hand method until you have developed good vehicle control.

**Tracking to the Rear** Learning to track to the rear is also difficult for many new drivers. You have to learn where to look and how to control steering and speed. Always back up slowly. Steering requires less effort and is more abrupt when you go backward. You must carefully control your speed of travel and steering-wheel movement, especially if there is not much room in which to maneuver.

You cannot see a great deal through the rear window. Head restraints and passengers block parts of your view. But if you backed up while looking into the rear-view mirror, the mirror would restrict your view even more. The best way to back up is to place yourself so that you can look in the direction you wish to go. Then move the steering wheel in the direction you want the car to go. Keep in mind that when you back up, the rear of the car will move in the direction the steering wheel is turned and the front of your car will swing in the opposite direction. The two high-hazard points on the car when you turn while backing it are the rear side in the direction you are turning and the front side opposite the direction you are turning.

1. With your foot on the brake, shift into *reverse* gear.

2. Keep your foot on the brake until you are ready to move.

3. If you are backing straight, place your left hand at the top of the steering wheel and your right arm across the top of the seat. Look over your right shoulder. If you are backing to the right or left, keep your hands at 9 o'clock and 3 o'clock on the wheel and look over your shoulder in the direction you want to go.

4. Ease pressure from the brake slowly. You will need the time to monitor the rear and front of your car and correct any steering mistakes.

5. Use slight pressure on the accelerator only if needed to move the car slowly.

6. Look where you want to go so you can identify steering errors early. As when you go forward, turn the wheel in the direction you want to go. If the car wanders left, turn

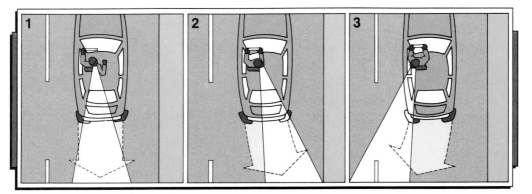

When backing, turn your head so that you can see through the rear window. (1) When backing in a straight line, brace yourself by placing your right arm and hand over the back of the seat. (2–3) When backing to the right or left, grasp the wheel in the 9- and 3-o'clock position and look over your shoulder in the direction you want to go.

**In some manual-shift cars, the gear-shift is on the steering column.**

**This gear-shift lever is on the floor.**

the wheel slightly to the right and back to center.

7. Look mostly out the rear window with alternating, quick, repeated glances to the front to make sure the car is moving in the direction you want and the front end is not about to hit anything.

8. Make sure you are looking out the rear window as you come to a complete stop. If you turn your attention to the front before you

are finished backing up, you could hit something with the rear end of the car.

## Driving a Car with a Manual Shift

Learning to drive a car with a **manual shift** (hand-operated gear shift) is not difficult after you have learned to drive a car with an automatic transmission. What will be new is learning to use the clutch pedal with the gear-shift lever and the gas pedal at the same time. When you start to drive a car with a manual shift, you will need longer gaps in traffic. This space will give you time to use the clutch smoothly, both when starting from a full stop and when shifting gears while the car is moving. To shift smoothly, you must listen to the sound and feel the vibration of the engine and check the speedometer. In short, you have more things to do when you drive a car with a manual shift.

Shifting gears **manually** (by hand) takes extra time and effort. When you drive a manual-shift car and you see a hazard ahead, you must act early. Be sure to keep your eyes up and give your full attention to driving. Give yourself extra time to shift gears up or down and change speed or lane position. Otherwise, driving a manual shift is the same as driving a car with an automatic transmission.

The transmission is made of a set of gears. The direction in which the motor vehicle moves and its speed are determined by the choice of gears. There are several gears for forward movement and one gear for reverse movement.

When you drive a car with an automatic transmission, you move a gear selector lever to the position you want. The transmission then changes gears automatically. When you drive a car with a manual shift, you must change gears by hand. You have to start in low gear and shift to higher gears as you pick up speed. You then have to shift from high to low as you slow or stop.

The gear-shift lever can be found either on the steering column or on the floor over the transmission. When and how often you shift gears depends on the size of the engine and the type of manual transmission in your car. Some cars have a three-speed transmission, with three forward gears plus a reverse gear. A car with a four-speed transmission has four forward gears and a reverse. Some cars and many trucks have more forward gears.

To shift gears when the engine is running, you push the **clutch pedal** to the floor and hold it there. This disconnects the engine from the transmission, which is in turn connected to the drive shaft, which provides the power to make the wheels turn. When the clutch pedal is up and the transmission is in gear, the engine is, in a sense, locked to the transmission and drive shaft. When the clutch is pressed to the floor, the connection is broken and you can shift from one gear to another.

The clutch pedal must be depressed to move the gear-shift lever. There are times when you may use the clutch pedal alone, such as when you stop from a very low speed. *Never try to move the shift lever without pushing down the clutch pedal.*

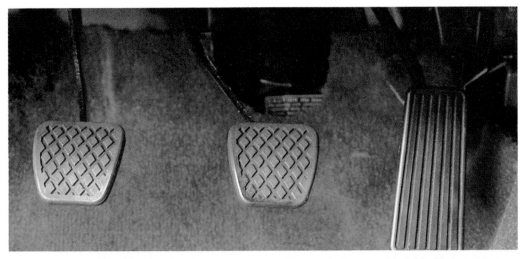

**When you want to shift gears, push the clutch pedal to the floor and hold it. You must use the clutch pedal along with the gear-shift lever.**

The secret of smooth clutch operation is to sense the **friction point**. This is the point where, as you let the clutch pedal up, the clutch and the other parts of the power train begin to work together. At this point, be very careful as you continue to let the clutch pedal up. You must now match the upward movement of the clutch with an increase in pressure on the gas pedal.

The easiest way to get a "feel" for the friction point is to start by using the reverse gear. Since *reverse* is the lowest gear, a lesser sense of feel is needed to control the friction point. Once you have developed this feel, shifting from one gear to another is quite simple.

**Getting Ready to Drive** When you are settled in the driver's seat, look down for the foot pedals. You must learn where they are so that you do not have to look to find them

as you drive. There are three pedals. The clutch pedal is on the far left. The brake pedal is in the middle. The gas pedal is the long, thin one on the right. Remember, the clutch pedal must be pressed and held to the floor each time you start the car, shift gears, or stop. You must be able to reach it and the other pedals easily. If you need pedal extenders, do not hesitate to use them.

## Starting the Engine

1. Make sure parking brake is set.

2. With your left foot, press the clutch pedal to the floor and hold it there. In general, if the engine is cold, push the accelerator pedal to the floor and let it up to set the automatic choke. Check the owner's manual for the correct procedure in your car.

3. Make sure the gear-shift lever is in *neutral*.

**Starting the Engine in a Manual-Shift Car**

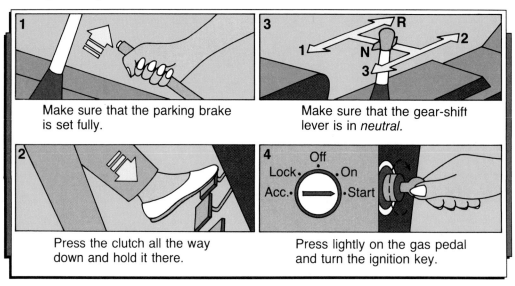

Make sure that the parking brake is set fully.

Make sure that the gear-shift lever is in *neutral*.

Press the clutch all the way down and hold it there.

Press lightly on the gas pedal and turn the ignition key.

## Putting a Manual-Shift Car in Motion

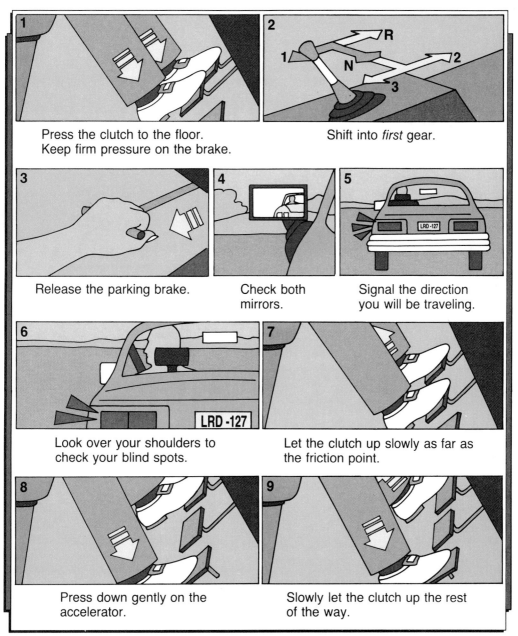

**1** Press the clutch to the floor. Keep firm pressure on the brake.

**2** Shift into *first* gear.

**3** Release the parking brake.

**4** Check both mirrors.

**5** Signal the direction you will be traveling.

**6** Look over your shoulders to check your blind spots.

**7** Let the clutch up slowly as far as the friction point.

**8** Press down gently on the accelerator.

**9** Slowly let the clutch up the rest of the way.

## Shifting to a Higher Gear

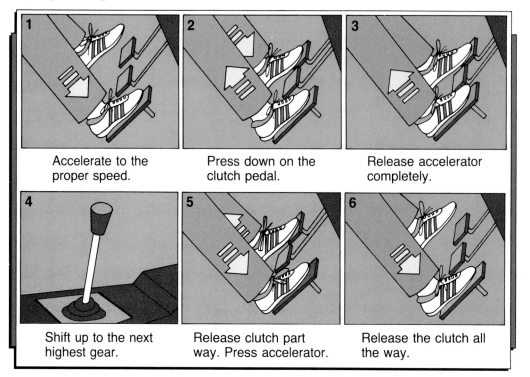

**1** Accelerate to the proper speed.

**2** Press down on the clutch pedal.

**3** Release accelerator completely.

**4** Shift up to the next highest gear.

**5** Release clutch part way. Press accelerator.

**6** Release the clutch all the way.

4. Press lightly on the accelerator and turn the ignition key to the right as far as it will go. Let go of the key as soon as you hear the engine start. Then take your feet off the accelerator and clutch pedal.

## Putting the Car in Motion

1. With your right foot, press the brake pedal. With your left foot, press the clutch pedal to the floor.

2. Shift into *first* gear.

3. Release the parking brake.

4. Check the mirrors for traffic.

5. Signal your intention to move. Look ahead through the path of travel. Do not look at your feet.

6. Look over your shoulders to check your blind spots.

7. Let the clutch pedal up slowly until it reaches the friction point, and hold it there a moment.

8. Move your right foot from the brake to the accelerator and press down gently.

9. At the same time, slowly let the clutch pedal up all the way.

If the car jerks forward, you have made one of two errors: either you have not let up the clutch pedal the right way or your right foot is bouncing on the gas pedal. In either case, press the clutch pedal to the floor.

Again, bring the clutch pedal up as far as the friction point and press on the gas pedal. Practice letting the clutch pedal up to the friction point until you can make the car move smoothly. If you feed too little gas to the engine, the car will stall and you will have to start again. If you feed too much gas to the engine, it will "race." This can damage the clutch and engine.

**Selecting Gears** The gear positions let you choose the power and speed needed for various kinds of driving.

*Low,* or *first,* gear gives the power needed to get the car in motion. This gear can also move your car through mud, sand, water, or deep snow.

*Second* gear lets you go as fast as 15 to 25 mph, depending on the size (horsepower) of the engine and whether the car has a three-, four-, or five-speed transmission. *Second* gear can also be used to start on ice or to drive in heavy snow. This gear works to brake the car as it goes down hills, as long as the road is not slippery.

**Downshifting**

*Third* gear, in cars with a three-speed transmission, is used for all speeds over approximately 25 mph. If a vehicle has a four- or five-speed transmission and a small engine, *third* gear is used at speeds up to 30 or 40 mph.

*Fourth* gear is used for driving at speeds above 35 mph on flat roads. When driving up hills, you may have to wait until you reach 40 mph before you shift to *fourth* or *fifth* gear.

**Shifting to a Higher Gear**

1. Accelerate to the proper speed for the gear you want to be in.

2. Press in the clutch pedal.

3. Release the accelerator.

4. Shift to the next highest gear.

5. Release the clutch pedal part of the way. Wait an instant while you press the accelerator.

6. Release the clutch pedal all the way.

**Downshifting**

1. Release the accelerator and press the brake pedal.

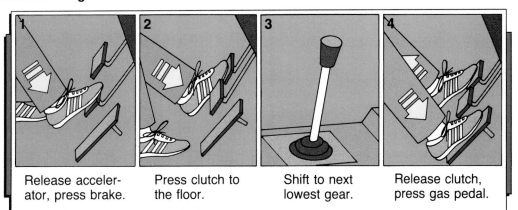

| 1 | 2 | 3 | 4 |
|---|---|---|---|
| Release accelerator, press brake. | Press clutch to the floor. | Shift to next lowest gear. | Release clutch, press gas pedal. |

**Stopping from Low Gear**

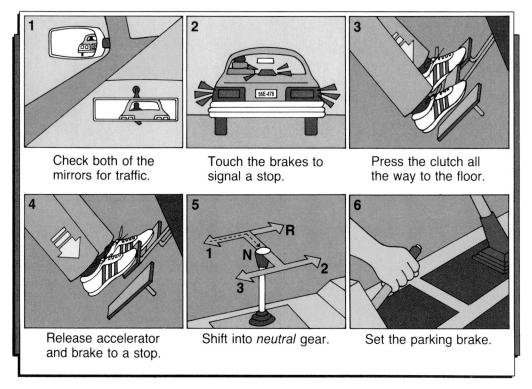

**1** Check both of the mirrors for traffic.

**2** Touch the brakes to signal a stop.

**3** Press the clutch all the way to the floor.

**4** Release accelerator and brake to a stop.

**5** Shift into *neutral* gear.

**6** Set the parking brake.

2. Press the clutch pedal to the floor.

3. Shift to the next lowest gear.

4. Release the clutch pedal to the friction point. Press down on the accelerator as necessary.

## Stopping from Low Gear

1. Check the mirrors for traffic.

2. Signal for a stop with the brake lights or by a hand signal.

3. Press the clutch pedal to the floor. Doing this will keep the car from jerking.

4. Take your foot from the accelerator and move it to the brake pedal.

Push down slowly until the car comes to a stop.

5. Keep your foot on the brake pedal and shift to *neutral*.

6. Set the parking brake. Take your foot off the brake pedal.

## The Emergency Downshift

Downshifting from *second* to *low* gear is difficult unless you are moving very slowly. You can shift down into *second* or *third* gear, though, at almost any time or speed. When you shift from *third* to *second* gear to slow your speed on a long or steep hill, you still will have to use your brakes. The braking power of your engine will not be enough.

1. Take your foot off the accelerator and press down on the brake pedal to slow your speed.

2. Press the clutch pedal to the floor.

3. Shift quickly to *second* gear.

4. Move your right foot to the accelerator. Let the clutch pedal up. Move smoothly through the friction point.

5. Adjust pressure on the accelerator as needed.

It is best to practice shifting gears, up or down, away from traffic. It is important that you learn to shift smoothly before you try to drive a manual-shift car in heavy traffic.

## Starting on an Uphill Grade

Your car may roll backward when you stop uphill. In a vehicle with an automatic transmission, you just step on the brake as needed with your left foot. When you are ready to move, step on the gas until the engine starts to pull the car forward. Then you take your foot from the brake pedal and move ahead. In a car with a manual shift, rolling back is more of a problem.

The parking brake should be set.

1. When you are ready to move, press the clutch pedal to the floor and shift into *first* gear.

2. With one hand on the steering wheel, grasp the parking brake release.

3. Let the clutch pedal up to the friction point and press gently on the accelerator.

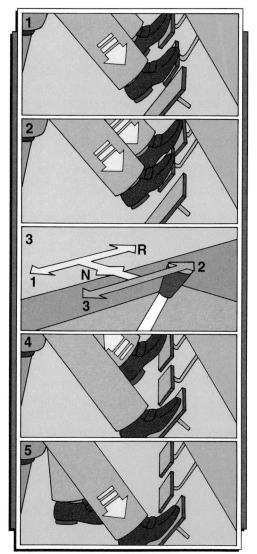

**Quick downshift: (1) Step on brake. (2) Press clutch in. (3) Shift to *second*. (4) Let clutch up. (5) Adjust pressure on accelerator.**

4. Release the parking brake when you begin to feel the car pulling forward.

5. Press on the accelerator as you let up on the clutch pedal.

6. Accelerate in *first* gear until you have gained enough speed to shift to the next gear.

*Important:* You must accelerate just enough to move the car forward the instant that the clutch pedal is at the friction point and the parking brake is let go. If you let the parking brake go too soon, the car will roll backward. If you do not feed the engine enough gas, the car will stall. If the car stalls or starts to roll back, push the brake pedal down and set the parking brake. Then shift to *neutral* and begin again.

## Parking Downgrade

Parking a car with an automatic transmission on a hill is the same as parking it on level ground. Parking a manual-shift car on a hill adds one more step to your parking procedure. Before you turn off the engine, shift into *reverse* gear and set the parking brake. Let the clutch pedal up after you turn off the ignition. The clutch and transmission, working together

**Starting on a Hill**

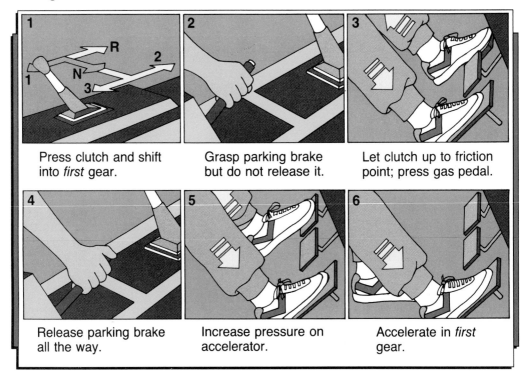

1. Press clutch and shift into *first* gear.

2. Grasp parking brake but do not release it.

3. Let clutch up to friction point; press gas pedal.

4. Release parking brake all the way.

5. Increase pressure on accelerator.

6. Accelerate in *first* gear.

## Parking on a Hill

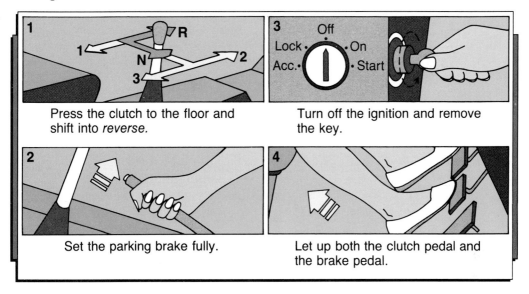

**1** Press the clutch to the floor and shift into *reverse.*

**3** Turn off the ignition and remove the key.

**2** Set the parking brake fully.

**4** Let up both the clutch pedal and the brake pedal.

in a manual-shift car, do the same thing that the *park* gear does in a car with an automatic transmission. The power train is "locked." Even if the parking brake should fail, the car will not move.

1. With your left foot pressing the clutch pedal to the floor and your right foot on the brake, shift into *reverse* gear.

2. Set the parking brake firmly.

3. Turn off the ignition and remove the key.

4. Let up both the clutch and the brake pedal.

## Projects

1. Question 3 drivers of cars that have manual transmissions and 3 drivers of cars that have automatic transmissions. Ask them to describe the advantages and disadvantages of driving their type of car. If they could make the choice again, which type of car would they select?

2. Make a checklist of things drivers should do to maintain the best control of their cars. Observe the driving of someone who you feel is a good driver. How closely does the person follow guidelines for accelerating, braking, and backing? Has the person become careless? Report your findings.

## Words to Know

acceleration          friction point          rate of acceleration
controlled slipping    manually               tracking

## Stop and Review

1. List and explain the steps you should always follow when starting your car.
2. What 4 factors affect acceleration?
3. What factors can make you aware of your car's speed without looking at the speedometer?
4. What steps should you follow to avoid braking errors?
5. List 5 factors that affect the amount of brake pressure needed to bring a vehicle to a stop.
6. What skills do you need for good tracking? What are some common tracking errors?
7. Explain why tracking on a turn is more difficult than tracking on a straight road.
8. Describe the hand-over-hand steering method.
9. Describe the controlled slipping method.
10. Why is it harder to steer when backing up?
11. What can you do to compensate for the difficulty of steering when you back up?
12. What factors make driving a car with a manual shift more complex than driving a car with an automatic transmission?
13. Why might a beginning driver need longer time gaps in traffic for maneuvers in a manual-shift car than in one with an automatic transmission?
14. Define the *friction point*.
15. What is the easiest way to get a "feel" for the friction point?
16. What 2 errors can make the car jerk forward?
17. What is *fourth* gear normally used for?
18. Name two situations when you should downshift.
19. List the steps taken to make an emergency downshift.
20. If you are stopped or parked on an uphill part of the road in a manual-shift car, what should you do to get your car moving without rolling back?

You are driving 2 friends to the shopping mall. The 3 of you are in the front seat of your parents' car. You have been catching a lot of red lights, but you have hardly noticed, thanks to the nonstop conversation in the car. Suddenly, Ann says: "Hey, please, I'm really getting bounced around. All I've got is a lap belt in the middle, remember?"

1. What have you been doing wrong? What corrections can you make?
2. Ann's seat belt does not have a shoulder harness. What could a sudden stop do?
3. What are the dangers of waiting until the last minute to brake?
4. What do you do to avoid jerky stops in a manual-shift car?

Complete the sentences by filling in the blanks with the correct terms.

hand-over-hand    *reverse*         *neutral*
decreases         downshifting      friction point
*low* or *first*  rate of acceleration  speedometer
clutch pedal

1. The time it takes to accelerate from one speed to another is called the _____ .

2. The _____ tells you how fast your car is traveling.

3. The _____ method of steering provides the most steering control on turns.

4. Every time you move the shift lever in a manual-shift car, you must first push down the _____ .

5. The clutch and the other parts of the power train begin to work together at the _____ .

6. Before you start the engine of a car with a manual transmission, make sure the shift lever is in _____ .

7. _____ gear provides power to move your car through sand, water, or deep snow.

8. When you park a car with a manual transmission on a downhill grade, you should leave it in _____ gear.

9. When you go from a higher gear to a lower gear, you are _____ .

10. As the speed of your car increases, the rate of acceleration _____ .

---

Decide whether each of the following sentences is true or false.

11. It is easiest to estimate your speed after a large change in speed.

12. In braking, timing and application of controlled brake pressure are critical factors.

13. When you make a turn, your front and rear wheel follow the same path.

14. When you back up, the rear of the car moves in the direction the steering wheel is turned.

15. The controlled slipping method is used to recover from a skid.

# Time-Space Management

## Chapter Objectives:

After reading this chapter, you will be able to:

■ select a safe position in traffic.

■ accurately judge the time-and-space gaps necessary for passing another vehicle, making turns, and braking to a stop.

To drive well in traffic, you need to position your car safely. Choose a spot that lets you see the best—and be seen the most. Learn how to use your space by deciding the amount of time you will need to maneuver the car. And learn to judge the time and space other drivers and vehicles need to perform their maneuvers. Then you will be able to answer such questions as these:

● Am I looking far enough ahead?

● Is there enough space between my car and the one ahead?

● Can I stop in time if the vehicle ahead of me stops suddenly?

● Can I avoid a crash if the vehicle ahead of me has a collision?

● Do I have time to pass the vehicle ahead?

Choose a position in traffic that will allow you to keep a safe time-and-space gap between your car and the car ahead of you.

- How much time or distance does it take to stop my car?

- Do I have time to make a turn or to cross this intersection before an oncoming car gets here?

Once you have learned to judge time and distance, you will find driving in traffic much easier and safer.

## Selecting a Position in Traffic

To avoid accidents, you need to choose a spot in traffic where you can see and be seen. You also need to allow yourself enough time to react to danger. The road and traffic conditions that endanger you the most are the ones in front of you. If you follow another vehicle too closely (**tailgate**), you may not have time and space enough to make a sudden stop or a fast change of lanes. So you need to keep a safe time-and-space gap between your car, the car ahead of you, and the car behind you.

The space gap between vehicles is called **following distance**. It is easy to convert following distances into seconds. Instead of car lengths, you use time to figure out whether you are far enough away from the car in front of or behind you. This system works whether you are driving fast or slowly.

**2-Second Following Distance**
In normal traffic and in good weather, a following distance of 2

This is a 2-second following distance, from the view of the driver and from outside the two vehicles. When the rear of the first car passes a fixed point, start to count from 1,001 to 1,002.

This is a 4-second following distance, from the view of the driver and from outside the two vehicles. When the rear of the first car passes a fixed point, start to count from 1,001 to 1,004.

seconds works well for cars. A gap of 2 seconds lets you see around the car ahead of you. It gives you time to change lanes fast if necessary. But if you are behind a van or a large truck, 2 seconds is not enough time. You cannot see as well around large vehicles, so stay at least 3 seconds behind them.

It is easy to judge a time gap of 2 seconds. Watch the vehicle directly ahead of you. Wait until the rear of that vehicle passes a fixed point, such as a tree, a sign, a post, or an overpass. Then begin counting with "one-thousand-one." The front of your car should not reach the fixed point before you have said "one-thousand-two." If it does, you are following too closely. If the road is rough or if it is raining, you should increase your following distance to at least 3 seconds. If there is ice or packed snow on the road or if it is raining hard, a gap of 5 or 6 seconds may be needed. You can practice counting seconds when you ride in a car as a passenger.

**4-Second Path of Travel** At a speed of 30 mph, you can stop in about 2 seconds, but if you are traveling at highway speeds and the road ahead is suddenly blocked by a crash, a 2-second following distance would not give you enough time to stop. Then the time needed to stop depends on your speed. If you are driving 55 mph, you will need nearly 4 seconds to stop. Also, to stay out of a collision, you would have to have an **escape route**. A 4-second path of travel gives you the time to take an escape route. Always have an escape route in mind when you choose a position in traffic. Ask yourself two questions:

- Considering road and traffic conditions, where do I want my car to be 4 seconds from now? This is called your **immediate path of travel**.

- Where would I place my car 4 seconds from now if my path of travel were suddenly blocked? This is called your **alternate path of travel**.

You can set up a 4-second path of travel by counting. Pick a point ahead of you. Then, after the car in front passes the point, count from "one-thousand-one" to "one-thousand-four." This distance you have traveled in 4 seconds is the *approximate* distance it will take to stop at speeds above 50 mph, considering perception time, reaction time, and braking time.

## Visual Lead Time

You have learned that steering is easier when you look farther ahead. You should look at least 12 seconds ahead when you drive on city streets. At 30 mph, you are moving at 44 feet per second. At this speed, with a visual lead time of 12 seconds, you

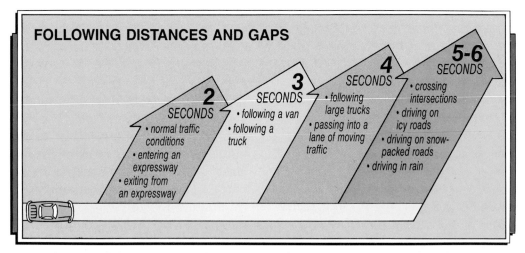

FOLLOWING DISTANCES AND GAPS

**5-6 SECONDS**
- crossing intersections
- driving on icy roads
- driving on snow-packed roads
- driving in rain

**4 SECONDS**
- following large trucks
- passing into a lane of moving traffic

**3 SECONDS**
- following a van
- following a truck

**2 SECONDS**
- normal traffic conditions
- entering an expressway
- exiting from an expressway

In certain cases, it is necessary to increase the minimum 2-second following distance.

would be searching about one block ahead. This is far enough in the city.

If you are on an expressway driving at 55 mph, you may need to look 20 to 30 seconds ahead. Such a visual lead provides the time you need to choose an immediate path of travel. It gives you time to search the areas beside the road. It allows you the time to adjust your speed or to make lane changes well in advance of any problems. And it lets you find alternate paths in an emergency.

You find the 12-second visual lead time the same way you find the 2-second following distance. Pick a point ahead of you. Start counting with "one-thousand-one" and count up to "one-thousand-twelve." If you get to the point you chose before you reach "one-thousand-twelve," you should look farther ahead. Remember, 12 seconds is a *minimum* visual lead for city driving.

## Actions to Avoid

There are two actions that often affect a driver's visual search. They are staring at a fixed point and distractions.

**Staring at a Fixed Point** Staring, no matter how far ahead, will not provide the information you need to plan a safe path of travel. It only results in a narrow visual-search pattern. Learn to **scan** the road and roadsides ahead by moving your eyes back and forth between your car and

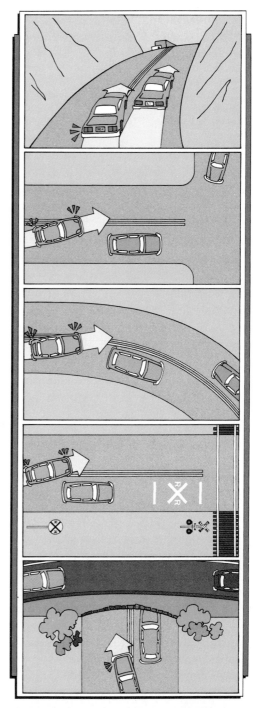

Do not pass on hills, at intersections, on curves, near railroad tracks, in tunnels.

your checkpoints. Look from one side of the roadway to the other. Search for clues that will help you select the safest and most efficient path of travel. Although the major source of problems is in front of you, you should also check to the rear. A simple rule exists for making such checks: Anytime anything in front of you indicates that you may need to adjust speed or position, check to the rear for possible conflicts.

**Distractions**   Many things may attract your attention. Unless you concentrate on driving, your visual lead may slip to as little as 3 or 4 seconds. A visual lead this short means that you are driving from crisis to crisis. The results of such visual habits can be observed when you see drivers making abrupt speed or lane changes or adjustments within their lane.

If you pass on a two-way road, make sure any car coming toward you is far enough away to allow you to pass and return to your lane.

## Judging the Time-and-Space Gap for Passing

Passing another vehicle on a two-way roadway can be dangerous. On a road that has only one lane going in each direction, you must check for cars that are coming toward you. You must also check behind, ahead, and to the side. Time and distance judgments are very critical for this type of maneuver.

When you start to pass a vehicle in front of you, any oncoming vehicle should be far enough away that it seems to be standing still. If the road is flat and straight, vehicles coming toward you will seem to be standing still when they are ½ mile or more from you.

There is another passing guide that involves counting seconds. It should take about 10 seconds to pass another car. Practice counting these seconds when you ride as a passenger. Start to count "one-thousand-one" when an oncoming car gets to the nearest point that you feel would still give you time to pass a car ahead. If you meet the oncoming car before you have reached at least "one-thousand-nine," it was too close. If you counted higher than "one-thousand-fourteen," you allowed too much time.

Waiting for too long a gap can place you in danger, too. If you do not pass when you have enough time, you may anger the driver behind you, who may try to pass both you and the car you are following. This increases the risk of collision for you and all the drivers near you.

## Judging the Time-and-Space Gap at Intersections

Up to now, you have learned to judge the time-and-space gap between cars traveling in the same or in the opposite direction. Intersections require a similar set of time-space judgments. At intersections, you must learn to judge gaps in traffic when vehicles are moving from the left and from the right of you. This is very important at intersec-

tions that have no signs or that have only yield or stop signs.

Most collisions at intersections occur when a car leaving a stop sign is struck from the right. This often happens because drivers approaching a stop sign look first to their left because that is the first lane of traffic they must cross. Drivers also tend to wait for a longer gap in traffic coming from the left than from the right. That habit places them in greater danger of being hit by a vehicle coming from the right.

From a stopped position, it usually takes about 4 seconds to cross a street that is 24 to 30 feet wide. This means that you need at least a 5- to 6-second gap in traffic from both directions in order to cross. There is no simple rule for judging intersection time gaps for all speeds. For vehicles moving at 30 mph, a time gap of 6 seconds equals about half a block.

Try to determine a 6-second time gap. Stand at a corner and pick a car coming from the right. Start at "one-thousand-one" and count as the car

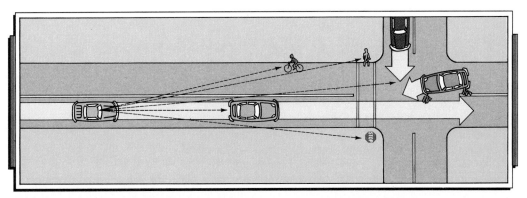

**Watch your following distance and estimate how long it will take you to reach the intersection. Look for pedestrians and bicyclists as well as other cars in the intersection.**

passes through the intersection. How far does it travel by the time you count to "one-thousand-six"? Practice this a few times at the same place. What is the average distance that cars travel in 6 seconds? Cars coming toward the intersection from the right should be this far away before you would start to drive across the street.

When you have learned to spot a checkpoint for cars coming from the right, find a point in the same way for cars coming from the left. These two points can serve as a reference for streets where speeds and traffic conditions are similar. You will need to find different checkpoints for places with different traffic patterns and speeds.

## Time Gap for a Right-Hand Turn

To safely make a right turn at an intersection, you will need a longer time gap than you would need just to cross the intersection. From a full stop, it takes about 6 seconds to turn right and get your car's speed up to 30 mph. To be safe, you need a gap of 7 to 8 seconds between you and a vehicle coming from the left. This allows the driver of that vehicle to keep a 2-second following distance once you have turned into the lane and are traveling at traffic speed.

On the open highway, traffic may be moving at up to 55 mph. It takes more time to reach the speed of traffic after you complete a turn, and you may have to increase the time gap for a right turn to 11 seconds or more. Use the method you have already learned. Pick a car that is passing through the intersection from the left. Find how far it goes in 11 seconds. That distance is the gap you will need between your car and cars coming from the left.

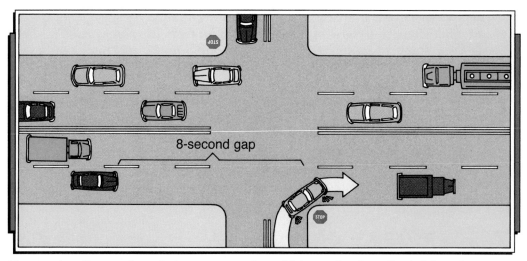

You need an 8-second gap between you and a vehicle coming from the left in order to make a right turn at an intersection. This gap will allow the vehicle behind you to keep a 2-second following distance when you are both in the same lane.

When leaving an expressway, begin to slow down in advance of the exit ramp. That way, you will not have to brake hard or suddenly when you enter the ramp.

### Time Gap for a Left-Hand Turn

A left turn is more dangerous than a right turn because you are faced with two hazards. Vehicles are moving toward you from the left and from the right. You must turn into the far lane while speeding up but while still moving at a low rate of speed. This takes time and increases the gap you need. At 30 mph you need about 9 seconds. It will take 7 seconds to turn into the far lane and come back up to speed, and 2 seconds more to make a following-distance gap between you and the vehicle that is closing in from the right.

To turn left onto a highway where traffic is moving as fast as 55 mph,

you will need a gap of 13 or 14 seconds. This gives you time to accelerate to highway speeds and allow a 2-second following distance for the vehicle behind you.

## Braking and Deceleration

Many factors influence stopping time and distance. Among them are the road surface, speed, and the condition of a car's brakes and suspension system. But too few drivers realize how big a role perception, reaction time, and braking time play.

**Braking Distance**

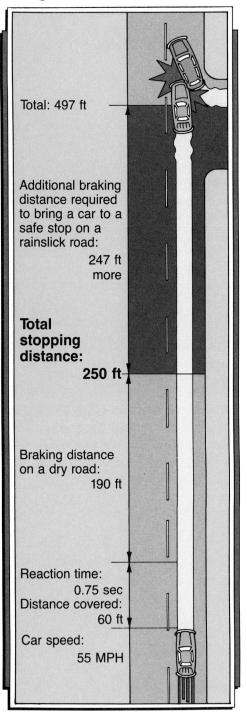

Total: 497 ft

Additional braking distance required to bring a car to a safe stop on a rainslick road:

247 ft more

**Total stopping distance:**

**250 ft**

Braking distance on a dry road:
190 ft

Reaction time:
0.75 sec
Distance covered:
60 ft

Car speed:
55 MPH

To bring a vehicle to a stop, a driver must do three things:

- Become aware of a need to stop.

- React by releasing the gas pedal and moving a foot to the brake pedal.

- Press the brake pedal, and brake the vehicle to a stop.

Each of these actions takes time: time to see (and decide), time to react, and time to brake. Time means distance. All drivers should be aware of the relationship between speed and braking distance.

- The braking-distance increase equals the square of the increase in speed. So if the speed of a vehicle is doubled, its braking distance is four times as great.

- The time needed to stop increases from approximately 2 seconds at 30 mph to nearly 4 seconds at 55 mph. But 2 to 4 seconds' time offers little room for error when the time you need to identify a hazardous situation is not known. Try to plan your immediate path of travel at least 4 seconds ahead.

**Braking to a Stop** Controlled stopping is a result of friction between the brake linings and wheel drums or wheel discs and pads. This friction slows the rotation of the wheels and tires and increases the amount of friction between the tires and the road.

There are a number of factors that determine the distance needed to

**The weight as well as the speed of a vehicle affects stopping time and distance. A truck needs more time and space to come to a stop than a small car moving at the same speed.**

stop after the brakes are applied. Among these are the area of the braking surface (the drum and brake linings) and vehicle size, weight, height, and load. The tire size, tread, and inflation, and the type of road surface also are factors.

Maximum braking occurs just before the tires start to slide on a roadway surface. At this point, the friction from the brakes and the friction between the tires and the road are nearly equal. More pressure on the brake pedal locks the wheels and causes them to skid. Locked wheels do not increase braking force. In fact, the heat that comes from the friction between the tires and the road surface melts the rubber. This lengthens the stopping distance a bit.

## Projects

1. While riding as a passenger in a car, identify alternate paths of travel. Then ask the driver where he or she would go if the road ahead were blocked. Repeat the question in several driving situations. Do you and the driver always agree?

2. Stand near an intersection that is controlled by a stop sign or a yield sign. Watch to see if the drivers who are turning or driving through the intersection allow themselves gaps in the cross traffic that are long enough. Report your findings to the class.

# Words to Know

alternate path of travel    immediate path of travel    tailgate
following distance    escape route    scan

# Stop and Review

1. What are the 2 major features of a good position in traffic?
2. Why is it important to keep an adequate time gap between your car and the vehicle ahead of you?
3. What is the space gap between vehicles called?
4. How many seconds of space should you allow when driving behind large vehicles?
5. Describe the method explained in the text for keeping a 2-second following distance.
6. In what weather conditions should you increase your following distance?
7. What is visual lead time? How can it be determined?
8. How far ahead should your visual lead time be on city streets?
9. What is a safe visual lead time for expressway driving?
10. Explain 2 actions that affect a driver's visual search.
11. What are 2 time-space guides that you should use when passing other vehicles on a two-way road?
12. How can waiting too long for a gap in traffic before passing another vehicle on a two-way road place you in danger?
13. Explain how you can judge the time gap needed when crossing an intersection.
14. Which turn requires a longer time gap: a left-hand turn or a right-hand turn? Give reasons for your answer.
15. Name 3 factors that influence stopping time and distance.
16. List the 3 things a driver must do to bring a vehicle to a stop.
17. What is the relationship between speed and braking distance? Explain.
18. What is the purpose of the 4-second path-of-travel rule?
19. List 4 factors that determine the distance needed to stop after the brakes are applied.
20. What happens when too much pressure on the brake pedal locks the wheels?

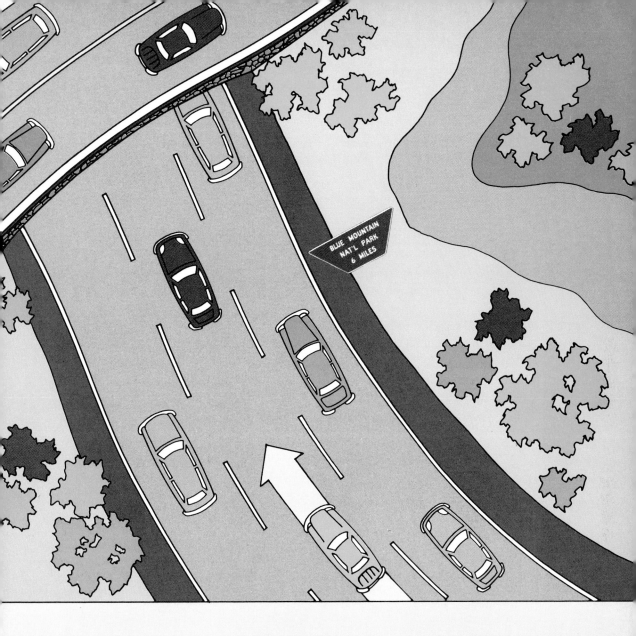

## What if...

It is threatening rain. You enter the expressway and accelerate to 55 mph. There are cars ahead of and behind you.

1. What should your following distance be? How can you check it?

2. What should your visual lead time be? Why?

3. How far ahead do you plan your immediate path of travel? Why?

4. It starts to rain. How should you adjust your following distance? Why?

# CHAPTER 5 TEST

Complete the sentences by filling in the blanks with the correct terms.

scanning   tailgating   rear   visual lead time   front
time-space   10   square   increases   2

1. The braking-distance increase equals the _____ of the increase in speed.

2. _____ decisions are a major part of safe driving.

3. The traffic conditions that endanger you the most are the ones in _____ of you.

4. Following another vehicle too closely is called _____ .

5. The distance in seconds that you look ahead when driving is called _____ .

6. In normal traffic and in good weather, a following distance of _____ seconds works well for cars.

7. Reduced traction _____ stopping distance.

8. Moving your eyes in a visual search pattern is called _____ .

9. Anytime anything in front of you indicates that you may need to adjust speed or position, check to the _____ for possible conflicts.

10. It should take about _____ seconds to pass another car.

---

Select the one best answer to each of the following questions.

11. Which of the following influences stopping time and distance?
    (a) road surface   (b) speed
    (c) condition of a car's brakes
    (d) all of the above

12. Locked wheels when braking:
    (a) increase braking force.
    (b) lengthen stopping distance.
    (c) equalize the friction between the tires and the road.   (d) provide maximum braking.

13. A following distance of 2 seconds does not give you time to:
    (a) change lanes.   (b) stop from a speed of 30 mph.   (c) see around the car in front of you.   (d) see around large vehicles in front of you.

14. When you drive on city streets, you should look ahead at least:
    (a) 6 seconds.   (b) 12 seconds.
    (c) 20 seconds.   (d) 2 seconds.

15. When you make a right turn at an intersection, you:
    (a) need less time than you would need to cross the intersection.
    (b) need a longer time than you would need just to cross an intersection.   (c) do not need to use your turn signal.   (d) should turn from the left lane.

# Lateral Maneuvers

## Chapter Objectives:

In this chapter you will learn how to:

■ enter a roadway from the curb.

■ change lanes on the highway.

■ pass another vehicle on the highway.

■ enter onto and exit from a highway.

■ parallel park.

A sideways motion, either to the front or to the rear, is called a **lateral maneuver**. Lateral maneuvers can be within, into, out of, or across a traffic lane. They are basic to driving. You may adjust your position by moving left or right within a lane. You may also move to another lane. These are the most common lateral maneuvers. Specific examples of lateral maneuvers are steering to the curb, entering a roadway from the curb, changing lanes, passing, merging onto or exiting from an express-

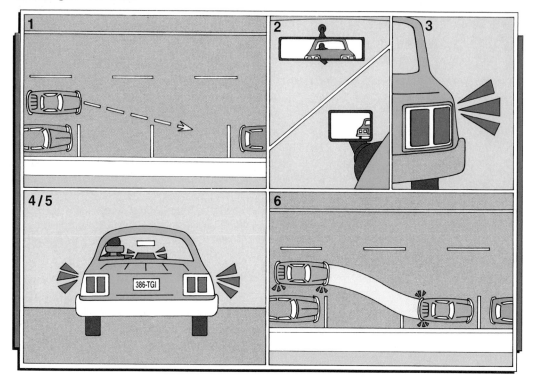

way, and parallel parking. When making a lateral maneuver, give special attention to:

- the traffic conditions around your car.
- speed adjustment, either through the use of the gas pedal or the brake.
- the amount of steering that has to be done.
- the time and space needed to enter or leave traffic.

## Steering to the Curb

1. Move into the proper lane well in advance. Make sure your in-tended path of travel is clear of any type of obstruction.

2. Check in both mirrors for any traffic behind you.

3. Signal your intentions to move right or left.

4. Pump the brakes lightly several times as a signal to drivers behind you.

5. Apply gradual pressure on the brakes to reduce speed.

6. Steer out of the traffic lane to where you want to go, and apply the brakes as needed to stop the car.

You must use great care if you choose a parking space just past an

**When you enter a roadway from a parallel parking space, check the posted speed limit. Always check traffic to be sure you have enough room to make the maneuver.**

intersection. If you signal as you approach the intersection, you could lead other drivers to think that you intend to turn. A car could pull out into your path as you go straight ahead. If other cars are near the intersection, just place your car in the correct lane and slow down. Do not use your turn signals until your car has entered the intersection.

## Entering a Roadway from the Curb

The simplest situation in which to move from the curb is shown in photograph A, above. The driver is about to enter a roadway where there is little or no traffic. The speed limit is 25 mph. Entering the roadway requires

When changing lanes on a highway, you need a 4-second gap in the traffic to safely enter the other lane.

only slight steering. There is room to accelerate and very little traffic.

In B, a truck is parked right behind the car. The driver must move forward in order to check traffic to the side and rear. Is there enough space to enter the roadway? The speed limit is 30 mph, but there is ample room to pick up speed. Little steering is needed because of the clear path ahead.

Situation C requires more accurate time and space judgments. The cars parked in front and behind limit the space in which the driver can maneuver. The speed limit is 45 mph. To allow the driver time to clear the car parked ahead, the gap in traffic must be much greater and

time is needed to accelerate to the speed of the traffic in the lane.

## Lateral Highway Maneuvers

On a multiple-lane highway, the same checks are required for positioning within a lane, lane changing, and passing.

Assume that there is something close to the roadside 12 seconds ahead, or that a slow-moving vehicle is blocking your view. What should you do if you decide to change lanes? First, you must make some checks. Will other vehicles, either behind or in front of you, be making the same move? Is there anything now in, or going into, the lane you plan to enter? Will other vehicles beside you try to enter your lane as you try to move out of it? Is anything approaching you fast from the rear?

As you plan your move, keep at least a 2-second following distance. Plan at least a 4-second path ahead. Check your mirrors and signal your intention to move. Just before you move, check over your shoulder in the direction in which you want to go. Is there a 4-second gap in traffic in the lane you want to enter? (A 4-second gap will give both you and the car behind you in the new lane a 2-second following distance.) If everything is all right, increase your speed a bit and steer into the new lane.

If you want to go back to your lane after you pass the other vehicle, repeat all the checks and signals. Before you move back into the lane, look into your inside rear-view mirror to make sure you can see both headlights of the vehicle you just passed.

## Changing Lanes on the Highway

1. Check the path ahead in the lane you are in and in the lane you want to enter. Make sure no other vehicles are signaling to move into your lane.

2. Check the mirrors to see that there is enough time and space to perform the maneuver.

3. If the way is clear, signal your intent to move right or left.

4. Check over your shoulder for cars in your blind spot.

5. Adjust speed up or down as needed.

6. Move only when you have the time and space to do so.

7. Gradually steer into the proper lane. Make sure your directional signal is off.

## Passing

1. Check the path ahead in the lane you are in and in the lane you want to enter. Make sure no other

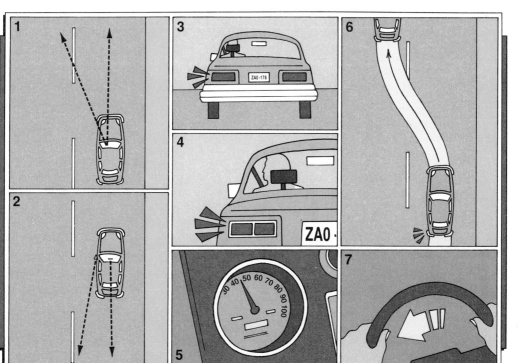

Changing lanes on the highway: (1) Check the path ahead. (2) Check the mirrors. (3) Signal. (4) Look over your shoulder. (5) Adjust speed. (6) Begin move. (7) Steer into proper lane.

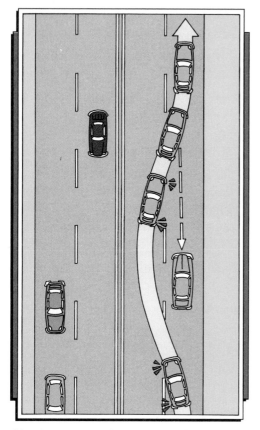

**Check your rear-view mirror before re-entering the right lane.**

7. Gradually steer into the proper lane. Make sure your directional signal is off.

8. Accelerate firmly. On a road with one lane in each direction, keep checking for oncoming traffic. Make sure your intended path is clear.

9. Check your rear-view mirror quickly. When you can see both headlights of the vehicle you have just passed, steer gradually back into the right lane.

## Entering and Leaving an Expressway

A lateral maneuver is harder to make when you are trying to enter or trying to leave an expressway. Often, drivers are slowing to exit as other drivers are speeding up to enter. The two groups of vehicles must cross in what is known as a **weaving lane** (the lane that leads to and from the expressway).

On some expressways, you will find a very short acceleration lane, or no lane at all. Signs will tell you to stop or yield to through traffic. In this case, you need a much longer gap in traffic and more time to accelerate to the speed of the traffic on the expressway.

In a few cases, the acceleration lane merges into the far left lane of an expressway. This lane usually is used by high-speed traffic. Here you

vehicles are signaling to move into your lane.

2. Check the mirrors to see that there is enough time and space to perform the maneuver.

3. If the way is clear, signal your intent to move to the left.

4. Check over your shoulder for cars in your blind spot.

5. Adjust speed up or down as needed.

6. Move only when you have the time and space to do so.

have to make quick, accurate time and distance judgments. You have to make early decisions and accelerate quickly to bring the car smoothly into the lane of traffic.

## Expressway Entry

1. Keep a 2-second following distance between your car and any vehicle ahead of you on the entrance ramp. If the driver ahead of you seems unsure, increase the distance. Be ready to stop.

2. Signal your intention to enter the expressway.

3. Use the acceleration lane to move up to expressway speed. Use quick, repeated glances in your mirror and to the side. Look for a gap in traffic sufficient to allow you to merge.

4. When you have identified a safe gap in the flow of traffic, accelerate and steer into the traffic lane.

5. Cancel your signal and continue to keep a safe following distance.

**Expressway Exit** To exit from an expressway, you have to plan ahead. Will you exit from the left or right side of the road? Can you make a simple lane change to a **deceleration** (slowing) lane and then reduce speed for the exit ramp? Will you have to pass through a weaving lane?

To help you to make these decisions, guide signs are placed about 1 mile ahead of the exits in urban areas, and 1 and 2 miles ahead of the exits in rural areas. They show if the exit is on the left or the right side of the expressway and also tell how many exit lanes there are. This should give you time to make changes in position and speed.

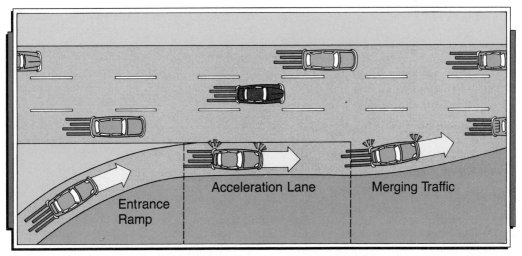

Use the acceleration lane to bring your speed up to that of the traffic flow. Check for a gap into which you can merge. Keep checking to the side and over your shoulder. You must merge into the lane of traffic before you reach the end of the acceleration lane.

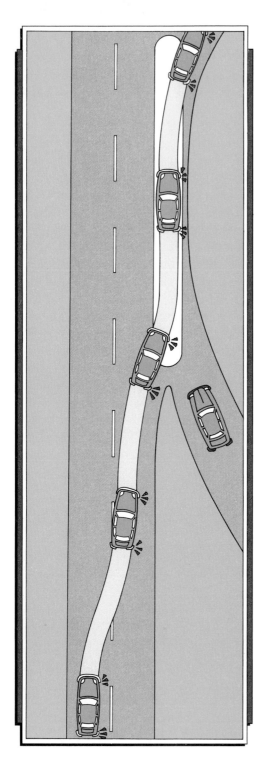

If you exit at a direct connection with a crossroad, just make the lane changes. Be sure you change only one lane at a time, though.

An exit through a weaving area is a more difficult task. You are trying to move into the weaving lane and slow down to exit. At the same time, drivers in the acceleration lane are entering the weaving lane and trying to speed up to join the traffic lane.

1. Use road signs to help you decide where you want to exit, and position your car in the proper lane well in advance.

2. Check traffic ahead and behind as you prepare for the exit.

3. Signal a right or left turn off the expressway.

4. If the deceleration lane is a weaving area, check your mirrors and look over your shoulder for a gap in the traffic on the entrance ramp. Adjust your speed and steer into that gap in the weaving lane. Remember to stay 2 seconds behind any vehicle in front of you.

5. Complete your merge into the deceleration lane. Move onto the exit ramp, and slow to the recommended speed.

## Parallel Parking

As you look for a parking space, keep an eye on the traffic around you. By concentrating only on finding a parking space, you could fail to see sudden changes in traffic. You could also forget to check or signal while making a maneuver.

Parallel parking may seem difficult at first, and it will require practice. Develop your own good parking procedure. Learn to judge if a space is large enough. You need at least 5 feet in addition to the length of your car. Look for restricting signs, fire hydrants, or obstructions such as broken glass close to the curb. As you become experienced, continue to use the check positions described in the Behind-the-Wheel Guide below. Remember to look forward with repeated glances because the front end of your car will swing out into traffic as you back into place. Learn to turn the steering wheel while you move the car slowly. Avoid turning the wheel when the car is not moving.

With practice, you will learn how fast you have to turn the wheel in order to arrive at each *check* position. If you start to park and find it is not working correctly, pull out of the space and start again.

The Behind-the-Wheel Guide below describes parallel parking on the right. If you park at the left-hand curb of a one-way street, follow the same steps but reverse the left and right directions.

1. Approach the parking space in the proper lane.

2. Check traffic behind you as soon as you have found a parking space. Signal your intention to stop. Move over parallel to car B, leaving about 3 feet between cars. Stop when the center door post of your car is even with the center door post of car B. This is your first *check* position.

3. Make sure it is safe to back up. With your foot on the brake, shift into *reverse*. Back up very slowly, steering sharply to the right until the car is at about a 45° angle to the curb. Your center door post should be even with the rear bumper of car B. This is your second *check* position. (The inside headlight of car C should now be visible in your outside mirror.)

4. Start backing slowly again, straightening your front wheels. Continue backing up until your right front bumper is even with the left rear bumper of car B. This is your third *check* position. Stop here. The right rear wheel of your car should be about a foot from the curb.

5. Start backing up slowly again, turning the wheel rapidly to the left as far as it will go. Keep looking to the rear and stop before making contact with the front bumper of car C.

6. With your foot on the brake, shift into *drive* (*first* gear in a manual-shift car). Move forward very slowly, straightening the wheels, and stop when your car is centered between cars B and C.

7. Shift to *park* (*reverse* in a manual-shift car). Set the parking brake.

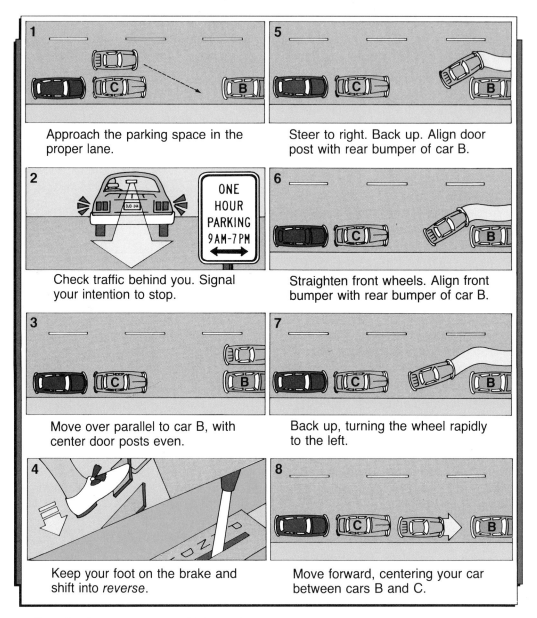

**1** Approach the parking space in the proper lane.

**2** Check traffic behind you. Signal your intention to stop.

ONE HOUR PARKING 9AM-7PM

**3** Move over parallel to car B, with center door posts even.

**4** Keep your foot on the brake and shift into *reverse*.

**5** Steer to right. Back up. Align door post with rear bumper of car B.

**6** Straighten front wheels. Align front bumper with rear bumper of car B.

**7** Back up, turning the wheel rapidly to the left.

**8** Move forward, centering your car between cars B and C.

The final step in parallel parking—turning the steering wheel to block the tire against the curb or toward the side of the road—is a safety measure, required by law in some states. This step may stop the car from rolling downhill.

### Exiting from a Parallel Parking Space

1. In preparing to leave, place your foot on the brake pedal, shift into *reverse* (if not already in that gear), and back up slowly.

## Parking on a Hill

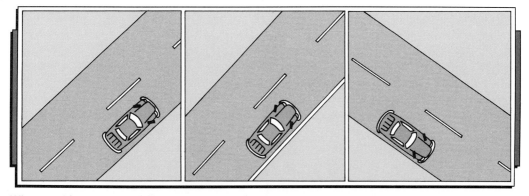

**When parking on an uphill grade where there is no curb, or on a downhill grade, turn wheels toward the side of the road (first and third pictures). On an uphill grade with a curb, turn wheels toward the center of the road (middle picture).**

2. Turn the wheel to the left when your car is about 1 foot from the car behind you.

3. Stop. With your foot on the brake, shift into *drive* or *first* gear.

4. Turn on the left directional signal and check both mirrors. Give an arm signal if required by your state or if your car's taillights are obscured by the vehicle parked behind you.

5. Before starting out, check over your left shoulder for traffic.

6. Move forward slowly, steering rapidly left. Try to pull out at an angle of about 45°.

7. When your center door post is even with the rear bumper of the car in front of you, start moving the wheel right to move in the direction of traffic.

8. Check the position of the car parked ahead of you, being careful not to scrape it on the way out. Continue to watch for traffic, especially to the rear.

## *Projects*

1. Observe traffic on an expressway entrance ramp for 15 minutes. Why are some vehicles unable to merge smoothly with traffic on the expressway? How could this problem have been avoided?

2. In an area with parallel parked cars, observe 5 to 10 drivers entering the traffic from a parked position. How many fail to make sure of an adequate gap to the rear? Make a record of your findings.

## Words to Know

lateral maneuvers        acceleration lane
weaving lane             deceleration lane

## Stop and Review

1. List 6 lateral maneuvers.
2. What 4 factors must you pay special attention to when you make a lateral maneuver?
3. How do you let other drivers know you are going to park along a curb?
4. Why is making a lateral maneuver harder when the time and space needed for the maneuver are limited?
5. List the checks required for positioning within a lane, lane changing, and passing.
6. Describe a situation in which you would have to make a lateral maneuver *within* your lane.
7. Why is it a good idea to wait for a 4-second gap in traffic in the lane you wish to enter before changing lanes?
8. List the steps you should follow to change lanes on an expressway.
9. As a general rule, should you slow down, keep the same speed, or increase your speed a bit when changing lanes on an expressway?
10. How much of the vehicle you are passing should you see in your rear-view mirror before you pull back in front of it?
11. Describe the hazards of making a lateral maneuver to enter onto or exit from an expressway.
12. List the steps to follow when entering an expressway.
13. How does a short acceleration lane affect the judgments you must make when entering an expressway?
14. What can help you to plan your expressway exit?
15. Why is exiting through an expressway's weaving area more difficult than exiting where there is no weaving area?
16. What must you always be aware of while looking for a parking space?
17. List the steps to take when parallel parking.
18. How do you judge whether a space is large enough for you to safely parallel park?
19. Why should you turn the steering wheel to block the tire against the curb as your last step in parallel parking?
20. In which direction do you move first when exiting from a parallel parking space?

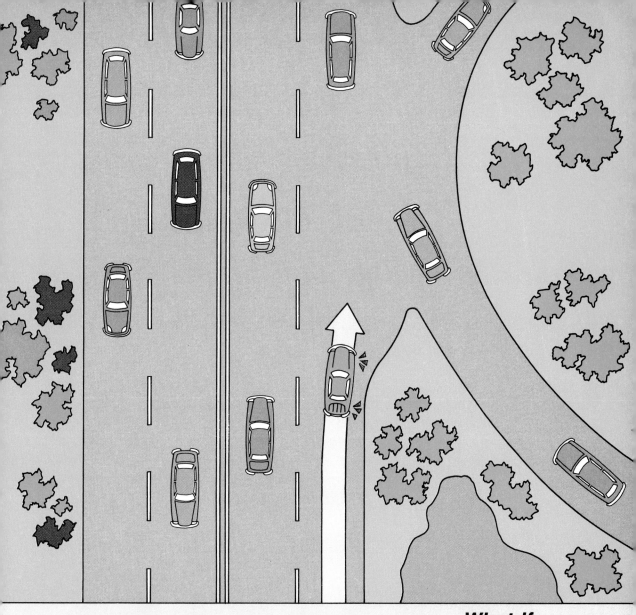

You are on the expressway, giving Karen a ride home. "Take the next exit," she tells you, "but watch for cars entering the road in front of you."

1. What situation must you deal with? What should you do?

You have made a safe exit from the expressway and driven to Karen's apartment house. "Look!" she says. "There's a parking place right in front. You can park and help me carry these packages upstairs."

2. What steps should you follow to park safely by the curb?

Complete the sentences by filling in the blanks with the correct terms.

> guide signs    far left    lateral maneuver    parallel    after
> 4-second    weaving    acceleration    turn signal    space

1. A sideways motion in an automobile is called a _____ .

2. Before changing lanes, check to see if you have enough time and _____ to perform the maneuver.

3. A lane that leads to and from a roadway, where entering and exiting cars cross, is called a _____ lane.

4. Before you change lanes, you must make sure that there is a _____ gap in traffic.

5. If you are going to park along a curb, use your _____ to let other drivers know you are leaving the road.

6. Aligning the center door post of your car with the center door post of the car you are parking behind is the first *check* position when you are _____ parking.

7. The _____ lane of an expressway is usually used by those vehicles traveling at the highest speeds.

8. If you choose a parking space just past an intersection, turn on your turn signal _____ you enter the intersection.

9. _____ are placed ahead of exits and tell you whether the exit is on the left or right side of the expressway.

10. If the _____ lane is short, you need a much longer gap in traffic to enter the expressway.

---

Select the one best answer to each of the following questions.

11. Which of the following is *not* a lateral maneuver?
    (a) parallel parking  (b) backing up  (c) leaving an expressway  (d) changing lanes

12. When you make a lateral maneuver, you should pay close attention to:
    (a) the amount of steering to be done.  (b) the speed adjustment.  (c) the space needed to make your move.  (d) all of the above.

13. Short acceleration lanes:
    (a) are more hazardous than long ones.  (b) give you more time to accelerate.  (c) always merge into the left lane of the expressway.  (d) are usually 1,500 feet in length.

14. You should parallel park in a space with _____ feet in addition to the length of your car.
    (a) 3  (b) 7  (c) 5  (d) 6

15. Which of the following is usually *not* done when changing lanes on an expressway?
    (a) Check traffic using mirrors.  (b) Adjust speed.  (c) Signal intention.  (d) Tap horn and flash headlights.

# Turns

## Chapter Objectives:

In this chapter you will learn how to:

- make right and left turns.
- perform angle parking and perpendicular parking.
- safely execute turnabouts.

Turns are another group of basic traffic movements. You must learn to judge the time and space you need to make turns under many different conditions. Although the basic steps are the same, turns may be simple or complicated. Pulling into an angle parking space when no other cars are present is easy. However, backing out of that same spot could be a problem when other cars are parked next to you and traffic is heavy. A turn from a one-way street onto another one-way street at an intersection controlled by a traffic signal is rather easy. But a turn into a multiple-lane, two-way highway without a traffic signal where traffic is moving at a high rate of speed requires difficult time and space decisions.

# Preparing for an Intersection Maneuver

You must let other drivers know what you plan to do as you come to an intersection. You can tell them in a number of ways. First, properly place your car in the correct lane well in advance. If you intend to turn, signal early. In the urban areas of many states, you must signal at least 100 feet before you reach the place where you intend to make a turn and in rural areas you must signal 200 feet ahead. It is best to warn other drivers even earlier, 150 to 200 feet ahead of your turn in town, and 300 to 500 feet on the open highway.

As you approach an intersection, check for signs that control your movement. Is there a traffic signal light? A yield right-of-way sign? A stop sign? Are turns allowed? If turns are allowed, may they be made only at certain hours of the day or days of the week? May they be made only by certain types of vehicles? Are there special lanes for turning? Even before you have determined that a turn is allowed, slow down by gradually pumping the brake pedal. The flashing brake light will warn the drivers in back of you that you plan to turn.

While all intersections are not the same, these rules apply to most:

- Unless you are told to do something else by a traffic sign, a signal, an officer, or road markings, make left turns from the farthest left lane of traffic. Make right turns from the farthest right lane of traffic.

- Unless a traffic sign, a signal, an officer, or road markings indicate something else, turn your vehicle

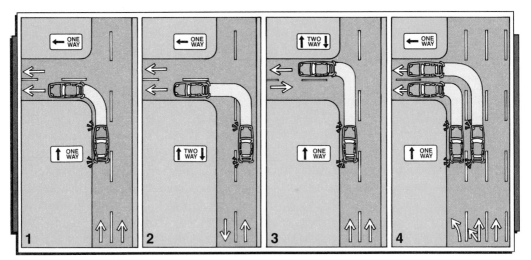

Correct lane placement for making a left turn: (1) from a one-way street onto a one-way street (2) from a two-way street onto a one-way street (3) from a one-way street onto a two-way street (4) from a multilane street onto a one-way street.

into the nearest lane moving in the direction you want to go.

- Where turns are allowed from more than one lane, turn into the lane corresponding to the lane you just left.

## Right Turns

The steps for a right turn are the same whether the street you are turning onto is one-way or two-way.

1. Move to the right lane well in advance.

2. Check conditions ahead and behind. Flash your brake lights.

3. Signal 100 to 200 feet before reaching the intersection.

4. Look for traffic controls, highway users, or conditions that could affect your movements.

5. Position your car 3 to 4 feet from the curb or line of parked cars.

6. Stop behind the crosswalk or stop sign. Be sure to allow sufficient room so the right rear tire will not hit the curb when you make your turn.

7. Make sure there are no obstacles in your path. Also be sure to check for cars across the intersection that may be signaling to make a left turn.

8. When you are ready to turn, move your car up until your front bumper is in line with the curb or edge of the road you intend to enter. Turn the wheels slightly to the right.

9. Find a 7- to 8-second gap in the traffic to your left. Just before you turn, sweep the intersection again, making your last check to the left.

10. Move forward slowly, yielding to

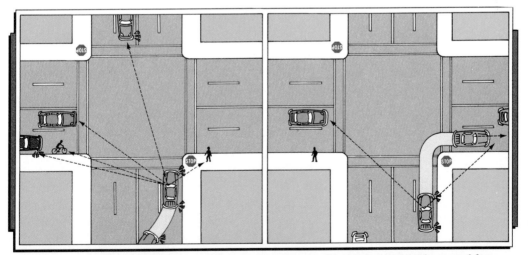

**To make a right turn, move to the right lane in advance. Check for pedestrians and for other vehicles, including those across the intersection. Turn into the farthest-right lane.**

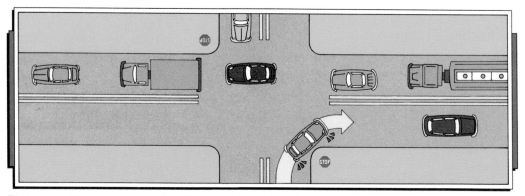

**The car making a right turn has the right to do so, since there is no oncoming traffic in the lane into which the car is turning. The car at the opposite stop sign must wait.**

pedestrians and other vehicles. Look through the turn to a point in the cross street where you want to go. You should enter the lane farthest to the right.

11. Accelerate to about 5 mph as you turn the steering wheel hand-over-hand to the right.

12. When the front of your car reaches a point about halfway through the turn, choose another point about 3 to 4 seconds ahead of your car and start to turn the steering wheel back to the straight-ahead position.

13. Accelerate to the speed of traffic and make sure the turn signal is turned off.

# Left Turns

### Left Turn on Two-Way Streets

The steps for a left turn vary. They depend on what type street you are turning from and what type street you are turning onto. Left turns from a one-way street onto a two-way street require that you cross the lanes of traffic coming from your left. Left turns from a two-way street require that you also cross a lane of traffic coming toward you from across the intersection.

1. Move your car into the left lane well in advance.

2. Check conditions ahead and behind. Flash your brake lights.

3. Signal 100 to 200 feet before you reach the intersection.

4. Look for traffic controls, highway users, or conditions that could affect your movements.

5. Stop next to the center line behind the crosswalk or stop sign. Keep the wheels straight.

6. Wait until there are no pedestrians or other obstacles in your path of travel. Check for cars across the intersection that may travel straight through the intersection or are signaling to turn right. Check for traffic from the left.

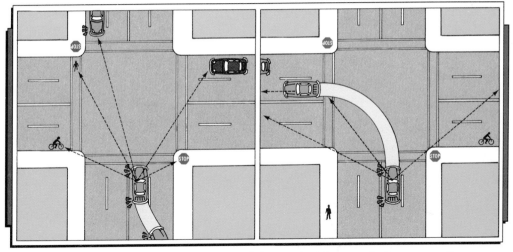

When making a left turn, check for other vehicles, pedestrians, and cars across the intersection. Look for a 9-second gap to your right and a 7-second gap to your left.

7. Find a 9-second gap to your right, and look through the turn to a point in the cross street where you want to go.

8. Find a 7-second gap to the left. (Steps 7 and 8 should be completed quickly. If more than 1 second elapses between them, return to step 7 and start again.)

9. Move your car forward until you are about 1 lane width away from the center of the intersection, then start to turn the wheel hand-over-hand to the left. Maintain a speed of 5 to 10 mph. Again check traffic to the left. Make your last check to the right.

10. Choose another point that is 3 to 4 seconds ahead of your car. Start to return your steering wheel to the straight-ahead position when the front of your car

enters the lane next to the center line.

11. Accelerate to the speed of traffic and make sure the turn signal is turned off.

## Left Turn from a One-Way Street

If you are making a left turn from a one-way street onto another one-way street, the procedure is similar to that followed for a right turn because you enter the first lane of traffic. If you are making a left turn from a one-way street onto a two-way street, the procedure is slightly different. You place your car in the far left-hand lane and turn into the first lane of traffic going in your direction.

# Angle Parking

In many parking lots and on some streets, angle parking is the only kind that is permitted. As a rule,

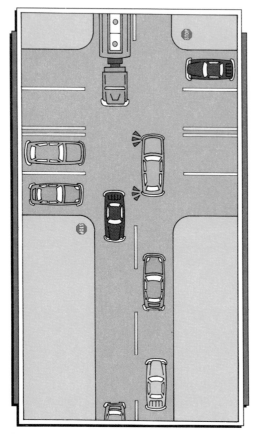

**Keep wheels pointed straight ahead when waiting to turn left. If hit from behind, you will not be pushed into oncoming traffic.**

when you park at an angle, you have little room and cannot see very much. You will have to be very careful getting in and out of an angle parking space.

## Angle Parking on the Right

1. When looking for a parking space, stay 5 or 6 feet from parked cars so that you can see as much as possible and have the most space for maneuvering. Watch for signs (brake lights, exhaust smoke) that tell you a

parked vehicle may be backing out. Remember to stay aware of other traffic around you at the same time.

2. As soon as you find a spot, turn on your right turn signal.

3. Check your mirrors and flash your brake lights, then slow to a speed of 3 to 5 mph.

4. Check to see that there are no obstructions, such as broken glass, shopping carts, or cars parked over dividing lines.

5. Drive forward until you can see along the left side of the car parked to the right of the space you want to enter.

6. Check approaching traffic.

7. Quickly turn the steering wheel hand-over-hand all the way to the right. Keep your speed slow. Check the left front and right rear of your car to make sure there is clearance.

8. As the front of your car moves into the center of the parking space, return the wheel to the straight-ahead position.

9. When the car is centered in the space, move up until the front of your car is aligned with those beside it.

10. Secure the car.

## Exiting from an Angle Parking Space

1. With your foot on the brake pedal, shift into *reverse* gear.

2. Check traffic all around your

7. As your car centers in the space, turn the steering wheel back to the straight-ahead position. Make sure your rear fender does not scrape the rear bumper of the car on your right.

8. Move forward slowly, positioning your car in the center of the space. Move up until the front of your car is aligned with those beside it.

9. Secure the car.

## Exiting from a Perpendicular Parking Space

1. With your foot on the brake pedal, shift into *reverse* gear.

2. Check traffic all around your car.

3. Move back very slowly with your wheels straight. Keep checking out the back and to the sides for possible obstacles.

4. When your windshield is in line with the rear bumpers of the cars parked on either side, start turning your wheel slightly to the right or left, depending on which way you want to back.

5. Make sure your front bumper does not hit the rear of the car opposite to the direction you are turning. Back up until your front bumper clears the rear bumper of the car beside you. Check to the rear and turn the wheel quickly in the direction you want to go.

6. As the car centers in the lane, turn the wheel quickly in the opposite direction to straighten the front wheels. Keep looking out the back window until the car is stopped.

7. Shift into *drive.*

8. Accelerate and move into the flow of traffic.

## Entering a Perpendicular Parking Space on the Left

Entering a perpendicular parking space on the left requires almost the same checks and steps used when entering a space on the right. These are the differences:

- You turn the steering wheel in the opposite direction.

- The danger points are your right front bumper and your left rear fender.

# Turnabouts

**Turnabouts** are moves that allow you to reverse direction. When they are done on a city street, they create potential hazards. The degree of hazard depends on several factors:

- the field of vision.
- width of the street.
- number of vehicles.
- speed of traffic.

Watch for signs that let you know where turnabouts are illegal. All turnabouts involve risks. In some cases, going around the block will be faster and safer. However, there are times when you will have to make a turnabout—for example, when you

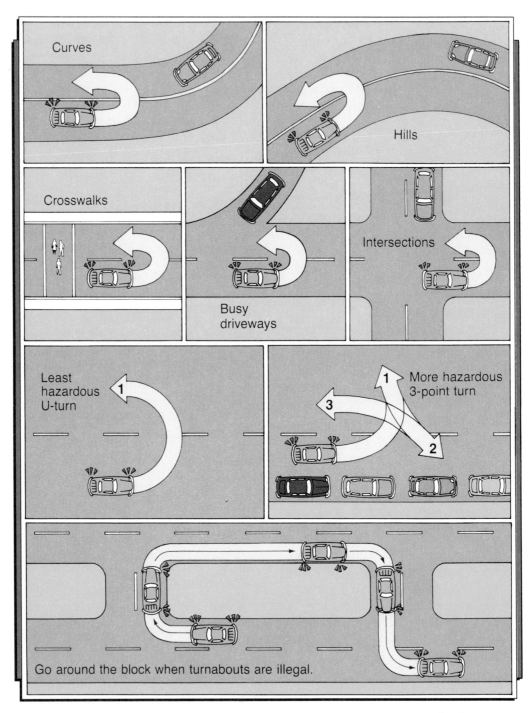

**It is dangerous and illegal to make turnabouts on curves or hills, at crosswalks, busy driveways, or intersections. Where turnabouts are legal, choose the safest kind possible.**

find yourself on a dead-end street or in other areas where you cannot circle the block.

**Two-Point Turn** The least hazardous way to reverse direction is to back into a driveway. This is called a **two-point turn.**

1. Signal early. Then check mirrors and flash brake lights.

2. Stop 2 to 3 feet from the curb, with the rear bumper of your car just past the driveway or alley that you want to back into.

3. With your foot on the brake, shift into *reverse* gear. Check to the rear for possible obstacles.

4. When the path is clear, look over your right shoulder into the driveway or alley. Then back up slowly, turning the steering wheel quickly all the way to the right. Check the front of your car with repeated glances to make sure it is not about to hit anything.

5. As the rear of the car enters the driveway or alley, start to turn the steering wheel back to the left. Stop when the front of the car is clear of the traffic lane. The front wheels should now point straight ahead.

6. With your foot on the brake, shift your car into *drive.* Signal a left turn, check traffic, and leave the driveway or alley when it is safe to do so.

There is another, more hazardous way to make a two-point turn. To do it, you head into an alley or drive-way. You then back into the street and come to a stop in the through-traffic lane. The steps in this maneuver are as follows:

Note: Steps 4–9 describe the procedure for backing out of a driveway.

1. Select a driveway or an alley on the left that allows a good field of vision.

**Reversing Direction
by Backing into
a Driveway**

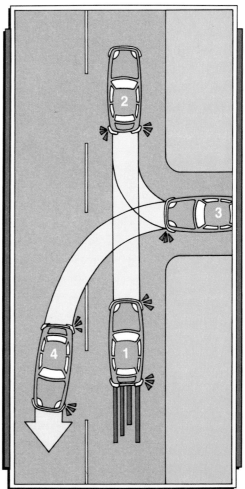

## Reversing Direction by Heading into a Driveway

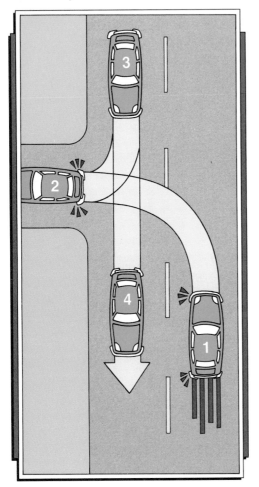

5. Check for traffic, and look over your right shoulder into your planned path of travel to the rear. Back slowly, stopping before the sidewalk and the street and re-checking traffic each time.

6. As you continue backing up your car, turn the steering wheel quickly all the way to the right. Be sure to keep the car in the first lane of traffic. Check the front of your car with repeated glances to make sure that it does not hit anything.

7. Halfway through the turn, start to straighten the steering wheel.

8. Stop with the front wheels turned straight ahead. Make sure you are looking out the rear window as you come to a complete stop.

9. Shift into *drive* and accelerate to traffic speed.

Reverse instructions in Steps 2, 5, and 6 if you choose a driveway or alley on the right. When making this type of turnabout, you must look for traffic in both directions. You must back across traffic in the first lane. Then, you must come to a full stop in the lane of traffic moving in the opposite direction. This type of turnabout must be done as quickly as possible. You must constantly look for cars in all directions while completing the maneuver. Steps 4–9 of this maneuver are also the steps to follow when backing out of a driveway.

**U-Turn** A U-turn is the easiest turnabout to make. But you need a wide street in which to do it. (Also, it

2. Turn on your left turn signal. Check traffic all around, flash your brake lights, and stop. When traffic is clear, turn into the driveway or alley.

3. Stop, with your front wheels straight, when the rear bumper clears the edge of the roadway.

4. With your foot on the brake, shift into *reverse* gear.

is illegal in some places.) If you must make a U-turn, pick a place where you can see well and other drivers can see you. To make a U-turn on a two-lane road, do the following:

1. Check your mirrors, turn on your right turn signal, flash your brake lights, and stop your car as far to the right of the road as you can.

2. Check for traffic in both directions; then signal for a left turn.

3. When there is a large time-space gap in both directions, move forward, turning the steering wheel quickly hand-over-hand all the way to the left.

4. As you complete the turn in the far right lane headed in the new direction, straighten your wheels. Check for traffic to the rear.

5. When the lane is clear, accelerate to the speed of traffic.

**Three-Point Turn** The hardest and most hazardous turnabout is a **three-point turn.** This turn should be used only when:

- the street is too narrow to make a U-turn.

- there are no driveways or alleys to turn into.

- traffic is very light.

- visibility is very good.

The three-point turn is hazardous because when you make it, you must stop your car twice. Each time you stop, you block a traffic lane. If you must make a three-point turn, make these checks first:

- Be sure that you are not near an intersection, a curve, or the crest of a hill. If a fast-moving car appeared suddenly, you would not be able to get out of the way, since you would be stopped in or across a lane of traffic.

- Check the height of any curbs at the side of the road. The front and rear of your car may go well over the curbs during this maneuver. High curbs could do damage to your car.

- Pick a spot without trees, telephone poles, fire hydrants, or other objects near the curb. Such objects

**U-turn**

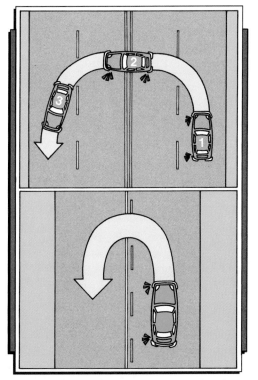

The U-turn is the easiest turnabout to make. It requires a wide street.

are hard to keep in sight while you back up and turn. You must also check for traffic from both ways.

- Be sure to move the car slowly and the steering wheel quickly.

Once you have made these checks, do as follows:

1. Find a safe spot to make the three-point turn.

2. Check traffic in both mirrors. Flash your brake lights.

3. Signal right and move over to the right edge of the roadway.

4. Watch for traffic in both directions. Wait until there is a gap that is long enough to complete the maneuver.

5. Turn on your left turn signal and look over your left shoulder for any cars in your blind spot.

6. Move the car forward, turning the wheel very quickly all the way to the left to bring the car into the opposite lane.

7. When the front wheels are about

4 feet from the edge of the pavement or curb, turn the steering wheel hard to the right. Stop the car just short of the road edge or the curb.

8. With your foot on the brake, shift into *reverse*. Check traffic. Back up slowly, holding the wheel in the extreme right position. During the last 4 feet or so before stopping, turn the steering wheel quickly to the left. Keep looking back until you have stopped the car. Check the front end with repeated glances.

9. Shift into *drive*. Check traffic. Move the car forward slowly, completing the turn to the left. Accelerate to traffic speed.

Both turns and turnabouts require close control of speed and steering. For each of these maneuvers, you must make accurate judgments of the time and space you need. You can start to develop these judgments by watching other drivers as you ride with them.

**Three-point turn**

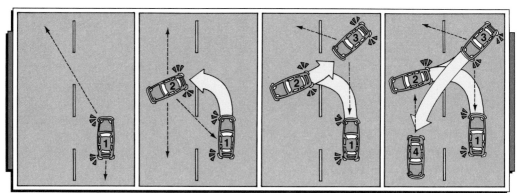

**The three-point turn is the most difficult and most dangerous type of turnabout.**

If you must make a three-point turn, choose a spot with good visibility and little traffic. Move the car slowly and the steering wheel quickly.

## *Projects*

1. Observe traffic turning left at a four-way, four-lane intersection. Identify the proper turns and the errors that different drivers make. Make a presentation to your class.

2. Observe a spot where turnabouts are allowed on a well-traveled roadway. Do the drivers seem to give themselves enough time and space for the turnabouts? Do any of them have any problems? If so, prepare a diagram showing the troublesome maneuver. Prepare a diagram showing a similar maneuver that was completed with no difficulty.

## Words to Know

three-point turn
U-turn

two-point turn
turnabouts

## Stop and Review

1. What are the steps you should take to let other drivers know that you are planning to turn at an intersection?
2. What information should you check for as you approach an intersection where you plan to turn?
3. Name 3 general rules that would apply to most intersection turns.
4. Steps for making a left turn vary. What factors influence how you make a left turn?
5. What is required when making a left turn from a one-way street onto a two-way street?
6. Which way should you keep your wheels pointed when you are waiting at an intersection to make a left-hand turn?
7. When making a left turn from a two-way street onto a two-way street, how fast should you be traveling?
8. Describe some hazards you should be alert for when making a left turn at a busy, four-way intersection.
9. List two signs that tell you a ve-hicle may be backing out of a parking space.
10. What are the 2 points on your car to be especially careful of when entering or leaving an angle parking space on the right?
11. What are the hazards of perpendicular parking?
12. List 5 places where you should not make turnabouts.
13. What factors determine the amount of risk there is in a turnabout?
14. List and describe 3 kinds of turnabouts.
15. What is the least hazardous way to reverse direction?
16. Describe the 2 different kinds of two-point turns.
17. What factors would you consider in choosing a place to make a U-turn?
18. Which turnabout is the most difficult and dangerous? Why?
19. List 4 factors that let you know that a three-point turn should be used.
20. List 2 checks you should make before executing a three-point turn.

You are going west on a two-way street with two lanes of traffic in each direction. You plan to turn right at the next intersection onto a one-way street. One block down, you want to turn left onto a two-way street with two lanes in each direction.

1. In which lane should you be for your turn to the right? Why? What else should you do?

2. In which lane should you be to make your left turn onto the two-way street? Which lane should you turn into?

Complete the sentences by filling in the blanks with the correct terms.

straight ahead U-turn left turnabouts back
parked cars 7 to 8 perpendicular 100 right

1. _____ parking is the most dangerous kind of parking.

2. Moves that allow you to reverse direction are called _____ .

3. When making a right turn, look for a _____ -second gap in the traffic to your left.

4. In the urban areas of many states, you must signal at least _____ feet before you reach the place where you intend to make a turn.

5. You should make left turns from the farthest _____ lane of traffic.

6. When you are waiting at an intersection to make a left-hand turn, keep your wheels pointed _____ .

7. In the less hazardous type of two-point turn, you _____ into a driveway or alley.

8. The easiest turnabout to make, provided you are on a street that is wide enough, is a _____ .

9. When looking for an angle parking space, stay 5 or 6 feet from _____ .

10. Unless you are told to do something else by a traffic sign, a signal, an officer, or road markings, make right turns from the farthest _____ lane of traffic.

Decide whether each of the following sentences is true or false.

11. The first step in making a turn is to check for signals that control your movement.

12. Steps for making a left turn depend on what type of street you are turning from and what type of street you are turning onto.

13. When you find an available parking space, you should slow down to a speed of about 10 mph.

14. When you are backing up, it is important to keep looking out your back window until you come to a complete stop.

15. Turnabouts are always illegal at intersections.

# Natural Laws

## Chapter Objectives:

In this chapter you will learn how to:

- understand the natural forces that affect your driving.
- take into account the effect of natural forces as you drive.
- recognize factors influencing traction, directional control, and cornering.

It is interesting to note the ways in which science and driver education are related. Many of the laws of natural science can be applied to an everyday situation like driving a car. Natural forces are involved in keeping a car on the road, turning a corner, moving around a curve in the road, and driving down or up a hill.

When you are driving, you should be aware of these forces. They are important in controlling the movement of your car on the road. Not all cars handle alike. Therefore, each car will react differently to these natural laws.

## Energy of Motion (Kinetic Energy)

An athlete is running a marathon race. A baseball is hit by the batter and soars into the air. A car is being driven down a highway. The athlete, the baseball, and the car have something in common. They all have **kinetic energy**. Kinetic energy is the energy of motion. The word *kinetic* comes from the Greek word meaning "to move." Kinetic energy, or energy of motion, is sometimes also called **momentum**.

The energy of motion, or the kinetic energy, of an object can change. For example, the kinetic energy of a moving car or other vehicle increases with **mass** (weight) and **velocity** (speed). The formula is $KE = \frac{1}{2}mv^2$. The kinetic energy of an object is equal to one-half the weight in pounds of that object times the square of its speed in **feet** per second. (A **square** is a number times itself.)

A dump truck filled with dirt weighs more than an empty dump truck. If the weight of the filled dump truck is double the weight of the empty dump truck, the kinetic energy of the filled moving dump truck is double that of the empty moving truck. Also, if one car weighs 4,000 pounds and another car weighs 2,000 pounds, the heavier car would have twice as much energy as the lighter car if both cars were traveling at the same speed.

While the doubling of the weight of a vehicle doubles the energy of motion, an increase in speed has an even greater effect on the energy of motion. The kinetic energy of a moving vehicle is increased by the square of its increase in speed. Therefore, if you double the speed of a car, its kinetic energy will be 4 times as great. If the speed of the car is tri-

The kinetic energy of this dump truck is increased when it is filled with soil.

pled, the kinetic energy is increased by a factor of 9 ($3 \times 3 = 9$ or $3^2 = 9$). If the speed is increased from 10 mph to 40 mph, how much greater will the energy of motion be?

The amount of energy of motion that builds up in a moving vehicle affects the way the vehicle handles. The faster a car is moving, the harder it is to turn safely. A fast-moving car also must travel a longer distance to stop than a slower moving car. For example, two cars of the same weight are moving on the road. One car is traveling at 25 mph. The other car is traveling at 50 mph. Since the car traveling at 50 mph is moving at twice the speed of the other car, the energy of motion that has built up in that car is 4 times greater than that of the car traveling at 25 mph. How much farther would the faster moving car have to travel to come to a stop than the car moving at 25 mph? If your answer is 4 times the distance, you are correct. The added kinetic energy must be changed to another form of energy. By applying the brakes, kinetic energy is changed to heat energy. This heat energy is given off into the air. This is why the brakes of a car get hot.

While driving, you should be aware of how changes in the kinetic energy of the car affect how the car steers, accelerates, and stops, and make the proper adjustments to control the car safely. Remember, you will need more room to stop while traveling at faster speeds. This is why it is so critical to keep a 2-second following distance.

You will have to adjust your speed to compensate for the effects of gravity when you drive uphill or downhill.

## Gravity

You have probably heard the saying "What goes up must come down." Whenever you toss a ball up into the air, it comes down. If you were to accidentally knock a drinking glass off a table, it would fall to the floor. The invisible force that pulls objects toward the ground is called **gravity**. Gravity also has an effect on the speed of your car.

If a vehicle is going downhill, the force of gravity will cause it to increase speed. If a vehicle is going uphill, the extra effort required to work against the force of gravity will

Your car will accelerate more slowly on an uphill grade. Downshifting will give a manual-shift car more climbing power.

When you are driving downhill, your speed will increase by itself. Downshift and use the brakes to control your speed.

cause it to lose speed. However, you should be able to use your car's controls to overcome or slow the effects of gravity.

When you drive downhill, you can use the brakes to keep the car from increasing speed too much. You can also use **engine braking** (releasing the amount of pressure placed on the accelerator), or you can downshift to slow the car.

Gravity also has an effect on the amount of time and space needed to stop a car going downhill. It will take longer to stop if you are moving downhill.

While driving uphill, your car is working against the force of gravity. To maintain speed on an uphill grade, you must accelerate more. Downshifting will give the car more climbing power. In a car with a manual shift, it may be necessary to downshift to drive up a steep hill. In

a vehicle with an automatic transmission, downshifting will occur by itself when drag on the engine and transmission reach a certain point.

Gravity gives objects their weight. **Weight** is the pull of gravity on an object. All the weight of an object such as your car is distributed evenly around a point called the object's **center of gravity**. Most cars have a low center of gravity. This enables a car to handle well on turns and on curves in the road.

Changes in a car's center of gravity affect the way a car handles. If a car-top carrier is placed on a car and loaded with heavy objects, the center of gravity is raised. The car will handle differently and will be less stable on turns and curves. This higher center of gravity makes the car less stable during sudden changes in direction, and also affects accelerating and braking.

# Friction

If you kick a ball across a field, the ball slows down as it moves, and eventually it stops. The ball does not slow down by itself, but rather is slowed down by a force called **friction**. Friction is a force which always acts in the opposite direction of the motion, or force, applied. One force pushes against another.

The control of a car or other vehicle depends in part on friction. In this case, friction is the resistance between the moving tires and the pavement. The friction between the tires and the road surface is typically called **traction**. Perhaps a better word for it is **adhesion,** which means "sticking together." Without traction, or adhesion, you would not be able to stop, turn, or even keep the car moving. The ability of the tires to "grip" the road, their traction, makes motion possible.

**Proper inflation and good treads help tires hug the road. Check the condition of your tires often.**

# Factors Affecting Traction

**Tires** The greater the traction is, the less chance there is that a car's tires will skid on the road. Tires are designed with grooved surfaces that touch the road. These are referred to as the **treads**. On a wet road, the grooved treads allow water to flow into the grooves and away from the tread, allowing it to have better contact with the road surface. Some tires have deeper grooves than others. Snow tires, for example, have very large, deep grooves, which provide traction by digging into the snow. On a snow-covered road, snow is pushed into the grooves as the car is moving, so the tire's treads make contact with the road surface and have greater adhesion. Some tires have studs, which dig into ice and snow to increase traction. Many people also put chains on their cars for added traction in snow and on ice-covered roads. Studded tires and chains should not be used on dry pavement. When there is nothing for them to dig into, metal studs and chains have less adhesion than rubber tires.

The condition of a car's tires affects the amount of traction they will have. "Bald" tires—that is, tires that have very little or no tread—provide very little or no traction on wet, icy, or snow-covered roads. Even on a dry road, bald or badly worn tires are hazardous. They will increase your stopping distance if there is sand or gravel on the road surface. They are also more apt to get punctured.

Tires should be inflated to the maximum pressure recommended by the manufacturer. When they are properly inflated, the tires can provide sufficient contact with the road. If tires are underinflated, tread is pressed together and only the outer edges grip the road. If they are over-inflated, only the center part of the tire comes in contact with the road. In both cases, the wear will be uneven.

**Rain** The amount of adhesion is not always the same, even with tires in excellent condition. Road conditions also affect the traction of the tires. Most drivers think they have more control than they really do when the road is wet. As a result, the number of accidents goes up when it rains. Wet surfaces give less adhesion than dry surfaces because of the reduced contact between the tires and the road. There are two types of dangers on wet roads:

- Roads are very slippery for 10 to 15 minutes after it starts to rain. This is caused by the mixture of water, dirt, rubber, dust, and oil that builds up on the road. The mixture, which creates a very slick surface, is soon splashed or washed away.

- Water on the road (caused by very

**Water reduces traction. Rainwater may collect at underpasses, near cliffs, in potholes, or at the foot of hills. If you drive through deep puddles, pump the brakes and drive slowly.**

Roads covered with snow, ice, and melting ice are slippery and extremely dangerous. To avoid skids, use snow tires or chains; drive slowly; never accelerate or brake suddenly.

heavy rains or poor drainage) is a special danger. Deep water on the roadway, or lesser amounts of water combined with worn or under-inflated tires, can cause your car's wheels to **hydroplane** (ride up on top of a film of water) even when you are driving at a moderate speed. This means that all contact between the road and the tires is lost.

You can reduce the level of danger when driving on these two kinds of wet roads. First, as soon as you notice water standing on the road or whenever it is raining so hard that raindrops are causing bubbles on the roadway's surface, reduce your speed. Second, drive in the tracks of the vehicle ahead of you. The vehicle ahead tends to wipe the water off the road for a few seconds and so improves your traction.

**Snow and Ice**  Snow and ice make roads very dangerous. The roads get even more dangerous as the snow and ice start to melt. (Wet ice is more slippery than ice that is dry.) Any change in speed or direction on a slick road may well result in a skid. The sharper the change, the more likely a skid will occur.

The wisest action to take in case of either water or wet ice on the road is to stop driving. Gradually reduce your speed, and leave the road as soon as you can find a safe place to stop.

**Other Road Conditions**  Other road conditions also reduce friction, or adhesion. Loose sand or gravel, oil droplets which have leaked from other vehicles, and wet leaves on the road all reduce traction. Bumpy or poorly maintained roads, such as roads with many potholes, also reduce traction, since the tires must bounce up and down to maintain contact with the road.

## Inertia

Sir Isaac Newton was a British scientist who founded the science of mechanics. Mechanics is the study of motion and the causes of changes in motion, which are very important in driving a car.

Newton stated three laws of motion. The first law of motion is called the **law of inertia**. Part of what the law of inertia states is that an object in motion will continue to move in a straight line unless some force acts against it. An object at rest will remain at rest unless some force acts on it. All things, including cars and other vehicles, have this property of inertia.

Vehicle control is affected by inertia. When you are driving a car, inertia is the tendency of a car in motion and the driver and passengers inside the car to resist any change in direction. You can feel this resistance when the car is making a turn. As you turn the steering wheel right

Loose dirt, pebbles, sand, and gravel on the road reduce traction. If you drive too fast or if you turn or stop too suddenly on this type of surface, your car could go into a skid.

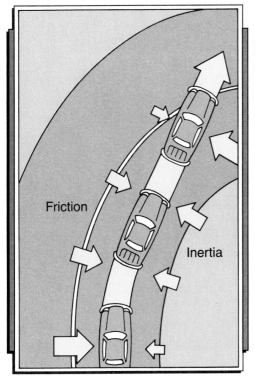

**The friction of the tires on the road acts against inertia. As long as there is more friction than inertia, you can make a turn.**

and the car turns right, your body feels as if it were being pushed to the left. Your body is still trying to move in the direction in which the car was moving before you made the right turn. This is why it is so critical to wear your safety belt. It will hold you in place if you have to make an emergency maneuver.

To make a turn from a straight path of travel, forces must be used that will let you change your direction and reduce your speed. The steering wheel, brakes, and accelerator, as well as the friction between the tires and the road, create this force.

# Centrifugal Force

A car is moving down a straight road. The law of inertia states that a moving object tends to keep moving in a straight line. The moving object also resists having its motion changed. A force is needed to stop the moving object or change its position or path. In order to steer a car through a curve, you must overcome the effects of inertia.

**Centrifugal force** is the term used to describe the force that tends to push a moving object out of a curve or turn into a straight path. Actually, this tendency called centrifugal force is really caused by inertia.

Three factors determine the amount of centrifugal force in a turn:

- the sharpness of the turn.
- the speed of the vehicle.
- the size of the vehicle.

What happens as a car traveling in a straight line tries to go around a curve? As you slow down the car to enter the curve and turn the steering wheel, the adhesion of the tires with the road resists inertia and forces the car into a curved path. The force that pushes a moving object from a straight line into a curved path is called **centripetal force**. Centripetal force "pushes," or keeps, the car in a curved path.

The centripetal effect of traction is very important when a vehicle is being driven around a curve. If there is not enough traction, a car will skid

Curves on race tracks are steeply banked in order to give race cars the traction they need for high-speed turns.

## Road surface contour

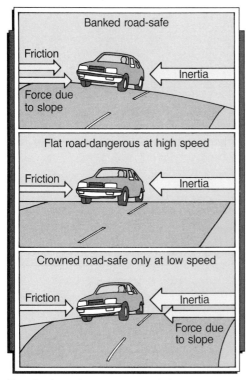

Roads that slope up toward the outside of a curve give better traction.

out of the curve and continue in a straight line.

Several factors affect the control that a driver has over a vehicle while it is rounding a curve. One factor is speed, and it is the only one of these factors that you can control while you are driving. The faster your car is going, the more the car will resist being turned from its straight path. The best way to maintain control while going around a curve is to slow down before you enter the curve so that there will be less inertia to overcome. Then you should accelerate slightly while you are starting to come out of the curve. Usually, a sign recommending a safe speed limit will be posted before you come to a sharp curve in a road.

The contour, or slope, of the road's surface also plays an important role in the ability of a car to travel through a turn or curve. When you are turning at higher speeds, you need more traction to keep your car from skidding toward the outside of the curve. That is why curves on a well-designed road are **banked** (sloped up toward the outside of the turn). When you make a turn on a banked curve, your car tilts down toward the inside. This tilt improves tracking. However, not all roads give you this advantage. Some roads are **crowned**. This means that they are higher in the center than at the edges. Such roads will aid you in a turn to the right because the lane is banked up toward the center of the road. Left turns on a crowned road can be dangerous, however, since the

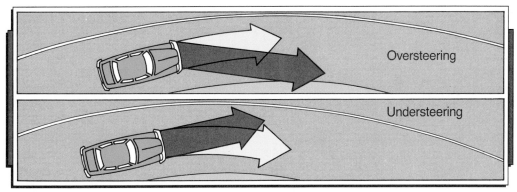

A car that has good cornering ability will not roll or stray when making a turn at a safe speed. It does not oversteer (move toward the inside of the curve) or understeer (move toward the outside of the curve).

slope then goes down toward the outside edge of the road.

The load, or weight, of a car helps determine how well the car will take a curve. Added weight increases a vehicle's kinetic energy, and cars that have added weight are harder to control on a curve. The condition of the road and tires are also factors that will affect the control you have over your car on a curve.

## Directional Control and Cornering Ability

The ability of a car to hold a straight line is called **directional control**. If a car has good directional control, very little correction is needed to keep the car moving in the direction in which you steer it. When you are driving straight ahead, the rear wheels should track in line behind the front wheels. A vehicle with good directional control does not change direction by itself, although steering corrections may be needed due to environmental conditions, such as road contour, traction, and wind.

On turns, some vehicles may move away from the path of travel. If the front of a car moves to the inside of a curve while the rear end slides out, the car is **oversteering**. If the front of a car moves towards the outside of a curve, the car is **understeering**. A car should have the ability to be steered around a curve without moving to the inside or outside of the curve. The ability to steer around a curve with control is called **cornering ability**. A car with good cornering ability will not roll or stray when making a turn at a safe speed.

Oversteering is more dangerous for most drivers than understeering. To correct oversteering during a turn, you must move the steering wheel slightly in the direction opposite to the desired path of travel. Understeering can also be dangerous if

**Larger rear tires and a raised rear suspension affect the balance of weight between front and rear tires, and can leave the fuel tank exposed.**

it is severe or if it is increased by high speed. Understeering in a turn can be corrected by reducing your speed and turning the steering wheel more in the desired direction.

## Factors Influencing Directional Control and Cornering

A problem with the suspension, steering, or tires decreases your ability to control a vehicle. Even under good roadway conditions, underinflated tires or tires out of balance affect vehicle handling. Worn shock absorbers or poor front-end alignment adds to the problem. A vehicle that is overloaded or loaded badly also has poor handling ability.

There are clues you can look for to tell you something about the directional control and cornering ability of the vehicles around you:

- Vehicles that sag to one side or to the front or rear may have worn shock absorbers or broken springs.

- Vehicles that are overloaded have an increased chance of skidding on sharp curves or turns. One sign of overload is that the back end of the vehicle is lower than normal.

- Heavy loads carried in a roof luggage carrier, especially when they are placed at the rear of the vehicle, will affect directional control. Also, vans or cars with full luggage racks are more seriously affected by winds.

- Wheels that shimmy, wobble, or bounce indicate a tire, steering, or suspension-system defect. Any of

144

these makes a vehicle harder to handle.

- Cars with raised or "raked" rear ends usually corner poorly. Their exposed fuel tanks are also a hazard because they increase the chance of fire in the event of a rear-end collision.

- Vehicles pulling other vehicles or trailers almost always suffer some loss of directional control. They also lose some cornering and acceleration ability.

- Most motorcycles driven at highway speeds need as much room as cars do to carry out lane-change and passing maneuvers. Motorcycles are highly maneuverable only when they are well controlled and driven at slow speeds.

## Force of Impact

The force with which a moving vehicle hits another object is called the **force of impact**. The force of impact is determined by three factors. Speed and the weight of the vehicle are two factors. The third factor is the distance a moving vehicle travels between the initial impact with an object and the point where the vehicle comes to a full stop.

The faster a car is moving, the greater will be the force of impact. Remember that if the speed of a moving vehicle is doubled the energy of motion is increased by a factor of 4, that is, the square of the increase in speed. Therefore, the force of impact

A vehicle's weight is one of the 3 factors that determine force of impact in a collision.

also is increased by the square of the increase in the vehicle's speed. In a collision, the greater the force of impact is, the greater will be the damage to the vehicle. The passengers and the driver also will generally be more seriously injured or are more likely to be killed in collisions at high speeds.

The force of the impact also will increase if the weight of a vehicle is increased. Doubling the weight of a vehicle doubles both the energy of motion and the force of impact. As a result, when a larger vehicle strikes a smaller vehicle, greater damage is generally inflicted on the smaller vehicle.

The force of impact varies with the kind of object a moving vehicle hits.

145

Hitting a brick wall will cause more damage to the vehicle than hitting a wooden fence. When a moving vehicle hits a solid stationary object, the distance between impact and full stop is very short. The solid stationary object does not "give," or yield. Therefore, the moving energy is expended immediately on impact, almost like an explosion. The shorter the distance between initial impact and full stop, the greater the damage will be.

Perhaps you have seen large yellow canisters in front of concrete barriers on highways. These are often filled with sand. If a car should hit these canisters, they would break apart and the sand would help reduce the force of impact of the car. Thus, the car would slow down more gradually than if it collided with the concrete barrier.

A wooden fence will give even more than a sand-filled canister. That is, the moving vehicle continues to move

upon impact. The distance between the initial impact and full stop will be greater. The fence will absorb most of the force of impact and the moving vehicle will slow gradually. As the distance between initial impact and full stop increases, the force of impact is reduced.

The design of many new cars also helps decrease the damage to the car and its occupants. All new cars have energy-absorbing bumpers which lengthen the time and distance in which the passenger area of the car comes to a stop in a collision. New cars also have energy-absorbing steering columns and steering wheels, windshields with safety glass, and padded dashboards. If a person strikes his or her head against the padded dashboard, the dashboard will give. Therefore, the distance from initial impact to full stop is increased, and the force of impact is lowered.

In a collision with a stationary, solid object, a car traveling at 40 miles per hour will come to a complete stop in a fraction of a second. Because of inertia, any loose objects, or the driver or passengers, if they are unrestrained, will continue traveling at 40 miles per hour. Remember, a force is needed to stop or change the motion. The driver or passenger could strike the dashboard, windshield, or other hard part of the car's interior with a force of several thousand pounds. Therefore, seat belts and other safety restraints may help prevent serious or even fatal injuries in a car accident.

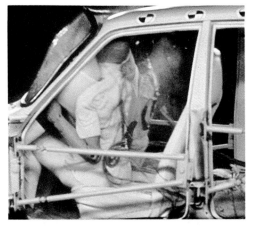

**In a collision, an unrestrained passenger could hit the dashboard with a force of thousands of pounds.**

| Natural Law | Definition | Application to Driving |
|---|---|---|
| **Kinetic Energy** | The energy of motion (momentum) | Kinetic energy increases with the weight and speed of the car. The more kinetic energy, the greater the stopping distance needed. |
| **Gravity** | The invisible force that pulls objects toward the ground | Gravity affects the speed of a vehicle, especially on hills. If a vehicle is improperly loaded, this contributes to unsteady handling. |
| **Friction** | The force that resists the motion of one surface against another | Friction makes vehicle control possible by giving tires their traction on the road. |
| **Inertia** | The force that resists any change of speed or direction of an object | The resistance you feel gradually being overcome every time you start, stop, or turn your car has an effect on vehicle control. |
| **Centrifugal Force** | The force that tends to push a moving vehicle out of a curve into a straight path | Centrifugal force makes it necessary to use the steering wheel and the friction of the tires to keep a car in a turn. |
| **Force of Impact** | The force with which one object collides with another | In a collision, the faster and heavier a vehicle, and the more solid the object it is colliding with, the more damage is done. |

## *Projects*

1. Make a photo display of hazardous low-traction areas in your community. Label each photo and list the potential hazard.
2. Sit a safe distance from a sharp curve in a busy road near your home. Take note of the way cars with directional-control problems make the turn. Report your findings to the class.

## Words to Know

friction
gravity
hydroplane
force of impact

inertia
square
kinetic energy
centripetal force

traction
treads
centrifugal force

## Stop and Review

1. How does doubling the weight of a vehicle affect its kinetic energy?
2. Why do the brakes of a car get hot?
3. How does driving uphill differ from driving downhill?
4. What is friction? How does your ability to control your car depend on friction?
5. How do snow tires act to increase traction?
6. What kinds of road conditions can reduce traction?
7. List the 2 dangers that exist on wet roads.
8. Explain why road surfaces are very slick just after a rain begins.
9. What is hydroplaning?
10. How can you reduce risk when driving on wet roads?
11. What are some steps you can take to improve traction on snow and ice?
12. Why do wet leaves, gravel, and sand reduce traction?
13. Describe road conditions that give the best traction.
14. How is vehicle control affected by inertia?
15. List some factors that affect the control a driver has over a vehicle while it is rounding a curve.
16. How are some curves designed to improve traction?
17. Why is oversteering more dangerous for most drivers than understeering?
18. List 4 factors that influence directional control and cornering.
19. How is the force of impact related to the speed of a vehicle?
20. List 3 energy-absorbing features found in many new cars.

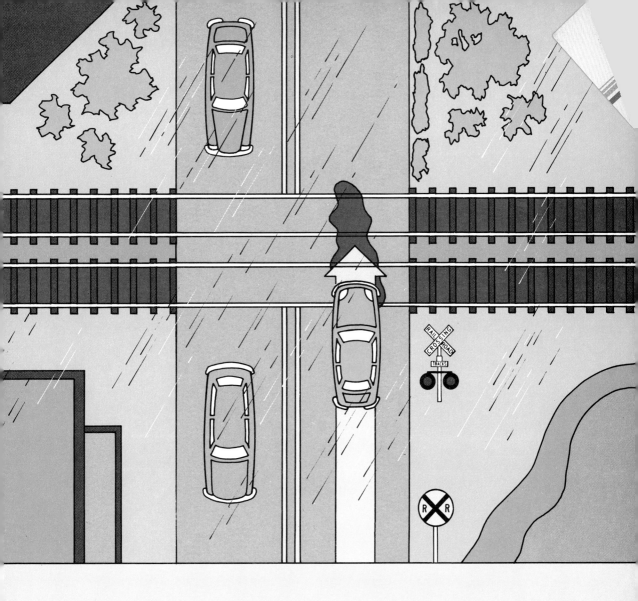

## What if...

You are at a railroad crossing. It is getting dark. It just began to rain. You slow, look both ways, and see no train coming. You accelerate to get across the tracks. As your car crosses the last rail, you feel the rear wheels skid.

1. Why did your car skid? How could you have prevented the skid? You see that you are going to hit some bushes.

2. What factors will affect your force of impact? What safety features can minimize your risk of injury?

3. Suppose you had hit a parked car. Would the damage be greater? Why?

Complete the sentences by filling in the blanks with the correct terms.

cornering ability    crowned    centripetal force
force of impact        square     inertia
friction              treads
traction           gravity

1. The invisible force that pulls objects toward the ground is called _____ .

2. _____ acts in the opposite direction of the force applied.

3. Friction between the tires and the road surface is called _____ .

4. The grooved surfaces of tires are called _____ .

5. The law of _____ states that an object at rest will remain at rest.

6. If a car has good _____ , it will not stray when making a turn at a safe speed.

7. Roads that are _____ are higher in the center than at the edges.

8. The kinetic energy of a moving vehicle is increased by the _____ of its increase in speed.

9. The force with which a moving vehicle hits another object is called the _____ .

10. The force that keeps an object in a curved path is called _____ .

Decide whether each of the following sentences is true or false.

11. If there were no traction, your car would skid each time you turned.

12. Roads that are crowned aid you in turning left and right.

13. Natural laws affect each car differently.

14. Luggage piled on your car's rooftop carrier lowers its center of gravity.

15. Bald tires provide little traction on wet roads.

# IPDE and the Smith System

## Chapter Objectives:

In this chapter you will learn how to:

- use the IPDE strategy for driving.
- make good driving decisions.
- minimize driving risks.

Driving is a complex task. You frequently have to keep track of and react to a number of things at the same time. This is easier to do with an organized procedure for gathering and processing information and making critical decisions concerning the selection of speed and the best position for your vehicle. One commonly used system is called IPDE—Identify, Predict, Decide, and Execute. Another, the Smith System, offers five good driving tips: aim high in steering, keep your eyes moving, get the big picture, make sure others see you, and leave yourself an out.

Many driving errors occur because drivers fail to identify what is happening on or near the roadway. Other errors occur because drivers interpret information incorrectly. As soon as you identify a potential traffic conflict, you must predict what might happen, consider the possible responses, and decide what action to take. The decision must often be executed in a matter of seconds.

# Identify

People often fail to notice what is going on around them. Basically, we tend to see those things that we expect to see. This can cause problems when we drive. We may not notice warning signs. We may also fail to respond appropriately to actions that other drivers take, because they are unexpected. Remember that other roadway users do not always act the way we think they will.

Good driving decisions depend on how well you gather and interpret information.

## What to Look For— Get the Big Picture

Our minds do not interpret everything we see. For this reason, we must learn to look at things selectively. When you drive, search for things with collision potential, things that would cause you to reduce speed or change lane position. Your first concern should be those things in or near your path with which you could collide—vehicles, pedestrians, animals, or fixed objects. Things near your path are more dangerous than those farther away. Things that move are more dangerous than those that do not. Remember, you must be aware of more than what is going on ahead of

In places where visibility is limited, such as on this blind curve, be alert to potential hazards hidden ahead. Reduce speed and search as far ahead as possible.

152

you. Vehicles that are tailgating or traveling beside you can create hazards, especially if you have to quickly slow down or change lanes.

Be aware of places where your vision is limited. Crests of hills, curves, large vehicles, shrubbery, and buildings can keep you from seeing important objects. Limited visibility should alert you to the possibility of trouble as you drive.

You can improve your ability to gather information by grouping like objects into four basic categories.

- *Signs, signals, and roadway markings.* These provide information about the road and the driving environment. They guide you in making driving decisions by warning you of such hazards as curves or steep hills. This information is usually accurate and simple to understand.

- *The highway.* Search the road and the road shoulder for information about their design, construction, maintenance, and surface conditions. Check for visual obstructions. Look for objects other than vehicles on or near the road that could possibly cause a collision. Identify other paths of travel that you could take if you had to leave the road.

- *Motorized vehicles.* Information about motor vehicles is more difficult to gather and evaluate. Cars, motorcycles, trucks, and buses all handle differently. A driver near you on the road may not know how

**Search your intended path for other roadway users. Bicyclists or pedestrians might enter the road in front of you.**

his or her vehicle performs or may not drive well enough to deal with some situations. You can adjust your speed or position to protect yourself against the possible actions of other drivers. Keep in mind, too, that drivers of certain kinds of vehicles are less predictable than others. For example, a driver ahead of you with out-of-state license plates who is moving slowly and looking at street signs can be expected to stop or turn off suddenly.

- *Nonmotorized highway users.* Pedestrians, bicyclists, and animals are the least protected of all highway users. They should be watched carefully whenever they come near the roadway.

## How and Where to Look— Aim High and Keep Your Eyes Moving

Develop an effective search pattern and then use it. Identify objects or situations on, near, or approaching the roadway. What you find in your search should influence your selection of speed and position. First search the area in and near your intended path of travel at least 12 seconds ahead of your car. If there are possible conflicts, you will have time to decide how to respond. Then check to see whether your immediate path,

This car is following the car ahead too closely. Tailgating like this is dangerous because it does not leave enough time to identify and react to potential hazards.

4 seconds ahead, is clear. Problems in this area develop quickly. Has there been any change in the position of potential hazards that you identified earlier? Because you must allow time for searching, remember to keep a minimum of 2 seconds (more for larger vehicles) between you and vehicles ahead of you.

Visual checks in any direction other than your intended path should be brief. After a quick check of the mirror or a fast look over your shoulder to check the rear, return your attention to the path immediately ahead. If a brief glance behind you does not provide enough information, do not stare. If there is no immediate problem in the path ahead, you can check the mirrors or look over your shoulder again.

Be sure to check your rear-view and side-view mirrors before reducing speed or moving to the side. Also, take a quick look over your shoulders to check your blind spots. Checking traffic to the sides and rear should become a habit. Learn also to check the instrument panel while you drive. Note your speed, understand what the gauges tell you, and then quickly return your attention to your path of travel.

## Predict

Usually, highway users act as expected, but some of them may not and their errors can lead to collisions. Be prepared for sudden **closing movements** (actions by other

**Look over your shoulder occasionally to check blind spots. These cyclists are in the blind spot of the driver ahead of them.**

highway users that may lead them into or across your path). Learn to assess the **probability** (chances) and **consequences** (results) of a collision.

Be prepared for the unusual by answering the following questions: What actions by other highway users could lead to a collision? How would these actions affect my safety? How likely is it that any of these actions will occur? If a collision should occur, what are the possible consequences? When you identify possible dangers in advance, you are better able to prepare for them.

### Anticipate Closing Movements—Make Sure Others See You

Here are some situations you should learn to anticipate:

- *Possible rear-end collision.* If the vehicle ahead of you should slow suddenly, would you be able to

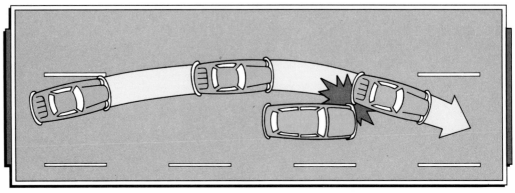

**A vehicle that is passing you could sideswipe you if it cuts back into your lane too soon. Learn to anticipate closing movements so that you can react in time to prevent a collision.**

steer around it? Following the vehicle ahead of you too closely reduces your possible paths of escape in an emergency.

- *Vehicles entering your path.* A vehicle parked at the curb or in a driveway with someone in the driver's seat could suddenly pull into your path. A vehicle at an intersection or in a merging lane may enter your path of travel. Is an adjustment of speed sufficient, or should you also communicate with the driver?

- *Possible head-on collision.* An oncoming vehicle may steer into your path. The other driver may make a turn, pass another vehicle, or simply drift into your lane.

- *Possible sideswipe.* Is the oncoming vehicle properly positioned in its lane? Will a passing driver have enough time to return to his or her lane, or should you adjust your speed and position?

- *Possibility of hitting a pedestrian or animal.* Will a pedestrian or an animal near the road step or dart into your path? What actions could you take to reduce the possibility of such behavior?

- *Possible collision with an off-road object.* A traffic situation may force you to leave the road. Are there light poles, trees, or traffic controls on the shoulder that would limit your alternate actions?

Closing movements are more likely to happen when your field of view is limited. Curves, hills, bushes, or other large objects or signs may hide hazards. So can fog, darkness, heavy rain, or snow. Be especially alert under these conditions.

## Decide

When you have gathered important information that is available from the road around you and interpreted it, predicting what effect it may have on your intended path of travel, quickly consider all of the possible courses of action and then choose the

156

best one. Your goal is to minimize your risks. You can do this by adjusting your speed and position. Your intentions must be communicated to other drivers.

## Estimate the Consequences— Leave Yourself an Out

When you are in a traffic situation that has closing potential, adjust your speed and/or position in response to the probability and consequences of a collision.

Suppose you are driving at 55 mph on a two-lane highway through gently rolling farm country. You notice a fenced field ahead to your right. Some cows in the field are running toward the fence. The consequences of a collision with a cow are usually severe. But the probability of the cows breaking through the fence is quite low. So the cows require little attention as a collision threat. Suppose now that several deer are heading toward the road. This situation has a different level of risk. The consequences of a collision with a deer are also severe. There is a high probability, too, that a deer will leap the fence. In this situation, you must adjust your speed to meet the threat. The difference in the level of risk is the difference in the probability that a collision will occur.

You will often be faced with several potential hazards at once. The difficulty this causes is shown in the following example. You are driving along at 30 mph on a two-way street.

**Be aware of potential hazards in and near construction areas. Reduce speed and watch for construction workers and vehicles, obstacles in the road, and damage to the road surface.**

**Drivers passing through this scenic area must cope with a narrow road, parked cars wanting to pull out, and pedestrians waiting to cross the street, all at the same time.**

Coming toward you in the other lane is a steady line of cars. A young child is riding a bicycle alongside the road. The child is having trouble steering and is weaving.

It is clear that you should slow down. You should also move as close to the center line as you can, but make sure that other drivers see you. Turn on your headlights. A car with its headlights on is much more visible. There is a chance that one of the cars may cross the center line, but the probability is now quite low. Of greater concern is the young bicyclist who is having trouble steering in a straight line. This increases the probability that the child may enter your path of travel. After slowing down, make sure the bicyclist sees you. Gently tap the horn. Give the child as much room as possible but be ready to stop quickly.

In judging the probability of a collision and deciding what to do, consider all likely consequences. Though the number of factors may seem almost unlimited, two should help you decide what to do. The most important is the extent of personal injury that may result: How many people are involved? How seriously would they be injured? The second is the amount of property damage that may occur.

## Execute

You can execute your decision by use of the steering wheel, either the accelerator or the brake, and/or the directional signal. In most cases, the maneuver you have to make to avoid conflict will be a routine one. Occasionally, an emergency action will be called for.

Remember, IPDE and the Smith System are ongoing processes. You may be deciding about and reacting to one situation at the same time as you are gathering information about a new one. With practice, you will learn to follow through and execute your decisions smoothly.

# Applying IPDE and the Smith System

Good drivers make safe driving decisions. As you apply the IPDE Process and the Smith System, you should learn to:

- **minimize** (reduce) the risk related to any hazard through responsible speed selection, proper management of time and space, and clear communication with other highway users.

- **separate** one hazard from another in order to simplify situations. Risk can be reduced by reducing the number of hazards you will have to respond to at one time. This will make most situations more manageable.

- **compromise**. Weigh the risks and react to your best advantage when you are faced with a number of conflicts. Try to minimize one risk without increasing another.

**Minimizing Risk** When events with collision potential develop well ahead of your car, you may need to respond with only a simple reduction in speed. Those that develop in your immediate path may be more difficult to handle. Dangerous events that can lead to a collision may be started by other roadway users or may arise from your own actions. One way to try to reduce the number of such events is to improve your ability to judge time-and-space gaps.

Too often, drivers fail to anticipate dangerous events. As a result, their

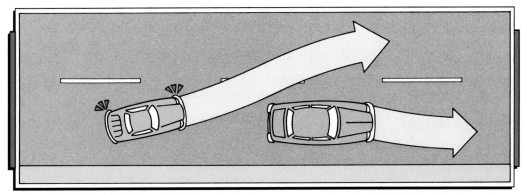

**If you signal your intention to pass in advance, the car you wish to pass can move to the right to give you more room to make the maneuver. This action minimizes risk.**

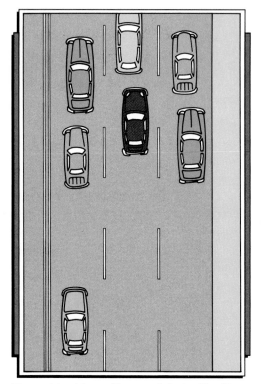

**Try not to drive with a pack in traffic. Keep a space margin around your car, as the car in the left lane is doing.**

speed and road position make it very difficult to respond.

An effective visual search is important in managing response time and minimizing risk. The sooner you are aware that you may be on a collision course, the sooner you can respond.

The time you have to respond can also be increased by keeping as much distance as possible between your car and potential hazards. These include other vehicles, pedestrians, animals, and fixed objects such as parked cars, road signs, walls, buildings, and fences. Keeping your distance from potential hazards is called maintaining a **space margin**.

Space is managed by using steering adjustments and controlling speed with skillful use of the brakes or the accelerator.

Keep a larger space margin around your vehicle at higher speeds and when there is limited traction or visibility. Also keep a space margin between your car and potentially hazardous places, such as a **blind driveway** (one that is blocked from view by trees or shrubbery). Anticipate hazards that may be hidden from view and provide a space margin for them. You may not notice anything in the driveway as you approach. But a driver may suddenly pull out just far enough to check traffic, partly blocking your path of travel. In the case of a hidden driveway, move into the left lane if there is one. If there is no left lane, move close to the center line. This enables people to see you more easily.

A conflict can arise when you are trying to maintain a sufficient time gap both in front and to the rear of your car. Suppose you are followed by a tailgater on a two-way highway. If you speed up, you may dangerously reduce the time-and-space gap ahead and the tailgater may simply continue tailgating. The best thing to do is slow down gradually. Keep these points in mind:

- Traffic flow rarely exceeds posted speeds by more than 5 mph. If you drive slightly slower, you will increase the gap in front of you without having much effect on the traffic behind.

- Rear-end collisions usually occur when vehicles reduce speed quickly, not when speed is reduced gradually or slightly.

- Under the law, you are generally more **liable** (legally responsible) for collisions that involve the front of your car than for those that involve the rear of your car.

Sometimes, a vehicle will follow you so closely that it becomes an extreme hazard. In this case, move well to the right and slow down gradually. This will encourage the tailgating driver to pass. If this does not work, look for a wide, clear road shoulder. You may have to pull off the road to allow the driver to pass you.

Usually, a slight adjustment of both speed and position is better than a major adjustment of one or the other. For example, if you are approaching parked vehicles, move a little farther away from them and slow down slightly. These actions will give you extra time to respond if a person or vehicle should move away from the curb.

Time-and-space gap problems can develop whenever you enter a stream of traffic. They can arise when you pull from a curb, change lanes, merge, or turn right or left at an intersection. You can influence the behavior of other highway users to reduce time-and-space problems through communication.

- Let other highway users know what you plan to do by using your directional signals and horn. The information you provide will help others avoid conflicts with you and reduce the chances of a collision.

- The placement of your vehicle can inform others of your intentions. By obeying traffic laws that regulate lane positioning, you can let other drivers know where you plan to go.

- Use hand signals and eye contact in cases where the other driver is close enough, and traveling slowly enough, to see. For example, you can wave to give another driver permission to merge into traffic ahead of you.

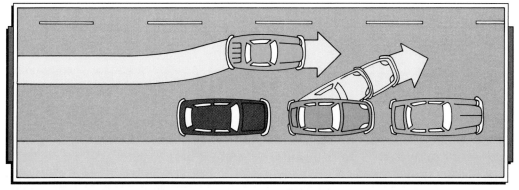

**Whenever you approach parked cars, slow down slightly and increase the space between your car and the parked cars. This will give you a little extra response time.**

This pothole presents a hazard, but swerving into traffic to avoid it could present a much more serious hazard.

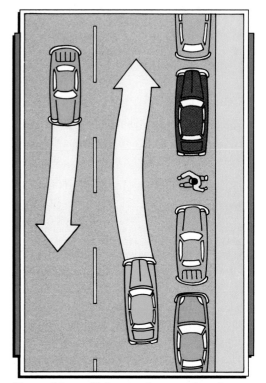

To avoid a collision, make speed and position adjustments as early and as gradually as possible.

- Make others aware of your presence any time you see a hazard or an emergency situation developing. You can signal danger by driving with your headlights on during daylight hours or by using hand signals or your car's emergency flashers. However, make sure that these signals do not confuse other motorists.

These actions can reduce the chance of trouble arising from the unexpected actions of others. They also offer protection against your own errors in judgment. But they cannot substitute for proper control of speed and position.

**Separating Hazards** Often, drivers have to deal with **multiple-hazard conditions** (several hazards at once). These conditions increase the chance of collision. Not all multiple-hazard conditions are difficult. For example, suppose you are driving on a residential street. There are a few potholes, one or two parked cars in each block, and a few pedestrians. Any of these elements could become a problem, so you must keep track of each. But there is no real danger here.

There are more difficult multiple-hazard situations. If possible, you should always try to avoid having to deal with too many hazards at one time because:

- the more hazards present, the greater the chance that difficulties will develop.

- the more hazards that occur at one time, the less likely it is that there will be enough space in which to maneuver.

- the more hazards that are present at once, the greater the chance of making bad decisions.

You cannot prevent all potentially hazardous situations from arising. But if at least one of the hazards is moving, you can usually simplify situations by separating hazards. You do this by adjusting your speed and position so that you will not have to deal with too many of them at one time.

You often have enough control over a situation to keep two or more high-risk situations from developing at once. You do this by anticipating multiple hazards. For example, you may be driving on a narrow, two-way road. You see a pedestrian walking on your side of the road. There is a

You can minimize risks by separating hazards. For example, passing a row of parked cars and passing a bicyclist both present hazards. Therefore, do not do both at the same time.

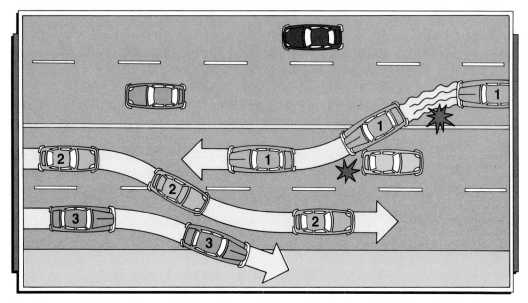

**Car 2 can avoid a head-on collision with car 1 by moving to the right instead of just braking. It may sideswipe car 3, but the consequences of that would be less severe.**

truck coming toward you. By adjusting your speed, you can avoid passing the pedestrian and the truck at the same time. If either does something unexpected, it will now be easier for you to move away from them. In another instance, a bicycle is traveling ahead of you on a narrow, two-way road. Farther ahead there is a blind curve. Adjust your speed so that you do not have to pass the bicycle on the curve, because doing so could bring you into conflict with an oncoming vehicle. In both cases, you have simplified the situation by separating the hazards.

When faced with two hazards at once, one on either side of your vehicle, position your vehicle according to how much danger each side presents. If the hazards are about the same, leave equal space on both sides. If the

hazards are not the same, give greater space to the one that presents the greater risk. When you adjust your position, take care not to surprise other drivers. Signal your movements early and change your position gradually. If possible, make the adjustments within your own lane. Whenever you leave your lane, you increase the risk of having a collision since there may be a vehicle in your blind spot.

If several hazards with collision potential occur at approximately the same point in your path of travel, decide which one would require the quickest response, then choose your speed accordingly.

**Compromise** The most difficult decisions occur when there is no chance of avoiding a collision. If you do not panic, however, you can often reduce the consequences of a collision. For example, you are driving at 55 mph on a road that has two 12-foot lanes in each direction. Traffic is heavy in all four lanes. You are driving in the inside lane 2 seconds behind the car ahead. Suddenly, the left front tire of an oncoming vehicle blows out. The driver slams on the brakes. The oncoming car skids across the center line and hits the left rear fender of the car ahead of you. It continues to skid straight down your lane toward you. If all you do is brake, you will not prevent a head-on collision. This is the worst kind of collision there is. To reduce the consequences of the collision, move as far as possible to the right. Ideally, any driver in the right lane will see the situation and move to the right as well. With 24 feet of roadway, there would be room for three cars to be side by side. With proper steering control and 1 to 2 seconds to respond, you could easily move 8 to 10 feet to the right. This would allow you either to avoid the skidding car or to be struck at an angle. If that car on your right does not move over, you may sideswipe it as you make your maneuver. But the consequences of a sideswipe are less serious than those of a head-on collision that might involve many vehicles.

In complex traffic situations, a decision about one hazard may conflict with a decision on another. For example, a conflict may arise when you try to simplify your path of travel. Suppose you are about to meet an oncoming car. At the point where you expect to meet the car, there are cars parked on the right. If you increase your speed, you will meet the oncoming car where a pedestrian is standing. If you decrease your speed, you will meet the oncoming car on a narrow bridge. What would you do?

Such situations point up the need for compromise. Your decision may not reduce risk as much as you like. But it should reduce risk as much as possible.

## Projects

1. Ride with someone over a frequently traveled road. Record everything you notice that has to do with driving, including traffic signs, pedestrians, and vehicles. Ask the driver which potential hazards she or he noticed. If the driver did not notice some that you saw, explain why you think this happened.

2. While riding in a car, try to predict what others on the highway will do. Take notes on what you see. Compare your predictions with what happens. How often were you correct?

## Words to Know

| | | |
|---|---|---|
| closing movements | tailgating | blind driveway |
| probability | minimize | liable |
| consequence | compromise | multiple-hazard |
| closing in on | space margin | conditions |

## Stop and Review

1. Why do drivers sometimes fail to notice a hazard? Why is it risky at times to assume that other drivers will act in a certain way?
2. How can a driver conduct a selective search?
3. What hazards should you be alert to when slowing down or changing lanes?
4. Why should you be more alert when you are driving in areas where visibility is limited?
5. What is the purpose of searching by category? Describe the 4 major categories.
6. Why do drivers of certain kinds of vehicles tend to be less predictable than others?
7. Describe an effective visual search pattern.
8. Define *closing movements*. What closing movements can result in a collision?
9. How can you judge the amount of risk that a closing movement will create? Where would closing movements most likely occur?
10. Describe 2 situations in which you are faced with several potential hazards at the same time. How would you handle them?
11. List the 5 parts of the Smith System.
12. Define the terms *minimizing risks* and *simplifying situations*. Give an example of each.
13. Discuss 3 techniques you can use to minimize risks.
14. How is space managed?
15. Why should you keep a space margin between your car and a blind driveway?
16. List some safe ways you can react to a tailgater.
17. How can you influence the behavior of other highway users?
18. Explain why it is best to avoid having to deal with multiple hazards at one time.
19. Give some examples of situations in which drivers should compromise by adjusting vehicle speed and position.
20. When there is no chance of avoiding a collision, what can you still aim to do?

You are heading north on a two-lane road. There is a driveway ahead on the right. You notice a car coming fast out of the driveway. The driver may not see you, since there are bushes partly blocking his view of the road. There is a car in the south-bound lane, and a car approximately 3 seconds behind you.

1. Analyze the situation and, using IPDE and the Smith System, describe your response. What options are open to you?

Now imagine a similar situation, except that there are houses on both sides of the street and parked cars on your right. Several young children are running on the sidewalk. You notice one of the children throwing a ball to a dog.

2. Apply IPDE and the Smith System. Having identified these conditions, make your predictions of the possible conflicts. What actions could you take to reduce the level of risk in this situation?

# CHAPTER 9 TEST

Complete the sentences by filling in the blanks with the correct terms.

reduce speed    bicyclists      roadway markings    animals
   sharply      closing movements    space margin      hazards
tailgating       Smith System       sideswipe        signs
blind           pedestrians        signals

1. _____ , _____ , and _____ provide information about the driving environment and the road.

2. _____ are actions that can lead to a collision.

3. A _____ is possible when a passing vehicle cuts back into your lane before completely passing you.

4. A vehicle that is following dangerously close to your car is _____ .

5. The _____ is a set of 5 driving behaviors that can help you keep a safe position in traffic.

6. _____ , _____ , _____ are the least protected highway users.

7. Keeping your distance from potential hazards is called maintaining a _____ .

8. A driveway that is blocked from view by trees or shrubbery is called a _____ driveway.

9. Rear-end collisions usually occur when vehicles _____ .

10. The more _____ present, the greater the chance that difficulties will develop.

---

Select the one best answer to each of the following questions.

11. IPDE is:
    (a) also called the Smith System.
    (b) short for Identify, Prepare, Decide, Execute. (c) an organized strategy for driving. (d) a response to an emergency situation.

12. Which of the following is *not* part of the Smith System?
    (a) Get the big picture. (b) Keep your eyes moving. (c) Make sure others see you. (d) Aim low in steering.

13. Closing movements:
    (a) can end up as accidents.
    (b) are less likely to occur when heavy rain or snow is present.
    (c) will become automatic as you gain experience as a driver.
    (d) result from using the IPDE strategy.

14. Multiple-hazard conditions:
    (a) increase the chance that difficulties will develop. (b) decrease the chance of making poor judgments. (c) increase the amount of maneuvering space. (d) are always difficult.

15. To help minimize risks, you should:
    (a) make closing movements early.
    (b) maintain a space margin around your car. (c) pull over and think whenever you have a tough driving decision to make. (d) none of the above.

# Cooperating with Other Highway Users

## Chapter Objectives

In this chapter you will learn how to:

■ become aware of and handle the special problems presented by bicycles, motorcycles, mopeds, snowmobiles, small cars, and trucks.

■ become aware of pedestrians and deal effectively with situations where pedestrians are present.

## Small Vehicles

There has been a marked increase in the number of bicycles, motorcycles, mopeds, and snowmobiles sold in the United States in recent years. People often use bicycles, motorcycles, and mopeds to travel to and from work. Basically, though, these vehicles are used mainly for leisure-time activities.

With the increased use of these vehicles, there has also been an increase in the number of accidents involving them. Most of the accidents are a result of errors made by the operators of these vehicles. These errors include lack of experience with

**169**

Many cities have special lanes for bicyclists. Be especially careful when crossing these lanes or driving near them. Never park in a bicycle lane.

the vehicle, failure to see possible hazards, and not being seen by other drivers. Improper use of the vehicle, failure to wear proper clothing, and violations of traffic laws are other errors. Knowledge of these errors helps drivers to be more aware and can help them make more accurate decisions.

**Bicycles** There are about 70 million bicycles in use in the United States today. For many years, bicycles were thought of as toys used mostly by children. However, many adults now ride bicycles, even in heavy commuter traffic, and sometimes where high speeds are allowed. They ride in all types of weather and after dark.

There are also more large tricycles in use. These are found mostly in retirement communities. Due to their size, these vehicles are easier to see than standard bicycles. However, they tip over more easily, particularly if they are moving too fast or are turned too quickly.

Bicycle injuries and fatalities among people over 15 years of age have risen sharply in the last decade. It is important to exercise special caution when sharing the road with bicyclists. They should observe traffic laws—ride on the right side of the road, stop at red lights, and signal turns—but they do not always do so.

As a driver, you must scan the roadway ahead of a bicyclist. You need to ask yourself if anything will require an adjustment in the bicyclist's position. Railroad crossings, stones, or storm drains may require little or no response from you. But to a bicyclist, they are critical and may call for a major adjustment. Storm drains are a particularly serious hazard. They are usually next to the curb, just where bicyclists ride. The front wheel of a bicycle may slip between the bars of the grating, stopping the bicycle and throwing the rider off. A bicyclist who sees such a drain ahead will steer around it, moving from the curb into the traffic lane. You must allow a bicyclist room and time to respond. Bicycles are more limited in their ability to turn or stop than is generally believed. Take this into account and adjust your speed or position accordingly. Never try to pass a bicycle rider in a tight space. Be sure to signal your intentions to bicyclists before stopping or turning, just as you do to other cars.

**Motorcycles** A motorcycle is a cross between an automobile and a bicycle. It has an engine and can travel the same roads at the same speeds as a car. However, like a bicycle, it has only two wheels.

By combining characteristics of both types of vehicles, the motorcycle takes on its own set of advantages and disadvantages. Even if you never drive a motorcycle, you should understand the special characteristics of the vehicles that share the road with you.

There are 5.8 million motorcycles in use in the United States today. One reason for their popularity is economic. A motorcycle costs less to purchase and gets much better gas mileage than a car.

However, a motorcycle is far less

This motorcyclist is illegally passing on a curve and forcing the van toward the shoulder of the road. Motorcycles should follow the same right-of-way laws as cars.

This motorcyclist should be on the left side of the lane so that he or she is visible in the rear-view mirror of the car ahead.

and gloves to reduce injury in case of accidents.

Other drivers on the road often do not realize how vulnerable the motorcycle is. Because it can move as quickly as a car and sounds so powerful, a motorcycle may seem to be quite sturdy. Many automobile drivers, therefore, don't allow for difficulties motorcyclists may have in avoiding obstacles or driving on slippery surfaces.

In fact, motorcycles should be given the same special consideration that bicyclists require. They need extra room to avoid rough surfaces and may have to reduce speed when crossing railroad tracks and following sharp curves.

Car drivers should also keep in mind that motorcycles require a longer stopping distance when traveling at high speeds.

In addition, because the motorcycle does not occupy a whole lane, it may easily disappear into another driver's blind spot. A motorcycle driver should ride on the left side of the lane in order to be visible in the rear-view mirror of the car ahead. Still, remember to check your blind spots before changing lanes.

stable than a car. Like bicycle riders, motorcyclists must avoid potholes and sewer gratings. They must also be very careful in situations where traction is reduced: an oil spill on the road, loose gravel, ice, wet leaves, or puddles can all cause skids. Strong winds, including drafts created by large vehicles passing in the opposite direction, can also affect a motorcycle's stability.

Since motorcycles travel at far greater speeds than bicycles, this instability can lead to dangerous accidents. Obviously, a motorcycle gives the driver and passenger far less protection than a car does. When a motorcycle skids and cannot be righted, the riders face the risk of hitting either the road or other vehicles with great impact.

Motorcycle riders should wear helmets, eye protection, heavy clothing,

**Mopeds** The word **moped** comes from the names of two vehicles: a motor-driven cycle and a pedal-driven cycle. A moped is like a bicycle because it is stopped by applying hand brakes and can be pedaled. It is like a motorcycle because it is run by an engine and operated with a hand throttle. The engine on a moped is small and produces only 1 to 2 horse-power of energy. For comparison, a motorcycle engine can be up to 24 times as large as a moped engine. Because of this small engine, mopeds can drive about 165 miles on a gallon of gasoline. State speed limits for mopeds are in the range of 30 mph.

It costs much less to buy and operate a moped than a motorcycle or a car. This is one reason for their popularity. There are about 1 million mopeds in use in the United States.

Although mopeds have their advantages, there are some problems connected with their use. In 1984, accidents involving mopeds, motor scooters, and small motor bikes accounted for 170 traffic deaths in the United States.

Since moped owners often use them to get to and from work, mopeds are found on roads with fast-moving traffic where they are often unable to keep up with the flow. Their slow speed causes conflicts which can lead to collisions. Drivers must be aware of the limitations of mopeds when sharing the road with them, and be ready to adjust speed or position to accommodate them. Always search the road ahead of a moped to see if any object in the roadway may force the operator to make an abrupt change in position. Be as cautious when you follow and pass a moped as you would be when you follow and pass a bicycle.

Both moped operators and bicyclists can make themselves more visible by wearing reflective clothing, by placing reflective devices on their

Bicyclists should use some device, such as a flag, to make themselves more visible to drivers.

These moped riders should be riding in the far right lane and wearing heavy clothes in addition to their helmets.

Snowmobiles are allowed on the road in some local communities. They are hard to control and to stop. Give them space.

vehicles and making sure that all lights are working well, and by traveling as far to the right in their traffic lane as possible. Also, moped riders should stay away from heavily traveled roads until they are skillful at operating their vehicles. To protect themselves against injury, they should wear helmets, leather gloves, heavy pants, jackets, and boots.

**Snowmobiles** A snowmobile is a motor-driven vehicle designed for travel on snow or ice. It moves on a revolving belt or tread. It is not generally considered a motor vehicle. Therefore, snowmobiles do not have to be registered with the Department of Motor Vehicles. There are anywhere from 2 million to 5 million snowmobiles in the United States.

Snowmobiles are usually not allowed on state highways. In some parts of the country, though, local communities allow them on certain roads.

Like many other special vehicles, snowmobiles are difficult to see because they are very close to the ground. They are often driven over ground that is covered with light, fluffy snow. This may create a cloud of snow that makes them even harder to see.

Snowmobiles can travel fast for long periods of time. This makes them very dangerous. They are hard to handle and to stop. Snowmobiles are often driven by young children. Therefore, as a driver, you must leave extra time and space to adjust to any maneuver that a snowmobile may make.

**Small Cars** During the fuel shortages of the 1970s, many Americans bought small cars as a way of getting more miles to a gallon of gasoline. What started as a fuel-saving measure then has turned into a national habit for many drivers. Today, there are more small cars on the road than ever before.

Small cars are generally less expensive to buy and cost less to operate than the larger models. In addition, many city dwellers like small cars because they fit into parking spaces that larger automobiles have to pass by.

However, small cars have their drawbacks. The fuel-efficient smaller engines in most small cars mean less power. This can be a problem on the highway, where it is important to keep up with the flow of traffic. It is often harder for a small car to pass another vehicle because it lacks the power to accelerate quickly to passing speed. When the road is a steep, upward hill, the small car may actually lose speed.

To overcome these problems, more drivers are purchasing cars with turbocharger engines. A turbocharger forces more air into the engine than it would normally take in on its own using either a carburetor or a fuel-injection system independently. The more air an engine takes in, the more power it can develop.

If you are driving a small car or are being passed by one, keep in mind that acceleration may be slower than in other cars. Allow extra room for the maneuver.

Strong crosswinds are also a problem. The lighter automobiles cannot hold to the road the way a heavier vehicle can. On a slippery road surface, particularly in rainy or snowy weather, a small car may skid more easily. Therefore, it is important to give a small car plenty of room when road conditions are poor.

**Recreational vehicles present some of the same hazards as trucks, especially when going uphill. Allow a 4-second following distance for better visibility.**

## Large Vehicles

**Trucks** Whether you do most of your traveling on city streets, country roads, or highways, you will probably come into frequent contact with large trucks. Understanding the special characteristics of the large vehicles will make sharing the road easier and safer.

The most obvious difference between a truck and other vehicles is size. Sitting high up above the road surface, the driver has excellent forward visibility. However, vehicles to the right of the truck may occupy the driver's blind spot.

In addition, the size of the truck causes visibility problems for other drivers. You may have difficulty seeing around a truck to hazards or obstructions ahead. Always allow at least a 4-second following distance when you are behind a truck to increase your visibility.

A truck loaded with cargo outweighs a car by many tons. This means slow acceleration and loss of speed on an uphill road, and generally a marked increase in speed on a downgrade.

If you find that a truck is bearing down on you as you head downhill, pull into a right-hand lane, if there is one, or pull over to allow the truck to pass.

The truck's size makes maneuvering more difficult. Trucks require a wide turning space. The driver may overlap parts of several lanes, particularly when making a sharp turn.

**Large, heavy vehicles may increase acceleration a great deal when going downhill. Keep this in mind when passing a truck.**

**Most accidents involving pedestrians happen in urban areas. However, pedestrian accidents in rural areas are more likely to be fatal.**

Leave the driver enough room so that you will not be in danger of contact.

In cities, trucks often have to operate within limited space. For example, they must often back into driveways along narrow streets. This may mean several adjustments that take time and block the street until the process is completed.

Be aware of stopped trucks with their engines running. They may just be in the middle of repositioning. If you move up too close behind a truck that is about to move in *reverse,* you may be out of sight of the driver. The key to driving among trucks is to leave the large vehicles plenty of room and make sure you remain visible to the drivers.

# Pedestrians

Eight thousand pedestrians are killed and 80,000 injured each year in the United States. Among adults, about one-third of the pedestrians killed had been drinking alcoholic beverages.

Research shows that many pedestrians killed by cars were never licensed to drive or did not understand problems related to vehicle control.

## Rural, Urban, and Suburban Areas

More than 85 percent of the pedestrians who get hurt are injured in urban areas. But accidents involving pedestrians in rural areas are often worse than those in cities. This is because vehicles travel faster in rural areas. The chance of a death in an urban pedestrian accident is 1 in 13. The chance in a rural area is about 1 in 5. Still, nearly 73 percent of the total number of pedestrians killed are in urban areas.

Most pedestrian accidents in business districts involve adults in intersections. Usually, the driver is looking at other vehicles or at traffic signals and does not see the pedestrian until the accident happens.

To make things worse, many pedestrians have difficulty judging the speed of traffic and the time needed to cross a street. They may run into the street or start across just as a traffic light is changing. Braking takes time, and heavy traffic does not let the driver swerve far enough to avoid pedestrians.

Most pedestrians struck at intersections are hit just as they step into the street. The vehicle is in the lane closest to the sidewalk. Usually, the car is driving straight through the intersection.

Pedestrians, like drivers, must learn to judge the gaps in traffic. The typical young adult can cross a two-lane street in a residential area in 4 to 6 seconds. A child needs 7 or more seconds. An old person may need from 7 to 10 seconds to cross the same street. As a driver, you should estimate how much time pedestrians

**Most pedestrian accidents in business districts involve adults in intersections. The driver may be watching other traffic; pedestrians may misjudge time-and-space gaps.**

will need to cross the street. Then you should adjust your speed to avoid hitting them.

People who live in the suburbs are not as aware of traffic hazards as people who live in cities. Since intersections are far apart and traffic is usually lighter, people often cross the street at places other than intersections. Other people may step into the street while mowing their lawns or sweeping sidewalks. If there are no sidewalks, people are likely to walk in the street. Parked cars and shrubbery limit both the driver's and the pedestrian's visibility. These factors combine to increase the chances of an accident.

Meter readers, postal employees, and people delivering packages have also been known to step into the path of moving vehicles. These people are usually thinking about their jobs, not about traffic.

Pedestrians and joggers are particularly hard to see at night and in rainy weather. They should wear light-colored or reflective clothing. Still, as a driver, you must be especially careful in these low-visibility situations.

**Ground Search** You have been taught to search at least 12 seconds ahead of your car. When you drive in residential areas, you must do a special type of scanning for young pedestrians. It is called a **ground search.**

**Before you back into or out of a driveway, search for children. They may be out of sight behind cars or shrubbery. Always check behind your car.**

**Be alert for children running to or home from school bus stops. They may forget to watch traffic.**

Parked vehicles or shrubbery may hide children from view. Look for movement under and around these obstructions. Look from one side of the road to the other. Look for shadows that may tell you a child is near the street. Any movement should warn you that there may soon be a conflict.

Since young children are small, it is hard to see them. They are also apt to dart into the street. In residential areas, keep your speed low and your car as far from the curb or parked cars as is safe. That way, you will be better able to see children before they move into the street.

Young children often do not act the way we expect. Even when they are near heavy traffic, they may run or play games or push each other. When they are playing, children often forget about traffic and run into the street. Parked cars limit the escape routes for both driver and child.

Their height keeps children from seeing over the trunks or hoods of parked cars. Small shrubs block their vision. Therefore, every driver must look for danger signals. The main one is children playing near the street or road. Be careful, also, if you see a ball bouncing into the street or notice a pet or any wheeled toy. Check for a single child who may run across the street to join a group of children. Be alert near construction sites and playgrounds. Children are likely to be there. Look for them also at bus stops, in school zones, and where you see crossing guards or school patrols.

Children also like to ride bicycles, tricycles, wagons, skateboards, and sleds down steep, sloping driveways. Take great care when you drive past such driveways. Anticipate the actions of children and be prepared to adjust speed or position to reduce potential conflict.

**The Elderly** Elderly people generally take longer than young people to cross a street. Sometimes, they fail to check traffic. They can also make errors in time-space judgment. In some cases, they need more time to cross than the "Walk" signal gives them. With this in mind, you should be careful as you come to a red light that is turning to green.

Slow-moving pedestrians can be a serious problem on wide streets. Vehicles stopped in other lanes may block your view. A pedestrian may suddenly step from behind a vehicle into your path. If you are not ready for this, you will have no place to go and no time to stop.

**Blind Pedestrians** Blind people often carry a white cane or have a seeing-eye dog to lead them. Most have learned to cope quite well with traffic. A driver must always yield the right-of-way to a blind person.

**Strollers and Carriages** A person who is pushing a stroller or baby carriage may have trouble getting down off the curb. Once in a while, a carriage goes out of control. It may even roll into the path of traffic. If you are not moving too fast and can see danger as it approaches, you may have the time and space to avoid it.

If you are not sure that a pedestrian sees you, slow down and move as far away as traffic allows. You may also tap the horn lightly. However, do not blast the horn. A blast of the horn may scare someone and cause her or him to do the wrong thing.

# Animals

**Small Animals** Pets often dart into the street or road. In trying not to hit the animal, a driver may swerve and strike a fixed object or another vehicle. A driver may also stop quickly and be struck from the rear. However, good visual search habits help to prevent accidents caused by animals. Use the same ground-search pattern that you use

**Blind people usually walk with a seeing-eye dog or carry a white cane. Give special consideration to blind pedestrians.**

when you suspect that small children may be near.

**Large Animals** If you see signs that say "Cattle Crossing" or "Open Range," look for farm animals on or near the road. Be cautious. A collision with a large animal can be very serious, even if you are not moving fast. Slow down as soon as animals come into view. It is hard to predict what they will do. Be prepared to stop and to give them as much space as you can. Move over and pass the animals at a low rate of speed.

**Wild Animals** You have probably seen small birds or animals hit and killed by cars. Many deer and other large animals are killed by cars as

**Slow down when you see signs that warn of animal crossings or announce scenic overlooks. Tourists, cars, and animals may cause unexpected congestion.**

well. A collision with such an animal can result in great damage to a car. It can cause injury or death to a driver or a passenger.

In some places, such as mountains, plains, and forests, wild animals are a major problem. They are not seen on the highway often. When an animal does come out, drivers often panic. Also, many animals come out at twilight or after dark. With little light to see by, drivers may not notice an animal until it moves into the path of the car.

There are very few steps you can take to avoid these accidents. All you can do is to slow your speed when you drive in places where you know deer or other wild animals may cross the road. You can also look for movement or the reflection of light off the eyes of animals when it is dark.

# *Projects*

1. Ask your local police department to supply some statistics and information about pedestrian accidents in your area. Are there any streets or intersections that have especially high numbers of such accidents? What age groups are most often involved? How often is alcohol a factor? Are weather conditions and time of day important? Report your findings to your class.

ground search               moped

## Stop and Review

1. Describe 3 users of the highway system that are not on foot or riding in cars or trucks.
2. Name a cause of most accidents involving mopeds and bicycles.
3. Name 3 roadway conditions that are not hazardous to motor vehicle operators but create extreme hazards for bicyclists. How can a driver compensate for these hazards?
4. What combination of characteristics gives the motorcycle its advantages and disadvantages?
5. What do mopeds and bicycles have in common? How are they different?
6. Describe the special problems that moped operators have while riding in traffic.
7. How can riders of bicycles and mopeds make themselves more visible?
8. Why are snowmobiles often difficult to see?
9. Why should drivers allow extra time and space to adjust to any maneuver a snowmobile might make?
10. Name some advantages and disadvantages of small cars.
11. In what ways do trucks handle differently from cars?
12. What does research show about many pedestrians killed by cars?
13. Why do rural pedestrian accidents result in fatalities more often than urban pedestrian accidents?
14. Why is it dangerous to drive through an intersection without carefully checking first, even when the traffic light is green and the crossing traffic is stopped?
15. Define the term *ground search*.
16. How is a ground search different from an ordinary visual search? When is it most important?
17. List some reasons why young children are often involved in pedestrian accidents.
18. Why are the elderly often involved in pedestrian accidents? What can drivers do to reduce the risks to older pedestrians?
19. What are some of the hazards pets create for drivers? If you were driving and saw a dog running near the roadway, what else would you look for? If a dog started to run in front of you, what would you do?
20. Discuss the bumper-sticker slogan "I brake for animals."

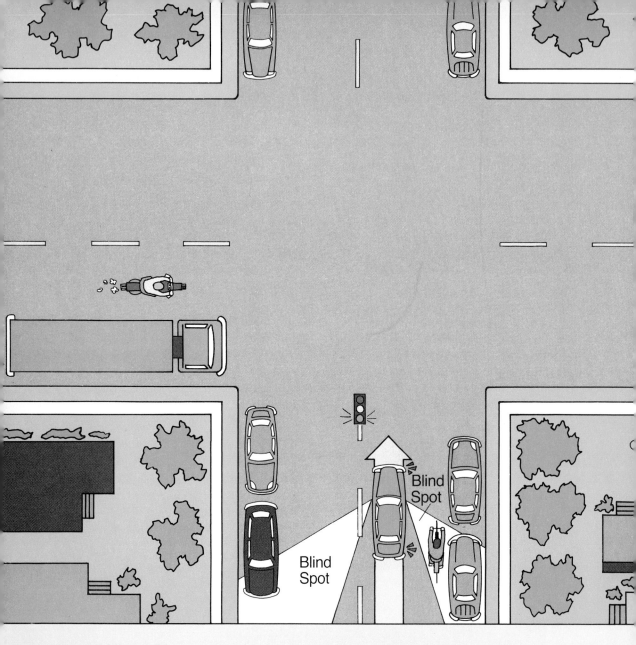

Blind Spot

Blind Spot

## *What if...*

You are driving down a tree-lined street with many homes. Cars are parked along both sides of the street. You see bicycles in one yard.

1. What should you do?
You are approaching an intersection.

You want to turn right onto the cross street.

2. What should you do first?
A large van parked to your left blocks your view of the left lane.

3. What should you do? Why?

Complete the sentences by filling in the blanks with the correct terms.

| | | | | |
|---|---|---|---|---|
| 7 to 10 | snowmobile | urban | helmets | mopeds |
| increase | ground search | operator | visible | tip over |

1. Most accidents involving bicycles, mopeds, and snowmobiles are the result of _____ errors.

2. _____ are a combination of motor-driven cycles and pedal-driven cycles.

3. Wearing reflective clothing makes bicyclists and moped drivers more _____ .

4. A _____ moves on a revolving belt or tread.

5. Most pedestrians who are injured are in _____ areas.

6. Motorcycle riders should wear _____ , eye protection, heavy clothing, and gloves to reduce injury in case of accidents.

7. A special type of scanning good for use in residential areas is called a _____ .

8. You should _____ your following distance to increase your visibility when you are behind a truck.

9. Large tricycles are likely to _____ , particularly if they are turned too quickly.

10. An older person may need from _____ seconds to cross the street.

---

Select the one best answer to each of the following questions.

11. Collisions with large wild animals: (a) are not serious. (b) are a major problem in some areas. (c) seldom happen at twilight. (d) could usually be avoided if drivers would not slow down where they know wild animals may cross the road.

12. Operators of mopeds can reduce the chance of collisions by: (a) keeping to roads with fast-moving traffic. (b) traveling as far to the left as possible. (c) wearing reflective clothing. (d) driving as slowly as possible.

13. Most pedestrians who are struck at intersections are hit by cars: (a) approaching from the left. (b) turning right. (c) turning left. (d) going straight through.

14. Which of the following is *not* true of pedestrian accidents? (a) Most of those occuring in business districts involve adults in intersections. (b) Most injuries occur in urban areas. (c) Those in urban areas are often worse than those in rural areas. (d) One-third of adults killed had been drinking alcoholic beverages.

15. A ground search is used: (a) to scan. (b) only in business districts. (c) before leaving a car. (d) to detect parked cars.

# Special Driving Conditions

## Chapter Objectives

In this chapter you will learn how to:

- be aware of atmospheric and environmental conditions and the demands they make on your driving patterns.
- take into account conditions that limit your visibility, and adjust your driving accordingly.
- be alert for on-road and off-road hazards.

Simply learning the mechanics of driving will not make you a good driver. In addition to controlling a car and being alert to others on the road, skilled drivers must learn to position their vehicles in a way that will allow them to manage time and space effectively under different types of driving conditions and to adapt to various situations.

# Atmospheric Conditions

**Nighttime or Darkness** It is always hard to see at night. Clean, properly aimed headlights do help you see straight ahead. But they are little help in lighting off-road areas or much of your path as you turn. When turning, look along your path beyond the area lit by the headlights.

Do not stare at the headlights of approaching vehicles. Look slightly to your right. Some roads have a road-edge line you can scan along. Switch your headlights to low beam when you meet or follow other vehicles. Low beams cut down the glare of your lights.

If a vehicle comes toward you with high-beam headlights on, signal the other driver to switch to low beams by flashing your headlights from low to high and back to low quickly.

**Fog and Smog** Fog, smog, and smoke can be so **dense** (thick) that they make it hard to see even the front of your car's hood. Because fog and smog make it harder to judge distances, you should reduce your speed and increase the space between you and the car ahead.

When you drive in fog, use your headlights on low beam. If you use high beams, the water in the fog will reflect your bright headlights back into your eyes.

Dense fog can cause moisture to gradually accumulate on the windshield without your realizing that visibility has been reduced. Use of wipers will prevent this.

Spots of fog are very bad because they can grow dense in an instant, cutting your field of vision with little warning. When this happens, reduce

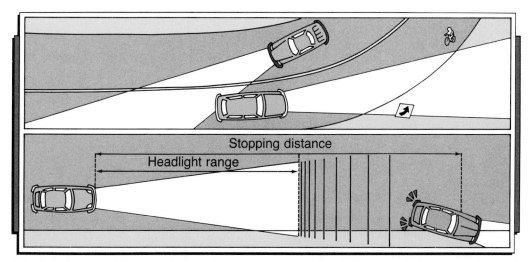

**Headlights do not fully light up the road on curves. If you drive too fast on straight roads, they will not shine so far ahead that you will have time to stop to avoid a hazard.**

**Fog can drastically reduce your visibility. Keep your speed down and use your headlights on low beam. Use your windshield wipers occasionally to keep your windshield clear.**

your speed gradually. Keep in mind the reduced visibility of drivers behind you, who may fail to see your brake lights.

If fog becomes too dense for you to see at all, pull off the road as soon as you safely can.

**Rain** Rain reduces visibility and traction. Oil that has left a thin film on the road surface, wet leaves, and dirt combine with the water to make the road slippery. As you drive, be aware that your stopping distances on a wet road can be four or more times as long as on a dry road.

Reduce your speed to minimize the possibility of losing vehicle control. For greatest control while driving in a rainstorm, follow these pointers:

- Drive in the tracks of other cars.

- Drive with the left tires near the center line. The road is usually crowned or built to be higher in the center, so there will be less water there.

- Make sure your headlights are on so others can see you more easily.

- Allow a greater following distance.

- Use your wipers to clear rain from the windshield. You may also need the defroster to keep condensation from forming on the insides of the windows.

It may be necessary to pull off the road until the rain eases off. If you do, remember to check all around you, choose a safe and level spot on the shoulder, and turn on your emergency flashers while you are stopped.

Traction is greatly reduced when the road surface is wet. Your car can hydroplane even at low speeds. Drive in the tracks of other cars and allow for greater stopping distances.

**Snow and Ice** Snow and ice also present the driving hazards of reduced visibility and traction. You need to be alert and cautious when driving in the snow, particularly when crossing over bridges because they tend to freeze more quickly than the rest of the road surface. Icy patches, strong winds, and glare from the sun reflecting off the snow are additional driving hazards in the winter.

Before setting out, scrape ice and brush snow off all windows, mirrors, headlights, and taillights. Also remove snow from your car's roof and hood so that it will not cover your windows as you begin to travel.

Use your wipers to keep the windshield clear from the outside and your defrosters to keep the windows from fogging up. Turn on your headlights to a low-beam setting to make you more visible to other drivers.

Falling snow reduces visibility. Use the windshield wipers. If the blades ice up, pull over and clean them.

Driving toward the sun at sunrise or sunset, you get sun glare. Reduce speed, wear sunglasses, and use sun visors.

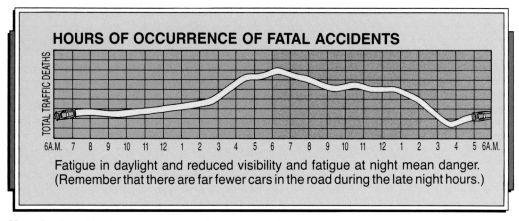

## HOURS OF OCCURRENCE OF FATAL ACCIDENTS

TOTAL TRAFFIC DEATHS

6A.M. 7 8 9 10 11 12 1 2 3 4 5 6 7 8 9 10 11 12 1 2 3 4 5 6A.M.

Fatigue in daylight and reduced visibility and fatigue at night mean danger. (Remember that there are far fewer cars in the road during the late night hours.)

More fatal accidents occur at dusk than at any other time of day or night. Use your headlights at that hour to make your car more visible to other drivers.

**Sun Glare** At sunrise and sunset, there can be a strong glare from the sun. If you are driving toward the sun, it may be very hard to see the road ahead. Sun glare is worse if your car's windshield is dirty or scratched. Sun visors or sunglasses can help. The sun visors should be adjusted so that you can see 12 seconds ahead without changing your driving posture. When there is sun glare, you may not be able to see the brake lights of a car that is slowing down, so you should reduce your speed in general. Remember that if the sun is behind you, oncoming drivers have the glare problem and will have trouble seeing your car.

# Environmental Conditions

Things often found on or near the road can also limit what you see. Any place on or near the highway where you have less than full vision should get special attention.

**Hills**  As you come to the top of a hill, your vision will be temporarily limited. The steeper the grade of the hill, the less you will be able to see, so choose a speed and position that will let you respond to hazards that may be just over the crest.

**Objects Adjacent to the Road**  Objects of almost any size may hide important things from your view. A tree trunk could hide an adult. Signboards or buildings could block a large vehicle.

**Bushes and Shrubbery**  Drivers often do not take note of shrubbery because it is not in their pathway. Bushes or shrubbery, however, could hide vehicles that may close in on your path of travel, or children who could dart into the road. When vision is limited, you should be prepared to cover your brake.

**Blind Turns**  On some turns, the driver's vision along the path of travel is blocked. Bushes, walls, or other things along the inside of the turn keep you from seeing as far as you need to. Drive cautiously.

**Other Vehicles**  Almost any other vehicle can limit your field of vision, especially a truck, bus, or van. The larger the vehicle, the more area it hides. In general, moving vehicles do not limit a driver's field of vision as much as parked ones do. Parked vehicles can keep you from seeing persons about to open a car door and step out. They can also hide pedestrians or cars that are about to move into your path. Look for clues, such as tire position, brake or backup lights, and exhaust smoke, that indicate a parked vehicle may move into your path of travel.

**Never pass on a hill. Be prepared for hazards that may be out of sight over the crest of a hill. Vehicles, animals, pedestrians, or other obstacles may be in your intended path.**

## Visual Obstructions Inside a Vehicle

Things inside your car can cut down your field of vision, too. Passengers may partly block your view in the rear-view mirror. Door posts, roof supports, and the rear-view mirror also limit what you can see. At some angles, they can hide other vehicles from your view. Packages piled on the rear seat, clothing hung on a rod, and an open trunk can also limit your vision.

## On-Road Hazards

There are many things with which you could collide on any road: bumps, bottles, boxes, tree branches, parts of vehicles, and so on. As you watch the road while driving, learn to spot anything that has collision potential. You must be able to judge not only the dangers involved in hitting something in the road but also the dangers involved in trying to avoid it.

As you drive, search the road for objects with which you could collide. Be aware of any potential dangers involved in avoiding them.

# Off-Road Objects and Hazards

Most of the things that cause hazards on the road (such as holes, bumps, or litter) also occur in off-road areas. Some other common off-road hazards are light poles, sign posts, fire hydrants, trees, bushes, fences, ditches, and embankments.

Although fixed objects off the road are not as hazardous as those on the road, you must not ignore them. Scan conditions off the road ahead to get important information about the shoulder of the road. Scanning ahead and planning a safe escape route will reduce hazards if you must leave the road in a hurry. The right information about off-road areas will help you recover smoothly if you are forced to steer onto the shoulder of the road.

Objects within 9 feet of the road are a problem not only because drivers might hit them when leaving the road but because such objects nearly always cause drivers to move away from them. Drivers who feel threatened by light poles, trees, signs, and bridge railings may move too close to the middle of the road, thus placing themselves on a collision course with oncoming drivers.

# Busy City Streets

What generally sets city driving apart from other types of driving is

After a storm, watch for fallen trees or branches on the road. Use your headlights to warn other drivers of hazards.

the density of vehicle and pedestrian traffic and the lack of space to maneuver. Conditions do vary from city to city and among different neighborhoods. However, city streets generally have more cars, trucks, buses, and people on them than do rural roads or highways.

High traffic density means slower traffic. Cars parked along the curb make the usable part of the street even narrower. This further limits the time and space there is to respond to traffic situations.

Frequent intersections, road signs, and traffic lights provide interruptions to the flow of traffic. City drivers must regulate their speed when they are behind buses or taxis making stops for their riders. They must also be more alert to pedestrians stepping out into traffic illegally, and bicyclists, who travel at much slower speeds, sharing the road. Unfortunately, bicyclists too frequently ignore traffic control devices when riding in the city.

Finally, even when traffic is not heavy, particularly late at night and on Sundays, city drivers must still obey speed limits, which are generally much lower than limits in rural areas or on highways.

**Keeping Alert** Concentration is important for all drivers, but city drivers must make a special effort to be alert to hazards. Never stare at a single distracting event. Keep your eyes moving so that you will notice dangerous situations as they develop and be ready to react to them. Frequently the only non-collision response possible in dense traffic is to brake, so you must make sure to maintain a safe following distance.

Turns can be difficult in city traffic. You must be especially careful when making left turns where there are no turn lanes or traffic signals. Always signal your intentions and be aware of hazards all around you.

When you turn from one busy street onto another, you must check oncoming traffic—those vehicles proceeding straight toward you and those that are also making turns. In addition, pedestrians may be trying to cross the street as you enter it.

The best approach to city traffic is to be alert to rapidly changing situations, and to try not to become flustered by distractions.

City drivers must maintain their concentration. Often there are many things happening at once. Keep your eyes moving. Avoid staring at any one thing.

**Country driving presents hazards different from those of city or highway driving. Drivers must reduce speed and look out for oncoming traffic on this narrow country bridge.**

# Along Country Roads

As you drive from the city to the countryside, you will see striking differences in traffic conditions.

There are typically fewer vehicles and pedestrians traveling along country roads. You probably will not have to make frequent adjustments for slowing buses and taxis. And you will encounter fewer busy intersections with many lanes of traffic all moving at the same time.

Country driving, however, has its own hazards and requires its own skills. Visibility is sometimes limited due to tall crops growing near the road and ditch banks or fence lines overgrown with bushes. Since you may find few traffic control devices along country roads, you will have to depend more on your own judgment when making certain types of decisions. One particular skill you will need in the country involves passing slow-moving vehicles.

## Moving Ahead of Slower Traffic

Most country roads are only one lane wide in each direction. Since slow-moving farm vehicles and passenger cars both use this single lane, drivers may find themselves stuck behind a large piece of farm equipment, unable to see around it.

Slow-moving vehicles, such as this horse-drawn carriage, will often pull to the right to allow you to pass.

Overtaking, or passing, such a vehicle on a one-lane road can be dangerous if you are not alert to possible hazards. In many cases, the driver will pull to the side and/or stop to allow you to pass. In this case, you can simply move around the vehicle. Be sure you do not pass too close to the vehicle, but also make certain you will not be moving into the path of oncoming traffic.

If the vehicle ahead of you does not pull to the side, and you feel you must pass, you may have to pull out into the opposing lane to see around it. Do so only when three conditions are met:

- It is legal to pass. You cannot pass when the dividing line on your side of the road is solid or in an area designated a no passing zone.

- You must have a clear view of oncoming traffic at least 10 seconds ahead of your car. You must also be sure there is no obstruction on the right side of the road that will force the driver of the farm equipment to move left, blocking the whole road. Never pass as you approach the crest of a hill or when the opposite side of the road is hidden around a curve.

- You must be certain you will have enough time to pull out, accelerate to a point far enough ahead of the slower vehicle, and pull safely back in *before* oncoming traffic gets close.

Remember to signal your intention to pass. Also remember to check for possible conflicts all around, using your mirrors and turning your head.

**Unexpected Animals** Like city streets, country roads have unexpected hazards which require quick driver decisions. Deer or smaller animals, such as skunks and raccoons, may dart out suddenly in front of you.

Naturally you will not want to hit an animal, and in the case of the larger creatures, you might well damage your vehicle and injure yourself or your passengers if you do make contact. However, you must use judgment in stopping or swerving to avoid animals. Be sure the vehicles behind you will be able to stop without hitting you. Never swerve into oncoming traffic or make a fast lane-change without looking.

**Railroad Crossings** Railroad tracks present another possible hazard. Heed warning signs. Slow down as you approach a crossing and never cross a track when a warning light is flashing. Check to see that there is no train coming before you cross a track even if the warning lights are not flashing.

In the unlikely event that you stall on a track, check immediately in both directions. If a train is coming, don't hesitate. Leave your vehicle at once. If there is no train approaching, *and* if you have a clear view of the track in both directions, try to start the vehicle, but continue to check for trains. If you can't start the car and you are certain there is no train coming, try pushing your car off the track.

**Unfamiliar Roads** Curves on country roads can be a hazard, particularly if you are driving along a road for the first time or driving at night. You may reach moderately high speeds on straight, uncrowded roads, but you will have to be prepared to reduce your speed before entering sharp curves.

Stay alert to road signs that warn of upcoming curves, and follow posted reduced speed limits. Be aware, too, that speed limits change frequently as you enter and leave towns.

# Highway Driving

As a highway driver, you will generally travel more quickly than you

Before passing a wide vehicle, check the shoulder. An obstruction there may cause that driver to move left.

would on city streets or on small country roads. Also, except in the case of traffic jams caused by obstructions, you will encounter far fewer interruptions.

Highway driving can be a smooth, efficient experience, but you will need certain special skills to ensure a safe trip.

Highway drivers travel at high speeds. Vehicles pass each other quickly and sudden moves can have dangerous results. Collisions at high speeds are far more damaging than those occurring at lower city-street speeds. For this reason, it is essential for you to maintain a safe following distance.

Since there are few opportunities to stop on a highway, it is important that you be able to respond immediately when decisions must be made. Be sure you know your route before

**Before you enter a highway, try to know what route and what exit you will be taking. Once you are on the highway, you will not have much time to make navigational decisions.**

your trip is underway so that you will know which exit you need.

If you encounter unexpected detours or confusing signs, make a quick choice based on what you think is the right decision. Never stop in your lane or attempt to back up while on a highway. Correct navigation mistakes after you have exited from the highway.

## Projects

1. Observe traffic at night. Do drivers cooperate with each other by switching on low-beam headlights when they meet, pass, or follow other vehicles? What percentage of drivers cooperate in each case? How many drivers have burned-out or poorly aimed headlights? Share your findings in class.

2. When you are riding as a passenger in a car, make a list of all the objects you see that are located with 9 feet of the roadway on a 5-mile stretch of road. Describe each object to your classmates and discuss with them the kind of hazard—if any—that it is likely to cause.

dense          overtaking          scan

## Stop and Review

1. How do different kinds of reduced visibility affect your ability to avoid collisions?
2. Headlights are of little help in lighting 2 areas. What are they?
3. How can you improve your visibility at night?
4. Why is it better to use your headlights on low beam in fog rather than on high beam?
5. How is your stopping distance affected by wet roads?
6. Describe some ways you can maximize vehicle control while driving in a rainstorm.
7. If you must pull off the road and stop because of heavy rain or fog, how can you make your car more visible?
8. What steps can you take to compensate for sun glare?
9. Name an area that tends to freeze more quickly than the road surface.
10. If your car has been out in a snowstorm, what areas should you clean off before driving?
11. Describe 3 situations in which visibility would be limited by fixed objects or geography.
12. Why should you never pass on a hill?
13. Explain why you must be aware of fixed objects on the shoulder of the road.
14. List 2 potentially dangerous situations that can be hidden by bushes and shrubbery.
15. How can visibility be limited by other vehicles?
16. How can you reduce visual obstructions inside your car?
17. Once you have spotted something with collision potential on the road ahead, you must be able to judge the dangers involved in what two alternatives?
18. Explain how scanning can reduce hazards if you are forced to leave the road.
19. What is one potentially dangerous situation that may occur when an off-road object is within 9 feet of the roadway?
20. Describe a special hazard of city driving. Describe a special hazard of country driving. What can you do to reduce the risks involved in driving in these areas?

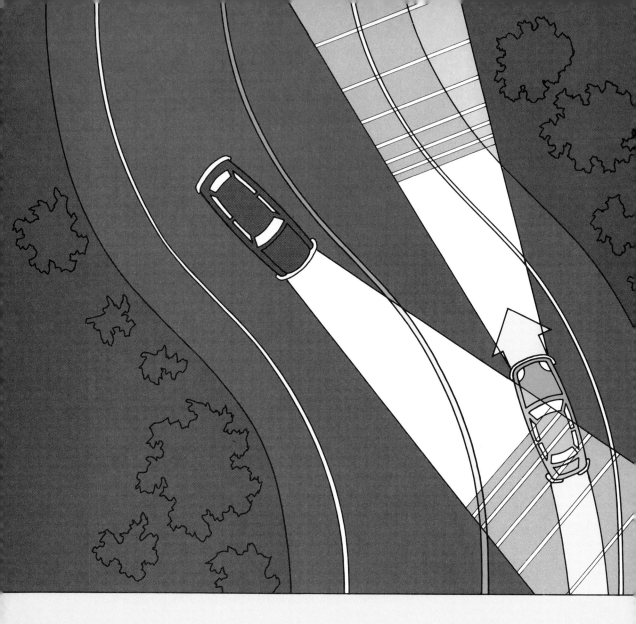

## What if...

You have to drive home from the lake going east on a winding, 2-lane road. You start at sunset.

1. What should you do before you leave? What should you do while driving?

2. Now it is dark. An oncoming car is blinding you with high-beam headlights. What will you do?

3. It has started to rain. What extra precautions should you take?

Complete the sentences by filling in the blanks with the correct terms.

| | | | | |
|---|---|---|---|---|
| bumps | ice | passengers | scan | tree branches |
| low | snow | sunset | roof supports | parts of vehicles |
| rain | traffic signals | less | low | |
| door posts | sunrise | city | | |

1. Your headlights should be on _____ beam when you follow other vehicles.

2. When driving in fog, your headlights should be on _____ beam.

3. Strong glare from the sun occurs at _____ and _____ .

4. You should _____ conditions off the road ahead to gather information about the shoulder of the road.

5. Frequent intersections and many pedestrians are features of _____ driving.

6. When driving up hills, you should remember that the steeper the grade of the hill, the _____ you will be able to see.

7. Since there are few _____ along country roads, a driver must often rely on personal judgment.

8. Traction and visibility are reduced by _____ , _____ , and _____ .

9. Visual obstructions inside a vehicle include _____ , _____ , and _____ .

10. Three examples of on-road hazards are _____ , _____ , and _____ .

---

Select the one best answer to each of the following questions.

11. Headlights:
    (a) help in lighting off-road areas.
    (b) enable you to see your path as you turn.   (c) should be kept clean.   (d) usually have 4 settings.

12. Which of the following is *not* an off-road hazard?
    (a) fire hydrant   (b) fence
    (c) door post   (d) light pole

13. Scanning:
    (a) can provide you with important information about the shoulder of the road.   (b) is unnecessary in most situations.   (c) should be done only in your rear-view mirror.
    (d) places you on a collision course.

14. Reduced visibility is a result of:
    (a) snow.   (b) rain.   (c) fog.
    (d) all of these.

15. Practices essential to safe highway driving include:
    (a) keeping a safe following distance.   (b) stopping whenever you are unsure of what your next move should be.   (c) choosing a speed slower than you would drive at in the city or on winding country roads.   (d) making sure you take enough time to make the right decision when you encounter unexpected detours or confusing signs.

# Evasive Action

## Chapter Objectives

In this chapter you will learn how to:

- take evasive action to avoid collisions.
- control skids and quickly regain control of the car.
- minimize the consequences of a collision.

To avoid a collision, you may have to make an **evasive action**. An evasive action is a quick change in speed or direction made when necessary to avoid a hazard. Depending on the situation you encounter, one of a number of different evasive actions may be necessary. The different types discussed in this chapter include quickly moving laterally (to the left or right), accelerating, and braking. In the case of a skid, the key to avoiding a collision is steering control and moderate speed changes.

If a collision is unavoidable, there are measures you can take while you are in the situation that can make the consequences less severe.

# Lateral Evasive

You make a **lateral evasive maneuver** when you turn the steering wheel quickly and accurately, swerving sharply to avoid a collision. This is easiest to do if the driver's seat is properly adjusted, your hands are at the 9 and 3 o'clock positions on the steering wheel, and safety belts are fastened and properly adjusted.

Remember, it takes about 4 seconds to stop when you are driving at highway speed. To avoid crashing into an object less than 4 seconds from you, you have to turn the steering wheel several times:

1. Turn it rapidly as much as ½ of a turn to the left or right.

2. Immediately turn it a full turn back in the opposite direction.

3. Then turn it left or right to bring the vehicle back to a path that is parallel to the original path of travel.

You must complete a lateral evasive maneuver quickly. If you do not, you may be on a collision course with an object off the road. You must assume that you will not have time to look for an escape route after an emergency develops. Therefore, while you are driving, you should always scan the road and off-road areas ahead to find possible escape routes. For example, suppose you are driving at 55 mph on a two-way road. As you reach the top of a hill, you see

For a quick evasive movement to the right, steer right, then left, then right again. Your hands should start at the 9-and-3 position. Your safety belt should be properly adjusted.

**Making difficult driving decisions requires experience as well as knowledge. Try to log as much practice time behind the wheel as you can.**

a car with a flat tire stopped in your lane about 3 seconds ahead. You know that it is too late to brake to a stop. You must make a lateral evasive maneuver. Which way do you go? Are there vehicles following or coming toward you? Are there any off-road obstacles? How far are they from the road? What would happen if you crashed into these obstacles? What is the condition of the surface of the off-road areas?

Obviously, you cannot answer all these questions in the time you have. But you can make some fast decisions. If you have gathered information in advance, you will be able to assume certain things. For instance, you can assume that the shoulder on both sides of the hill will be more or less the same. You can assume that

you could use controlled braking and steer off to the right if you are faced with an emergency.

It will be harder to make a decision if the escape routes both to the left and the right are blocked. For example, suppose the right shoulder is lined with shrubs and there is on-coming traffic in the left lane. In such a situation, you should choose the route that holds the lesser consequences. A move toward the oncoming traffic may result in a head-on collision. Even if you are fortunate enough to make it to the left shoulder, an oncoming driver may panic and possibly steer off the road or into your car. Your evasive move should, therefore, be to the right, even though the shrubs may hide some object.

# Off-Road Recovery

At times, you may have to steer part or all the way off the road to avoid a hazard. **Off-road recovery** (returning to the road from a shoulder), however, can be a dangerous maneuver.

**Shoulder Hazards** Steering may be difficult if the shoulder area is not solid or smooth. Soft or loose sand, mud, and grass reduce traction, which is needed to control the car. If the shoulder area and the roadway have different types of surfaces, traction will suddenly change. The result may be loss of control.

Steering may also become difficult if there is a difference in the level of the roadway and that of the road shoulder. The road surface is sometimes several inches higher than the shoulder. When you try to come back on the road in such a case, the left front tire may drag against the edge of the road, making control difficult. Or, the inside sidewall of the right front (off-road) tire may get caught on the edge of the pavement, stretching the tire out of shape. The bottom of that front tire then continues to point straight ahead, while the wheel points toward the road. Finally, the caught tire snaps up onto the roadway. If the steering angle is great enough, the vehicle will shoot across the road.

Sometimes the shoulder is lower than the road surface. This can make it difficult to control your car when you are getting back on the road.

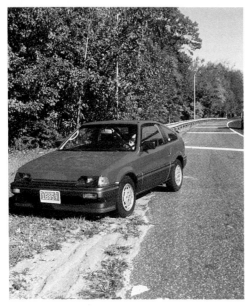

You may have to steer almost completely off the pavement to avoid an on-road hazard. This is not dangerous if the shoulder is wide and firm.

Reduce speed. Steer right until your left wheels are 1 to 2 feet from the pavement edge. Straighten your wheels. Choose a spot where the shoulder and road are level.

Check traffic and signal a left turn. Steer quickly to the left by making a 1/4 turn of the steering wheel.

As the right front tire strikes the pavement edge, turn the steering wheel almost 1/2 a turn to the right. Then straighten your wheels and move ahead.

## Controlled Off-Road Recovery

Sometimes you must drive across the emergency lane (if there is one) onto the shoulder to avoid a hazard. The best way to maintain control of your vehicle and return to the road is this:

1. Hold the steering wheel firmly, hands at the 9 and 3 o'clock positions. Reduce speed to 20 or 25 mph by letting up on the accelerator and braking gently.

2. Steer to the right until you are completely on the shoulder. Straighten your wheels. Choose a spot where the shoulder and road are as level as possible.

3. Check traffic and signal a left turn. Steer quickly to the left by making a ¼ turn of the steering wheel.

4. As the *right* front wheel touches the edge of the pavement, turn the wheel almost ½ a turn to the right. This steering reversal prevents your car from entering the oncoming lane. Straighten your wheels and move ahead.

## Emergency Off-Road Recovery

If you have driven onto the right shoulder to avoid a collision, you may find yourself headed toward some other object. A bridge abutment, a large tree, or a pedestrian may force you to return to the road immediately. You will not have time for a routine off-road recovery. However, if you have both hands firmly on the steering wheel in the proper position, you should still be able to control your car and recover.

Avoid hard braking, as this will result in a skid and cause new problems. Move your car far enough off the road so that the right front and right rear wheels are off the road and free of the pavement edge. Then do the following:

1. Take your foot off the accelerator and brake pedals. Quickly turn the steering wheel ¼ of a turn or slightly more to the left.

2. As the *right* front wheel strikes the edge of the road, turn the wheel smoothly and quickly ½ of a turn or more back to the right. Immediately steer straight ahead.

In either a controlled or an emergency off-road recovery, you must remember to do three things:

- Steer smoothly and quickly back onto the road.
- **Countersteer** (turn the steering wheel back in the opposite direction in order to straighten the car and control your lane position).
- Brake gently if at all.

The quickness and smoothness of steering must be precise to keep your car within a single lane. Quick, sharp steering back onto the road allows the leading edge of the front tire to climb up onto the edge of the pavement. Thus, the tire keeps its shape and continues to maintain contact with the pavement.

## Acceleration Evasive

The accelerator is the control device most often overlooked in an emergency. There are times, though, when speeding up may be your only means of escaping danger. These situations most often occur at intersections and in merging traffic. For example, you may be in an intersection when a car comes at you rapidly from one side. Braking will leave you directly in the car's path. A lateral maneuver will take too much time or be impossible because there are objects on both sides of you. If the road ahead is clear, a quick increase in speed may bring you to safety.

## Braking Evasive

In some emergency situations, a lateral evasive or acceleration evasive maneuver may not be possible.

There may be no place to steer to. At speeds under 20 mph, it takes less time and distance to stop than to steer to another lane.

If you evaluate situations accurately and brake in time, you should be able to bring your car to a quick stop without losing control of steering. Press the brake pedal hard enough to stop fast without making the wheels **lock** (stop turning). Slamming on the brakes and locking the wheels may *increase* stopping distance, will cause a complete loss of steering control, and may result in a skid. Use the threshold braking method. With this method, you use your whole body to sense how the brakes are working. "Squeeze" the pedal down with a steady, moderate pressure until just *before* the brakes lock, then ease off, but not completely. Immediately squeeze again. Continue in this way until you reach your desired speed.

Optional equipment that elimi-

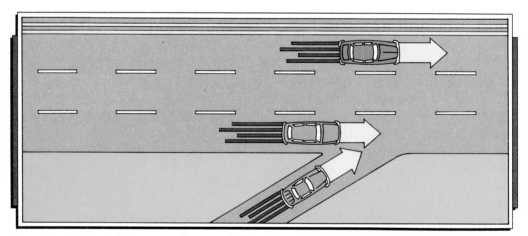

The driver in the left lane saw the possibility of a collision developing in the right lane and accelerated to pass it. This is called an acceleration evasive maneuver.

nates the problem of locked brakes is becoming more readily available. It is identified as an **antilock brake system.** When such a system is used, sensors detect if a wheel stops turning under braking conditions and signal for a reduction in hydraulic pressure to that wheel's brakes until the wheel starts turning again. This reduction in braking-system pressure is independent of the amount of pressure the driver is exerting on the brake pedal. Such antilock systems eliminate the need to modulate the brake and permit maximum brake pressure application while retaining steering control.

Always anticipate the possibility of a skid in conditions such as these. Stay alert, but try not to become tense.

# Skid Control

**Skidding** is loss of control over the direction in which your car is moving, because of reduced traction. Your tires lose their grip on the road's surface and begin to slide. You can go into a skid any time there is not enough traction to start, stop, or change the car's position.

Watch for conditions that cause skids. If you are prepared for a skid, you will be less likely to panic. Among the most common causes of skidding are changing speed or direction too quickly and changing speed or position when traction is poor. To prevent skids, make *gradual* and *smooth* changes in direction and speed, particularly when driving on slippery surfaces. For safe braking on a slick road, shift to *neutral* gear and press the brake pedal down gradually. In *neutral,* all 4 wheels brake equally, since none of them are receiving power. This helps balance braking efficiency and prevent skids.

If a skid does occur, you are not helpless. If you stay calm, you should be able to use the time and space available to regain control of the car. It is important to try to keep the car from swerving out of the lane or spinning around and facing in the wrong direction.

## Responding to a Skid— General Rules

There are several things to keep in mind to help you to recover from any skid:

- The sooner you respond to a skid, the easier it will be to correct it.

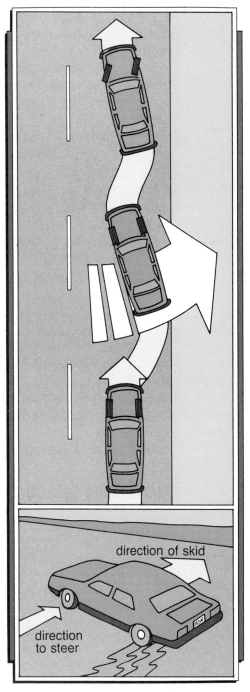

**If the rear of the car slides right, the front moves left, so you steer right. This is also called steering "into" the skid.**

- Keep your eyes up so that you are aware of conditions ahead and to the sides.

- Do not brake. This will only make the skid worse.

- Make steering corrections quickly and smoothly. Do not steer so abruptly that you cause a skid in the opposite direction.

If your car begins to skid, do not step on the brakes. Braking would cause the nondrive wheels (in a rear-wheel-drive vehicle, the front wheels; in a front-wheel-drive vehicle, the rear ones) to lock before the drive wheels, increasing the skid. Stay off the brake and ease your foot off the accelerator.

With your feet off the pedals, steer in the direction in which you want the front of the car to go. As soon as the skid begins to change direction, change the direction in which you are steering. You should start steering to straighten your car as soon as you start to skid. The longer you wait, the more the car will slide out of your intended path. Be careful not to **overcorrect** (oversteer). This could result in a **counterskid**—either a **fishtail** (a skidding back and forth of the rear wheels) or a **spinout** (a breaking of the traction of the rear wheels that will send the car spinning around). To avoid overcorrecting, you must steer smoothly and quickly. Each time the car changes direction, you must turn the wheel in the direction in which you want to go. Steering corrections should be continuous until you are out of the skid

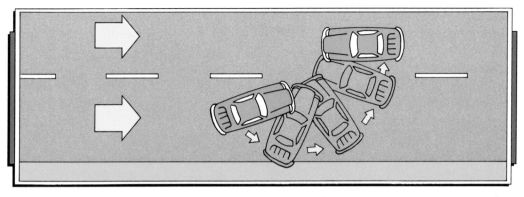

If only the rear wheels lock in a braking skid, they will slide sideways. The car could spin all the way around. Take your foot off the brake to regain control of the car.

and you have fully regained control of the car.

An added corrective measure that can be used in a skid is shifting to *neutral* gear immediately. When you release the accelerator in *neutral,* there will be no sudden decrease in speed to make the skid worse. Also, if you need to slow down after you have regained traction, braking efficiency will be balanced.

**Braking Skid** A braking skid occurs when the brakes are applied so hard that one or more wheels lock. If one or more wheels lock, you will lose control of the steering. Your car may go into a braking skid if you stop suddenly. This skid can also occur if you brake too hard on a wet road or on a road covered with sand, gravel, wet leaves, ice, or snow. Keep in mind that traction is reduced on all of these surfaces.

When all four wheels or only the front wheels lock, a car will skid straight ahead. It will keep going straight unless something (such as a slope in the road) changes its direction. If only the rear wheels lock, the loss of traction makes the rear wheels slide sideways. The car could go into a 180-degree spin so that you end up facing the opposite direction.

To get out of a braking skid, ease your foot off the brake pedal. When the wheels start to turn and traction is regained, steering control will return. Then turn the wheel in the direction you want the front of the car to go. If you have to use the brakes again, use less pressure. This way, the wheels will continue to turn, and the car will slow down. You reduce your chances of a braking skid by applying your brakes in plenty of time in a smooth manner when there is reduced traction.

**Power Skid** A power skid occurs when you suddenly press on the accelerator too hard. A power skid is much like a braking skid. If power is sent to the drive wheels in the rear too quickly, the sudden acceleration may cause the rear wheels to lose traction. The back end can then skid to the side. In a bad skid, the car may spin out. If the drive wheels are in the front, the car will simply plow straight ahead, out of control. Power skids occur most often when a driver accelerates quickly on a slippery surface. But they can happen even on a dry surface when there is a sudden, hard acceleration.

To correct a power skid, ease up on the gas until the wheels stop spinning. Steer in the direction you want the front of the car to go. You may have to countersteer if the car starts to spin around.

To prevent power skids, sustain traction between the road surface and your tires by accelerating slowly and smoothly.

**Cornering Skid**  A loss of steering control in a turn is called a **cornering skid**. A cornering skid can occur at any speed. If traction is reduced by worn tires or by a slippery road surface, you could go into a cornering skid even if you are traveling at a low speed. If you try to turn a corner very fast, the car will be likely to skid. In a cornering skid, your car continues to move straight ahead no matter which way you turn the wheel.

To correct a cornering skid, ease up on the gas pedal. Do not step on the brake. As always in a skid, steer in the direction you want to go as traction returns.

**Responding to a Blowout**  In a **blowout**, a tire suddenly loses air pressure. This can happen if the tire hits something on the road or goes into a pothole. Whenever a tire blows out, a car can go into a skid. This is most likely to happen if the driver applies the brakes hard. Even if no skid occurs, there will usually be a sharp change in the way the vehicle steers. If a front tire blows out, there will be a strong pull toward the side on which the tire has blown. If a rear tire blows, the car will sway from side to side, fishtail, or pull toward

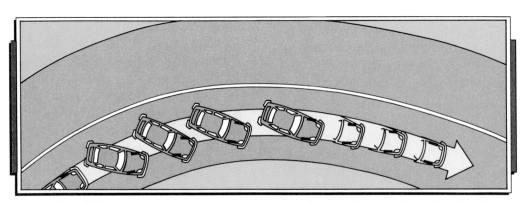

A cornering skid can occur at any speed. Ease up on the accelerator. Do not brake. Steer in the direction you want to go.

| Type | Braking skid | Power skid | Cornering skid | Blowout skid |
|------|-------------|-----------|----------------|--------------|
| Reason | The brakes are applied so hard that one or more wheels lock. | The gas pedal is pressed suddenly, too hard. | The rear tires lose traction in a turn. | A tire suddenly loses air pressure. |
| Conditions | a sudden stop<br><br>a wet, slippery, or uneven road | a sudden, hard acceleration<br><br>a slippery road surface | a turn made too fast<br><br>poor tires or a slippery road surface | a punctured, worn, or overinflated tire<br><br>an overloaded vehicle |
| What Can Happen | Steering control is lost. If the front wheels lock, the car skids straight ahead. If only the rear wheels lock, they slide sideways. The car might spin around. | A car with front-wheel drive plows straight ahead. In a car with rear-wheel drive, the back end can skid to the side. The car might spin around. | Steering control is lost. The rear wheels skid away from the turn. The car keeps going straight ahead. | There is a strong pull toward the side on which a front tire has blown out. A rear-tire blowout might cause a pull toward the blowout, side-to-side swaying, or fishtailing. |
| What To Do | Take your foot off the brake pedal. Steer. When the wheels start turning again and moving forward, steering control will return. | Ease up on the gas pedal until the wheels stop spinning. Steer to straighten the car. Countersteer if the car starts to spin. | Take your foot all the way off the accelerator. Steer to straighten the car. | Do not brake. Make firm, steady steering corrections. Do not change speed suddenly. Slow down gradually and drive off the road. |

**Be aware of the conditions that cause skids. If you skid anyway, do not panic. The sooner you respond to a skid the better.**

the side of the blowout. Remember that any blowout can cause a major skid or spinout.

If a tire blows, ease your foot off the accelerator. Do not step on the brake pedal. Maintain a firm grip on the steering wheel and steer to correct any change in direction caused by the blowout. Be very careful to avoid any abrupt changes in speed. As soon as you regain control of the steering, gradually reduce your speed. Turn on your hazard flashers, look for a safe place to pull over, and drive off the road.

# Reducing the Consequences of a Collision

The goal of any driver is to avoid collisions and injuries. Unfortunately, this is not always possible. You should know what to do *before* you find yourself in a situation where a collision appears inevitable.

When you think of an automobile collision, you must be aware that there are really two collisions. The first occurs between the car and the object it strikes. The second occurs a fraction of a second later between the occupants of the car and some part of the car's interior. Remember that the vehicle decelerates rapidly in a collision and the occupants, if not properly secured, will continue to move forward at the speed of the vehicle. The first collision causes damage to the car. The second may result in occupant injury or death. This is why it is so important to lock doors and use safety belts.

If a collision seems unavoidable, you may be able to choose an off-road path. A head-on collision with another vehicle and hitting an immovable object, such as a large tree or a bridge abutment, are the worst types of collisions.

If you are able to reduce speed before the collision, the impact will be less severe. If you can choose what object you will collide with, try to choose something that will give. A bush, a shrub, or a snowbank can absorb energy, and that will reduce impact forces.

Many collisions are more serious than they have to be because drivers freeze when they see that they are going to hit something. If you are on a collision path with another vehicle, try to make impact behind the passenger compartment for minimal damage. For example, if you are about to be struck broadside in an intersection, accelerate so that the other car will make contact with the rear end of your car rather than with the passenger compartment.

Try to follow these suggestions if a collision is unavoidable:

- Never hit anything head-on.
- Hit something soft instead of something hard.
- Hit something traveling in the same direction as you are instead of something stationary.
- Hit something stationary with a **glancing** (slanted) blow.
- Hit a stationary object instead of something coming toward you.
- Dodge trouble by heading right, away from oncoming traffic.

## Projects

1. Watch several drivers—including friends and members of your family—as they prepare to drive. How many of them make predriving checks and adjustments that will help them deal with emergency situations? Report your findings to the class.

2. Check the shoulders and off-road areas of some local highways. Are they well designed and maintained? Do they provide an escape path in an emergency? What hazards do they present to drivers? How do you think could they be improved?

# Words to Know

evasive action
lateral evasive maneuver
off-road recovery
countersteer
threshold braking

skidding
overcorrect
counterskid
fishtail
spinout

braking skid
power skid
cornering skid
blowout
lock

# Stop and Review

1. What 3 factors make it easier for a driver to perform an evasive maneuver?
2. Name 3 evasive actions. Give examples.
3. How do you make a lateral evasive maneuver?
4. Why are soft shoulders next to the road a serious hazard?
5. If you are forced to go off the road and onto the shoulder in a lateral evasive maneuver, what steps do you take to get your car safely back onto the road? What problems should you watch for?
6. In what situations can speeding up be a useful means of escaping danger? Give examples.
7. Why should you *not* lock the wheels when braking? What should you do if you overbrake and lock the wheels?
8. Describe threshold braking.
9. Define *skidding*.
10. Explain what causes each of the four types of skids.
11. How would you respond to each type of skid?
12. What are the most common causes of skidding? If your car begins to skid, what must you try to do? List the five general rules for responding to a skid.
13. Which way should you steer if you find yourself skidding?
14. What can cause a counterskid? How can you avoid it?
15. Why does braking increase a skid?
16. How does shifting to *neutral* during a skid help minimize loss of control?
17. In what ways is a power skid like a braking skid? In a power skid, how will a front-wheel-drive vehicle react? How will a rear-wheel-drive vehicle react? How do you correct a power skid?
18. What happens in a cornering skid? How should you respond?
19. If your car's front left tire blows out, which way will your car pull? How should you respond?
20. Explain why every automobile collision is really *2* collisions.

## What if...

You are driving a front-wheel-drive vehicle on a two-lane highway. As you reach the top of a hill, you see a car stopped in your lane. You do not have time to brake to a stop.

1. Suppose there is an oncoming car about to meet you in the other lane. What will you do?

In the same situation, suppose it is snowing and you think there *is* time to stop. You hit the brakes and the rear end slides to the right.

2. What will you do? How could you have avoided this situation?

Complete the sentences by filling in the blanks with the correct terms.

lateral evasive   accelerator   blowout   behind
  maneuver   speed   give   skidding
20   evasive action   braking skid   rear

1. A change in speed or direction to avoid a collision is called an _____ .

2. At speeds under _____ mph, it takes less time to stop than to steer to another lane.

3. Loss of control over the direction in which your car is moving because of reduced traction is called _____ .

4. A _____ occurs when the brakes are applied so hard that the wheels lock.

5. In a _____ , a tire suddenly loses air pressure.

6. Skids are made worse by abrupt changes in _____ .

7. When you turn the steering wheel quickly, swerving sharply to avoid a collision, you are making a _____ .

8. The control device most often overlooked in an emergency is the _____ .

9. If a collision seems unavoidable but you can choose what object you will collide with, try to choose something that will _____ .

10. If you are on a collision course with another vehicle, try to make impact _____ the _____ wheels.

---

Decide whether each of the following sentences is true or false.

11. Cornering skids may occur when you turn, regardless of your speed.

12. A blowout can happen if a tire hits something on the road.

13. A tire blowout is always followed by a skid.

14. In some situations, speeding up may be your only effective evasive action.

15. The worst types of collisions are head-on with another vehicle and hitting an immovable object.

# Vehicle Performance and Maintenance

## Chapter Objectives

In this chapter you will learn how to:

- understand how the major systems in your car provide its power and give you control over its movement.
- properly maintain the major systems in your car.
- drive in a fuel-efficient manner.

You do not have to be a mechanic to become more familiar with your car, but you do have to know something about how it works. You must know what to expect from it. You must be aware of the importance of keeping it in good condition.

Several major systems in your car provide its power and give you control over its movement. They are the engine, the power train, the fuel system, the electrical system, the exhaust system, the lubricating and cooling systems, the suspension and steering systems, and the braking system. Secondary, but still very important, are the lighting system and the tires.

Your vehicle should be serviced periodically by a licensed mechanic. There are a number of things you can easily check between tune-ups yourself. There are also ways to drive that will reduce fuel consumption and wear on your car.

# The Internal Combustion Engine

The **engine** produces the car's power by exploding an air-fuel mixture within its cylinders. The amount of power produced is determined by:

- the number and the size of the cylinders.

- the quality and quantity of the air-fuel mixture.

- the amount of pressure the mixture is placed under.

- the timing of the spark from the spark plug, which ignites the air-fuel mixture and causes that mixture to explode.

The engine operation starts with the **ignition switch**. When you turn the key in the ignition switch to *start,* power is drawn from the battery to the electric starter motor. This motor has a gear which turns the **flywheel** of the engine. When the flywheel turns, it turns the **crankshaft**, which causes the intake and exhaust valves to open and close. The **four-step** (or stroke) **cycle** of each piston gives your car its power.

1. When the piston goes down, a vacuum is created. This draws the

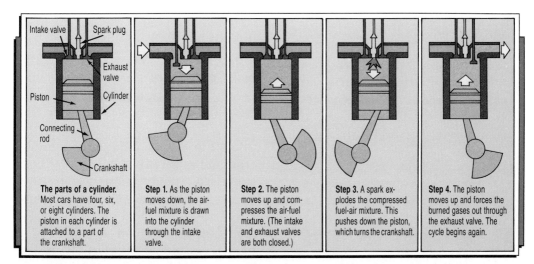

**The parts of a cylinder.** Most cars have four, six, or eight cylinders. The piston in each cylinder is attached to a part of the crankshaft.

**Step 1.** As the piston moves down, the air-fuel mixture is drawn into the cylinder through the intake valve.

**Step 2.** The piston moves up and compresses the air-fuel mixture. (The intake and exhaust valves are both closed.)

**Step 3.** A spark explodes the compressed fuel-air mixture. This pushes down the piston, which turns the crankshaft.

**Step 4.** The piston moves up and forces the burned gases out through the exhaust valve. The cycle begins again.

**The most common type of internal combustion engine is the four-step piston engine. The controlled explosion of an air-fuel mixture pushes the pistons up and down.**

The pistons and cylinders are a vital part of the internal combustion engine. Periodic maintenance is required to keep them operating smoothly and efficiently.

air-fuel mixture through the intake valve into the cylinder. The exhaust valve is closed during this downward motion. When the piston gets down as far as it can go, the intake valve closes, too.

2. The piston then starts to move upward in the cylinder, pushing the air-fuel mixture into about one-tenth of the space it had before. The **spark plug** (there is one for each cylinder) is then electrically charged. This sets off a spark which then causes the compressed air-fuel mixture to explode.

3. This explosion drives the piston back down. (All of this happens quickly. The speed of the engine depends on the number of explosions per minute.)

4. The exhaust valve now opens, and the piston rises, forcing the burned gases out.

This up-and-down motion of the pistons keeps the crankshaft turning. In a rear-wheel-drive car, this power, sent from the crankshaft to the rear axle, makes the vehicle move. In the case of a front-wheel-drive car, the power is sent from the crankshaft directly to the front wheels.

**Maintaining the Engine** The heart of your car is its engine. It is among those things that need the most frequent adjustment. The frequency for your car depends on the kind of driving you do. For instance, stop-and-go city traffic is harder on a car than steady highway driving. Learn to use an engine dipstick and check the oil each time you stop for gas. Change the oil every 3 to 4 months, or at least every 4,000 miles. The air filter must be changed more frequently in places where there is a lot of dust. Check your owner's manual for information on your car.

A car driven 12,000 miles per year generally should need one major and one minor tune-up in a 12-month period. An engine tune-up should include changing the oil and/or oil filter; checking the carburetor adjustment or fuel-injection system; cleaning the spark plugs and air filters and replacing them if necessary; checking the alternator, battery, and voltage regulator; and checking the ignition wires and timing or electronic ignition system. Various drive belts and hoses must be checked for wear. The fluid level in the radiator should also be checked. The battery terminals may need cleaning. Pollution-control devices must be checked or replaced. Any parts that are replaced must meet the manufacturer's specifications for the car you have.

If an engine needs major repairs, it may run unevenly after a tune-up. An engine compression check may be needed. A **compression check** can spot such problems as burned or badly seated intake or exhaust valves, worn piston rings, or damaged cylinder walls. These problems will require a major overhaul of the engine.

## The Power Train

In most cars, the engine sends power to only two of the four wheels, front or rear. These wheels are called the **drive wheels**. The power is sent to the **clutch** and **transmission**. (It is the clutch and transmission that allow the driver to change gears.) In a rear-wheel-drive vehicle, the transmission is connected by the **driveshaft** to the **differential**, **rear axles**,

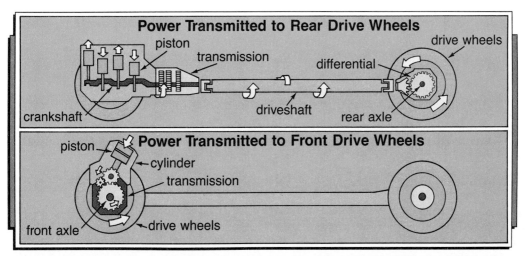

The power train delivers power from the engine to the drive wheels. With rear-wheel drive, the differential changes the angle of rotation between the driveshaft and the rear axles.

and **rear wheels**. The differential does two things:

- It changes by 90 degrees the direction of the power (rotation) supplied by the driveshaft. This power is used to turn the drive-wheel axles.
- It lets each of the drive wheels turn at a different rate of speed. This enables a car to turn a corner.

In a front-wheel-drive vehicle, power is delivered from the engine to a combination transmission and differential, and then directly to the front wheels.

**Maintaining the Power Train**

The fluid level in both automatic and manual transmissions must be checked at least every 6,000 miles. So should the fluid level in the rear-axle housing. Automatic transmission fluid should be changed every 24,000 miles or as indicated in your owner's manual.

Universal joints connect the driveshaft to the transmission and differential. If these joints are not sealed units, they should be greased every 6,000 to 8,000 miles. If the universal joints are sealed units, they should be checked for signs of leaks or damage. If there are such signs, the units should be replaced.

## The Fuel System

The **fuel system** is made up of the fuel tank, the fuel pump, the carburetor, and the intake manifold. The pump forces the fuel from the tank to the carburetor. There the fuel is mixed with air and then drawn into the intake manifold. Many new vehicles are equipped with a **fuel-injection system** instead of a carburetor. In such a system, the fuel is mixed with air and then the mixture is forced under pressure into the intake manifold. From there, the air-fuel mixture enters the engine cylinder through the intake valves.

Always use the proper fuel, which, in most cases, means using lead-free gasoline.

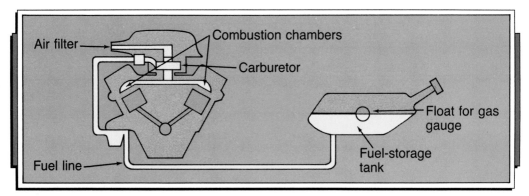

The fuel system has a twofold purpose. It stores fuel, and it delivers the correct air-fuel mixture to the engine.

# The Electrical System

The **electrical system** begins with an energy source: generally a 12-volt battery. The system also includes an alternator or a generator, a voltage regulator, and the wires that carry the electricity throughout the car.

The **battery** provides the power needed to start the engine. It also allows you to operate equipment, such as the lights and radio, for a short time when the engine is not running.

After the engine is started, the starter motor disengages when you release the ignition key. The **alternator** or **generator** provides electricity to keep the engine running, recharge the battery, and operate equipment. The **voltage regulator** controls the amount of electricity generated and the rate at which the battery is recharged. If the voltage regulator fails, the battery could receive too much electric charge and be damaged, or not be recharged at all.

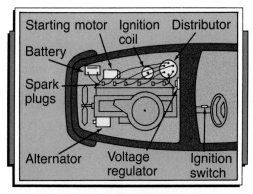

The electrical system supplies the energy to start the car. It also distributes electrical charges to the cylinders.

Just as the heart of your car is its engine, the heart of the electrical system is the battery. Check the battery as often as the manufacturer suggests. The fluid should be at the proper level, the cables should be tight, and the terminals should be kept free of corrosion.

# The Exhaust System

The exhaust system serves two purposes:

- It carries off water vapor, unburned fuel, and harmful gases, such as carbon monoxide, nitrous oxides, and lead oxides.
- It reduces the amount of noise coming to the outside from the explosions within the cylinders.

The **exhaust manifold** is a collecting system for the unburned gases as they exit from the cylinder. The exhaust pipe carries the gases to the muffler. The **muffler** helps to reduce the noise. The **tail pipe** carries the gases to the rear and away from the car.

## Exhaust Emission-Control System

Unburned fuel and other gases produced by the explosions in the cylinders collect in the engine crankcase. The **positive crankcase ventilation (PCV) system** was developed to reduce this problem. The PCV system recycles gases in the crankcase back into the cylinders to be burned again.

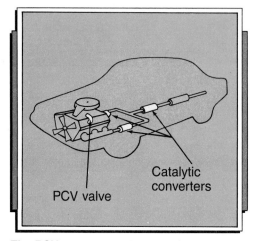

PCV valve

Catalytic converters

**The PCV system sends gases in the crankcase back to the cylinders. Catalytic converters reduce harmful exhaust gases.**

**Leaks in the exhaust system are very dangerous. They allow poisonous gases into the car.**

Since 1975, cars made for sale in the United States have been equipped with **catalytic converters**. These devices reduce the amount of harmful gases that goes into the outside air from the tail pipe. The use of leaded gasoline in the engine will destroy the catalytic converter. Other devices collect or control gasoline vapors that come from the fuel tank and carburetor.

Proper adjustment of an engine's timing and its carburetor will result in more efficient use of fuel. **Air-injection pumps** and **high-temperature thermostats** save even more fuel and reduce air pollution.

## Maintaining the Exhaust System

How long the exhaust system of your car will last depends on the conditions under which your car is driven. Stop-and-go, short-trip driving is hard on it. On short trips, acid and water collect in the system and corrode the metal. On long trips, heat

and evaporation get rid of the acid and moisture.

It is very dangerous to drive a vehicle with an exhaust leak or with a broken tail pipe. These defects allow exhaust gases to be trapped beneath the vehicle, even when the vehicle is moving. If there are any holes in the floor or wheel wells, the gases can be drawn up into the passenger compartment. The most dangerous of these gases, carbon monoxide, has no odor, color, or taste. Small amounts of carbon monoxide make you sleepy or give you a headache at first. Too much of it will kill you.

To guard against such problems, the exhaust system should be inspected, from the exhaust manifold to the tail pipe, every time the car is serviced. Points that need special attention are the connections at either end of the muffler, the muffler itself, and the tail pipe. Two places on the tail pipe that require special attention are the last 2 inches of pipe that carry the exhaust gases out from beneath the vehicle and the section of pipe that bends up over the rear axle.

There are times when the danger of carbon monoxide poisoning becomes a special hazard. These actions should be avoided:

- Driving with the rear window of a station wagon open or driving with the trunk lid up.

- Running a car's engine in a closed garage.

- Sitting in a parked car with the windows closed, the engine running, and the heater turned on.

# The Lubricating and Cooling Systems

Many parts of an engine move very fast and rub against each other, creating friction. Friction produces heat. This heat and the heat produced by the air-fuel explosions produce very high engine temperatures. The temperatures may be greater than 4,000 degrees Fahrenheit. If not cooled, the engine would soon weld itself into a solid chunk of steel. The lubricating and cooling systems deal with this heat.

**The purpose of the tail pipe is to carry off poisonous gases from the car. It is important that you have the tail pipe inspected every time your car is serviced.**

**The Lubricating System** The lubricating system reduces heat by coating the engine's parts with oil. Oil reduces friction and wear between moving parts and helps seal the joint between the piston rings and cylinder walls. It absorbs shock from the bearings, cleans internal engine surfaces, and prevents rust and corrosion.

Oil is stored in the oil pan attached to the bottom of the engine. An oil pump, operated by the engine, pumps oil from the oil pan to the

**Check the engine oil every time you fill your fuel tank. Your owner's manual will tell you how.**

moving parts of the engine. Other parts of the engine are lubricated by having oil splashed on them by the crankshaft and connecting rods.

**The Cooling System** The cooling system gets rid of engine heat. In cars with air-cooled engines, this is done by forcing air over metal cooling vanes that surround the cylinders.

The more common system is the so-called water-cooled engine. Few engines today are actually cooled by water. Instead, cars use a **coolant** (a special liquid that can withstand very high or very low temperatures). This liquid moves around the **water jacket**, a passageway that surrounds each of the cylinders, and absorbs heat.

Hoses connect the engine to the radiator. A pump forces the liquid from the engine to the radiator, where it flows through a network of tiny pipes. As the liquid circulates through the radiator, a fan driven by a belt forces air through the radiator to cool the liquid. A thermostat in the system acts as a gate to control the flow of liquid and maintain the best operating temperature. Then, the cooled liquid is circulated again to the engine. A radiator overflow tank is provided to catch and store coolant that flows from the radiator as it is heated and is drawn back into the radiator as it cools.

If the cooling system fails, the engine will overheat. In very cold weather, the liquid will freeze if there is not enough antifreeze in it. **Antifreeze** lowers the freezing point of engine coolant. Frozen coolant

**To prevent an overheated engine, make sure there is enough coolant in your car's radiator.**

cannot flow into the engine, and so the engine gets hot.

A temperature gauge or warning light on the dashboard gives information about engine temperature. If the light goes on or the gauge reads *hot,* stop the car in a safe place and turn off the engine. Great damage can occur if you drive with an overheated engine. Never remove the radiator cap from an engine that is hot. The boiling water could spill out and cause a severe burn. Let the engine cool first and then check for the problem.

To maintain the cooling system in your car, use the proper coolant and check the level each time the car is serviced. If necessary, add antifreeze before the onset of cold weather. Have the system thoroughly drained and refilled every 2 years.

## The Suspension and Steering Systems

You change the direction a car is going by turning the steering wheel. To respond properly to steering corrections, all the wheels must maintain contact with the roadway. Bouncing reduces the road contact. However, a good **suspension system**, made up of springs and shock absorbers, reduces the effect of bumps and provides better contact between the tires and the road.

### Springs and Shock Absorbers

Springs and shock absorbers connect the car's frame to the wheels. **Springs** "soften" the effect of bumps. But if a car had only springs, it would keep bouncing after going over a bump and would lose traction.

The suspension system reduces the effect of bumps in the road. It not only provides a smooth ride, it helps you to control the car.

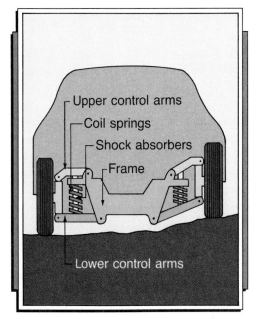

The suspension system is made up of springs and shock absorbers. They "cushion" the car's frame.

**Shock absorbers** are mounted between the frame and axle near each wheel. They act as a "cushion" for the car's frame, and they control bouncing. This produces a smoother ride. The result is better steering and braking control.

Shock absorbers wear out gradually. If your car bounces more than once after going over a small bump, the shock absorbers are wearing. If the vehicle sways or leans on a turn or curve, the shocks are worn. You can check your shock absorbers by pushing down hard on the trunk or hood a few times to make the car bounce. If the car bounces more than once after you stop pushing, the shocks should be checked by a mechanic to see if they need to be replaced.

**Steering Control** The steering system enables the driver to turn the front wheels. The steering wheel is connected to the front wheels by a steering shaft and movable rods.

To maintain their movement, the wheels must be held in an upright position. They must also be able to move up and down even when they are turned. Control arms hold the front wheels upright. Upper and lower control arms are hinged with ball joints to allow the wheels to move up and down over bumps while the vehicle is moving.

A failure in any part of the steering or suspension systems will drastically affect your ability to control a vehicle.

## Maintaining the Suspension and Steering Systems

Sudden failure of the suspension or steering systems is rare since most problems are the result of wear and usually develop gradually. You should have these systems checked and serviced every 6 months.

The suspension and steering systems are most easily checked when your car is up on a hoist for servicing. Shock absorbers should be checked for leaks and for the condition of the fasteners. The tie-rod fittings and ball joints should be greased every 4,000 to 6,000 miles or 4 to 6 months. If your car has power steering, check the fluid whenever you change your engine oil, about every 3 to 4 months. If any part shows signs of wear or looseness, it should be replaced.

Your tires can also tell you something about the condition of the steering and suspension systems. Heavy tread wear on one side of one or both front tires shows that there is need for front-end alignment. Flat spots in the tire tread show that the tires need to be balanced.

As you drive, you may notice that there is play in the steering wheel. (It can be turned quite a bit before

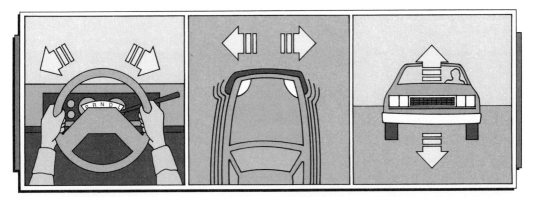

**Be alert for signs of wear in your car's steering and suspension systems. Signs include free play in the steering wheel, front-end wobble or shimmy, and excessive bouncing after the car has hit a bump.**

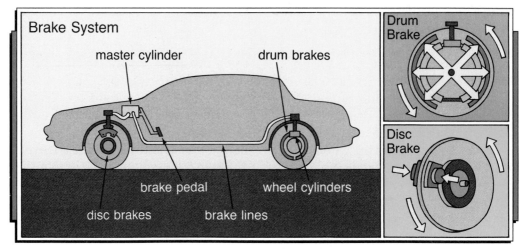

**The hydraulic brake system gives all 4 wheels stopping power. Drum brakes: brake shoes push on brake linings which push against wheel drums. Disc brakes: brake pads push on wheel discs.**

the wheels move.) Two inches or more of play in a manual system indicates a problem. Any play in a power-steering system is serious and should be checked right away. Other signs of trouble are front-end shimmy or wobbling, bumping as you turn the wheel on a smooth road, and pulling to the right or to the left as you drive. Pulling to the right or to the left can also mean that one or more tires are soft. Any of these signs may mean that the front end needs to be aligned or that the wheels need to be balanced.

## The Brake Systems

All passenger vehicles have at least two brake systems—a hydraulic brake system and the mechanically operated parking brake. The **hydraulic brake system** brings the moving vehicle to a stop. The **park-**

**ing brake** keeps the vehicle from moving after it has been stopped.

## The Hydraulic Brake System

The hydraulic brake system is made up of the brake pedal, a master brake cylinder, brake-fluid lines, wheel cylinders, brake shoes and linings, and wheel drums. (Cars with disc brakes are equipped with brake pads instead of brake linings, brake shoes, and wheel drums.)

When you push down on the brake pedal, a piston in the master brake cylinder moves forward. This movement forces fluid into the brake-fluid lines, which builds up pressure in the lines. This pressure forces pistons in the wheel cylinders to move out against the brake shoes. The brake shoes push against the brake linings, which get forced against the wheel drums. The dual master cylinder actually provides two separate brake systems. Both front-wheel brakes

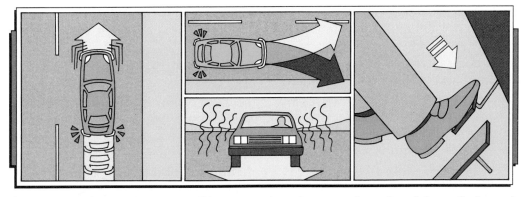

**Sudden grabbing, pulling to one side, a squeal or chatter, and a soft pedal are all signs of wear in the brake system. Have the system checked immediately at the first sign of wear.**

are controlled by one cylinder and both rear-wheel brakes are controlled by another. For this reason, a total brake failure is very rare. With disc brakes, the brake pads get forced against the wheel discs. The friction that develops, in either kind of brakes, slows the car. Letting up on the brake pedal takes the pressure off the wheel drum or discs. The pistons in the wheel cylinders then force the brake fluid back into the master brake cylinder.

Many cars are equipped with power brakes. The power assist reduces the force you must use on the brake pedal but does not shorten or increase stopping distance.

**The Parking Brake** The parking brake is operated by a foot pedal or by a hand lever. The pedal or lever is attached to a cable that is connected to the brake shoes of the rear wheels.

The main purpose of the parking brake is to hold the vehicle in place after it has stopped. You can try to stop a vehicle by using the parking brake. But, you should do so only under unusual conditions (such as hydraulic brake-system failure).

**Maintaining the Brake System**
When you press down on the brake pedal, you should feel firm resistance and your vehicle should come to a smooth, straight stop. The first sign of brake trouble may be that you have to press down farther than usual before the car begins to stop. Your car may pull to one side. The brakes may suddenly "grab" as you press down. If the brakes squeal or pull unevenly, they should be checked right away.

The level of fluid in the master brake cylinder should be checked every time the engine is serviced. In cars that have disc brakes, the fluid level may go down slightly as the brake pads wear down. If there is continued loss of fluid, have the whole system inspected for leaks.

Brake linings should generally be checked at 15,000 and at 25,000 miles, and then every 5,000 miles after that. If you make quick stops and brake hard, the brake linings will wear out faster, so more frequent checking and repair may be needed. It is very important that worn brake linings be changed before they wear through the brake shoes. Otherwise, wheel discs or drums can be damaged, and they may have to be replaced. Also, driving with worn brake linings is dangerous.

## The Lighting System

Your car's headlights help you to see when visibility is poor and always help others see you. The parking lights, signal lights, brake lights, and emergency flashers allow you to communicate with other drivers. It is

Even a fine film on the headlights will reduce the amount of light they provide. Check them before getting into the car.

essential that the lighting system in your car be kept in perfect working order.

**Maintaining the Lighting System**
The lenses of your headlights must be kept clean. Even a fine film will reduce the amount of light they provide and can reduce light by as much as 90 percent. Check also for **headlight alignment**. (This means directing the high and low beams to cover specific areas of the path ahead.) If your high-beam headlights do not seem to light up the roadway far enough ahead, they may need alignment. Your first sign of poor headlight alignment may come from other drivers. At night, oncoming drivers may flash their headlights from low to high beams as they drive toward you. If your headlights are on low beam, they may be poorly aligned and are blinding the other driver. The same is true if the driver in front of you reaches up to adjust the rear-view mirror as you drive closer. Another possible cause of poor headlight alignment is too heavy a load in the trunk of your car.

## The Tires

The general construction of tires, their tread depth, and their inflation are all important to vehicle control. If the tires on your car do not give enough traction, you are in trouble.

**Inspecting Your Tires** Check for cuts or blisters on the sidewalls and treads of your tires. Check, too, for

Check the depth of the tire treads. The minimum legal depth is ²⁄₃₂ inch. Tires have built-in tread-wear indicator bars.

Check to make sure the tires do not have bald spots. Worn spots are a symptom of more serious vehicle problems.

Check for cuts and blisters, both on the sidewalls and on the treads. Check for any embedded nails, glass, or metal.

Check the tires for bulges. If you see a bulge, it could mean that there is a serious defect in the tire.

nails, glass, or metal stuck anywhere in the tires. Your tires should not be **overinflated** (too much air pressure) or **underinflated** (too little air pressure). Underinflation is the more common and serious problem.

Tread depth can be critical in cer-

tain situations. The minimum legal tread depth is ²⁄₃₂ inch. Although that may be enough on a smooth, dry surface, it may be dangerous on a wet surface. The depth of a tread can be seen by the tread-wear indicator bar that is built into the tire.

**Tire Inflation**  Tires inflated to the pressure recommended for long-distance, high-speed driving improve vehicle control. Pressure should never be allowed to fall below the carmakers' and tiremakers' suggested minimum. Underinflation causes increased flexing of the sidewalls. This flexing produces heat, reduces vehicle control, and increases the chance of tire failure. Higher tire pressure will give you a ride that is not as smooth as that of a softer tire, but it will give more traction. Tires should not be inflated above the maximum that is recommended by the manufacturer. When a tire is overinflated, the center of its tread wears out quickly. Use a tire pressure gauge to check if your tires have the proper air pressure. This should be done when the tires are cold.

**Tire Rotation**  Tires on the front of the vehicle wear faster than those on the rear. To even out the wear, they should be rotated. Their positions on the car should be switched from front to rear and in some cases left to right. It is generally recommended that tires be rotated every 4,000 to 6,000 miles. Keep these two things in mind:

- Tire rotation plans differ, depending on the tire's construction. Check your owner's manual for the right plan for your tires.
- Tire rotation should not be used as a substitute for front-end alignment, wheel balancing, or new shock absorbers. Uneven tread

wear on the front tires means that your steering or suspension system needs attention.

# Having Your Car Serviced

Some kinds of maintenance are pretty much the same in most vehicles. However, the schedule of services is different for various cars. Which garage or mechanic you choose to service your car is very important, especially if you do not know much about how a car runs. If you do not know a good mechanic or service station, ask your family or friends. Certification by national agencies can also serve as a guide. Among these are the American Automobile Association, Approved Auto Repair Service, and the National Institute of Automotive Service Excellence.

When you bring your car in for service or repairs, give the mechanic any information you can about the car's performance. Get a written estimate of the cost and tell the mechanic to call before any work is done that will be more than the estimate. Ask that any parts that are replaced be held for you to look at.

# Making Your Own Inspection

There are a number of routine checks you should make inside and outside your car. Your owner's man-

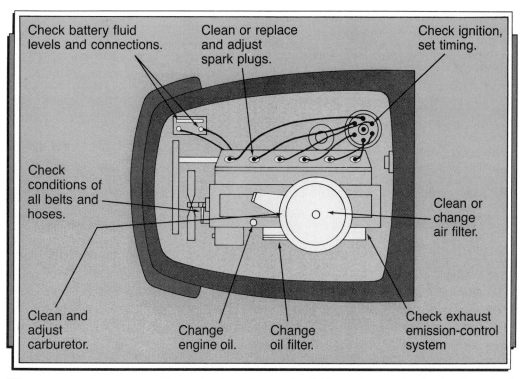

Check battery fluid levels and connections.

Clean or replace and adjust spark plugs.

Check ignition, set timing.

Check conditions of all belts and hoses.

Clean or change air filter.

Clean and adjust carburetor.

Change engine oil.

Change oil filter.

Check exhaust emission-control system

**Whenever you have your car's engine tuned, you should have the mechanic check each of the items shown above.**

ual has the information you need to make these checks. If you do not have an owner's manual, get one from a dealer or order one from the company that built your car.

**Outside the Vehicle** Always make these checks before you get in your car:

- Check under the car for leaking oil or radiator fluid.
- Check for damaged windows, windshields, mirrors, or lights.
- Check tire inflation, and look for tire damage or tire wear.
- Check for damage to the car body and trim.

- Check for burned-out or broken headlights, brake and signal lights, and side warning lights.
- Check to see that windshield, taillights, and headlights are clean.
- Check to make sure there are no objects on the ground that might damage the tires.

**Under the Hood** The following checks should be made at least once a month and before long trips:

- Check the amount of fluid in the radiator and radiator overflow tank, the battery, and the windshield-washer fluid tank. (Make sure the fluid in the radiator is cool

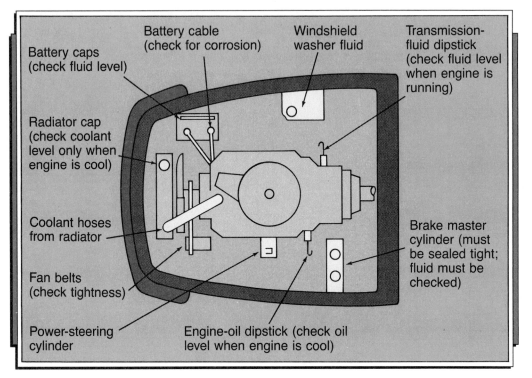

Battery caps
(check fluid level)

Battery cable
(check for corrosion)

Windshield
washer fluid

Transmission-
fluid dipstick
(check fluid level
when engine is
running)

Radiator cap
(check coolant
level only when
engine is cool)

Coolant hoses
from radiator

Brake master
cylinder (must
be sealed tight;
fluid must be
checked)

Fan belts
(check tightness)

Power-steering
cylinder

Engine-oil dipstick (check oil
level when engine is cool)

**You or a service station attendant should make the under-the-hood checks shown above at least once a month and before any long trips.**

before you remove the radiator cap.)

- Check the engine oil, power steering, and master-brake cylinder reservoirs.

- Check the fan belt and the belts that run the power steering, power brake, and air-conditioning units. They may need adjustment. Have any frayed or cracked belt replaced right away.

- Check all hoses and hose connections for leaks.

- Check for loose, broken, or disconnected wires. Check also for cracked insulation on wires.

- Check the transmission fluid. (This test usually must be made with the engine running and the gear selector in *park*. You will have to run the engine for a few moments to give the transmission fluid time to warm up.)

## Driving in a Fuel-Efficient Manner

**Fuel efficiency** refers to any methods that are used to cut down on the burning of gasoline. There are many things you can do to reduce fuel consumption and operating costs after

These people have parked their cars and will travel to their destination in one vehicle. Carpooling saves money and fuel.

you buy your car. These include trip planning, good driving practices, proper maintenance, and proper loading.

**Plan Your Trips** Most people drive many more miles per week, month, and year than is necessary. These miles could be reduced by simple trip planning. Too many drivers think of trip planning only in terms of vacations or long-distance driving. It can also be applied to everyday use of the car.

A number of short trips that add up to 30 miles a day take much more gasoline than one trip covering 30 miles. The engine does not have time to warm up when you are starting and stopping your car and this reduces fuel mileage. The way to cor-

rect this loss of mileage is to plan ahead.

**Use the Telephone** If you need a hard-to-find item, use the telephone to find out which stores have the item in stock. Then you can make one trip with fewer stops, saving both time and fuel.

**Carpooling** Carpooling can save you gasoline and money, even if you ride in a carpool only one or two days a week. Though it takes time to pick up and drop off passengers, the money and fuel you save can be worth the sacrifice.

**Don't Waste Fuel Idling** The way you drive makes a big difference in your transportation cost. Many drivers believe that they should let the engine **idle** (run while not in gear) for several minutes before moving their car in the morning. This is not true. Allow your engine to idle for no more than 30 seconds, even in cold weather. Start moving quickly. Then drive at a moderate speed for the first 5 to 10 minutes. During the first few minutes, you will improve your fuel mileage if you do not drive too slowly. Accelerate smoothly but briskly to reach driving speed. The more time you spend getting up to travel speed, the more fuel your engine will use. However, do not push the accelerator to the floor. This uses large amounts of fuel and may damage an engine that is cold.

**Anticipating** Driving at a smooth pace is one of the most important driving techniques you can develop. A 12-second visual lead will enable you to anticipate changes in the traffic around you. A 2-second following distance will allow you to make your moves smoothly. If you apply these principles when you drive, you will reduce the need to brake suddenly or accelerate suddenly. When you reduce the number of changes you make in your speed, you use less fuel.

Tailgating, besides being dangerous, also takes extra fuel because you constantly change your speed. This is even more of a problem if the vehicle ahead is a truck or a van which limits your area of vision.

When driving on hills, accelerate as you approach a hill. Do not wait until you are halfway up and then accelerate. As you drive down hills,

ease off on the accelerator. Let gravity help pull you down.

One of the most frequent fuel-wasting driving practices is the "jackrabbit" start when a red light turns green. To avoid wasting fuel, accelerate smoothly after stopping and when coming out of turns.

**Maintenance** Maintenance is critical to the safe performance of your vehicle. It is also critical to fuel economy. A properly tuned engine helps you to get maximum fuel mileage. A car's fuel mileage is the average number of miles it can travel on a gallon of fuel. There are a number of different ways to determine when your car needs attention. One way is to follow the manufacturer's recommendations. Another is to keep track of the fuel you buy. Every time you buy fuel, fill the tank all the way and write down the number of miles the odometer registers. You can then check your mileage by dividing the number of miles traveled between fill-ups by the number of gallons of fuel you buy. By recording this information every time you buy fuel, you will be able to tell when your miles per gallon start to drop. If you have been driving the same as usual and under normal conditions, a drop in mileage of 2 miles per gallon indicates that some part of the car needs attention.

In addition to buying the right fuel for your car, you should change the oil and oil filter as often as your car's owner's manual recommends, make sure your car's front wheels are correctly aligned, and have the brakes checked periodically.

**Tire Pressure** Tire pressure is very important to good mileage. Too often, people drive with underinflated tires. When tires are soft, they are more resistant to movement and this resistance reduces mileage. In fact, for each 2 pounds that your tires are underinflated, you will use about 1 percent more fuel.

**Checking Under the Hood** Whenever you check under the hood of your car, remember to check the alternator and fan drive belts. Also check the level of water in the battery, coolant in the radiator, and oil in the engine. Check the battery terminals to make sure there is no corrosion. Any one of these items may contribute very little by itself. Together, however, they aid in fuel savings by making certain of efficient engine operation.

**Loading Your Vehicle** Objects in the trunk add to the weight of the

Buying fuel at a self-service pump saves you money. Driving in a fuel-efficient manner saves both money and fuel.

car. Added weight means lower fuel mileage. Therefore, for everyday driving, keep in the trunk only those items necessary for the repair or operation of your car. When you are on a trip, keep your luggage in the trunk instead of on car-top carriers and luggage racks. Luggage on carriers and racks increases air resistance, which reduces mileage.

## Projects

1. Make an under-the-hood check of your family's or school's car. Identify as many of the parts of the engine as you can.

2. Make a list of the mechanical defects you would recognize after reading this chapter. Which de-

fects are the most dangerous and which would result in the most costly problems if neglected? Study the owner's manual of your school's or your family's car. Has your school or family followed the maintenance suggestions made in the manual?

## Words to Know

catalytic converter
compression check
coolant
fuel efficiency

headlight alignment
hydraulic brake system
idle
suspension system

transmission
underinflated
universal joints
voltage regulator

## Stop and Review

1. List the 8 major systems in your car that provide its power and give you control over its movement.
2. Why is it useful for a driver to know how the different parts of the car work?
3. Why is a complete program of vehicle maintenance important?
4. Explain the 4-step cycle of the pistons.
5. Explain what occurs during a complete engine tune-up. What determines how often you need a tune-up?
6. List 3 problems that can require a major overhaul of an engine.
7. How is the rotary motion of the driveshaft transmitted to the drive-wheel axle?
8. Describe the path that fuel takes in your car from the time it enters the tank to the time it is burned in the engine cylinder.
9. Identify the energy source of the electrical system.
10. Name two important functions of the exhaust system. What problems can occur if you drive with a worn-out exhaust system?
11. What does the positive crankcase ventilation system do?
12. What is the purpose of the engine oil?
13. What is the purpose of the cooling system?
14. What is the function of springs and shock absorbers, in addition to passenger comfort?
15. What test can you use to see if your shock absorbers need to be replaced?
16. What are some of the signs of trouble in the suspension and steering systems?
17. What are the differences between the hydraulic brake system and the parking brake?
18. Describe some signs of trouble in the braking system.
19. Explain why proper tire inflation is essential.
20. What steps must be taken before you can check the transmission fluid level?

## *What if...*

You are riding with Dave to the recreation center. He has been screeching to a stop at every red light, then "scratching off," with a squeal of tires, as soon as the light changes. He has been tailgating other cars and "lane-hopping" to pass whenever possible. Now he has started complaining that his car is a "gas-guzzler."

1. How does Dave's driving affect his car's use of fuel? How does it affect your safety?
At your request, Dave is driving more slowly and smoothly, but the car tends to bounce and you notice a thumping sound when he drives over a stretch of dirt road.
2. What might be wrong with Dave's car? What should he do?

# CHAPTER 13 TEST

Complete the sentences by filling in the blanks with the correct terms

parking brake    catalytic        attention      maintenance
reduce                      converters  compression  "jackrabbit" start
antifreeze        battery          check          differential

1. The _____ lets each of the drive wheels turn at a different rate of speed.

2. Worn piston rings or damaged cylinder walls may be discovered during a _____ .

3. The _____ provides power so that you can operate your lights or radio for a short time when the engine is not running.

4. _____ reduce the amount of harmful gases that goes into the outside air from the tail pipe.

5. The freezing point of engine coolant is lowered by _____ .

6. Flat spots in the tire tread show that the car's front end needs _____ .

7. A frequent gas-wasting driving practice is the _____ .

8. _____ is critical to the safe performance of your car as well as its fuel economy.

9. Trip planning, good driving practices, and proper maintenance help _____ gasoline consumption.

10. The _____ can hold the vehicle in place after it has stopped.

---

Decide whether each of the following sentences is true or false.

11. The engine of your car sends power to its 4 wheels.

12. City driving is harder on your car than highway driving.

13. In cold weather, you should let your engine idle for 5 minutes before driving.

14. A drop in your fuel mileage means that some part of your car may need attention.

15. Underinflated tires decrease rolling resistance and thus increase fuel mileage.

# Physical and Mental Impairments

## Chapter Objectives

In this chapter you will learn how to:

- recognize factors that can impair your mental and physical abilities.

- compensate for the effects of fatigue, emotions, and temporary illnesses.

- understand the effects of carbon monoxide and take steps to prevent problems involving it.

- understand the role played by vision and hearing in the making of good driving decisions.

Some factors that can impair your mental or physical abilities to drive a motor vehicle include fatigue, emotional stress, and a variety of physical problems. If one of these factors affects you, you must decide whether or not you are fit to drive. If you must drive, ask yourself whether there is any way to compensate for the disability.

**If you find yourself yawning or relying on such things as playing the radio to stay alert, stop driving.**

# Fatigue

Fatigue is a temporary condition that affects everyone. Fatigue impairs vision and the other senses. It weakens your judgment and your ability to make decisions. If you are tired, you may ignore or fail to recognize emergency situations. You may also misjudge speed and distance and take unusual chances. Many tired drivers become irritable and overreact to minor annoyances.

Fatigue can be caused by many things: a hard day at work, a day at the beach, emotional stress, or boredom. Other causes are the glare of the sun, illness, overeating, drinking alcoholic beverages, an overheated room or car, and nonstop driving over long distances.

Recent research indicates that fatigue is a major contributing factor in a high percentage of collisions involving tractor-trailer trucks. Fall-

ing asleep at the wheel also appears to be involved not only in early-morning single-car accidents but also many of those that occur during the late afternoon and early evening when people are driving home from work.

## What Can Be Done About Fatigue?

There is only one way to overcome fatigue. You must sleep. But there are a few things you can do to delay fatigue and maintain alertness:

- Let plenty of fresh air circulate in the car.
- Wear good-quality sunglasses in bright sunlight.
- Avoid heavy foods and alcoholic beverages before you drive.

Especially on long trips:

- Be well rested when starting the trip.
- Plan to eat light snacks and drink plenty of liquids. This will necessitate frequent stops.
- Stop periodically for rest and light exercise.

On long trips, 10-minute stops every 2 hours, plus regular stops to get fuel and food and to go to the restroom, can do a great deal to prevent fatigue and enable you to continue driving.

There is no fixed rule about the maximum amount of driving that should be done in one day. Just do not overexert yourself. When you have driven a reasonable distance, stop driving for the day. It is best when planning your trip to decide in advance how far you want to drive in one day and make hotel reservations before you leave. Your local travel agency or auto club can help you with these decisions.

It is usually not a good idea to sleep in a car at the side of the road. If you must stop along the roadway to rest, follow these practices to ensure your safety:

- Make sure you are as far off the highway as possible.
- Try to find a lighted area.
- Give yourself a little outside air, but keep the window closed far enough to prevent entry from the outside.
- Lock all the doors.
- Have parking lights on but all other electrical equipment off.
- Before beginning to drive again, get out of the car and make sure you are *completely awake.*

# Emotions

Our basic personality, our values, and our self-awareness all affect the way we drive. A recent study demonstrated that those persons who were lacking in self-awareness and exhibited less self-control in general had many more convictions for moving violations and collisions than those persons who had a strong self-image and reacted well with peers and authority figures.

Strong emotions, such as fear and

**Public rest areas are provided so that drivers may take a short rest and walk around before continuing their trips.**

anger, can also affect the way we grasp and use information. This impairs our ability to reason and make sound judgments. The experience of strong emotions is also draining, both physically and mentally. Therefore, emotions can and do affect the way we drive.

## How Do Strong Emotions Come About?

Strong emotions are responses to the things that happen to us. Quite often, one emotion leads to another. For example, you are driving on a highway when another motorist cuts in front of you. Your first response is fear. This quickly changes to anger, and you may honk your horn.

Any number of situations may leave a person too emotional to drive safely. For example, you have an argument with your parents. In your

Emotions such as depression, anger, worry, or fear can affect your ability to reason and make sound judgments. Such emotions can also impair your concentration. Delay or stop driving when you are emotionally upset.

anger, you slam out of the house, jump into the car, and drive off. Or you are excited about a closely played ball game. As you drive home, the events of the game race through your mind. Maybe you become impatient and frustrated while following a slow-moving car along a winding roadway. As the minutes tick by, you grow more and more eager to move out and pass.

## Guides for Controlling Emotions

The following guidelines can help you keep strong emotions from interfering with your driving:

- *Identify situations that can lead to upsets.* Anticipate likely traffic problems, such as congestion at rush hour. If it is not possible to use a less stressful route, prepare yourself to deal with problems calmly.

- *Plan trips to allow enough time.* Many common traffic situations become frustrating when you are late. Avoid such situations by planning a trip in advance.

- *Expect other drivers to make mistakes and have upsets.* All drivers make mistakes. Some may not have the skill or knowledge that they should have. But remember that the mistakes others make may be ones you have also made or may make in the future. Be alert and compensate for other drivers' mistakes without letting them upset you.

- *Direct your emotions to the driving errors of persons rather than to the persons themselves.* Rarely do other drivers have anything against you. They are only trying to meet their goals.

- *Delay driving when upset.* Most emotional upsets are temporary. It is best to wait until the emotion subsides before getting behind the wheel.

- *Stop driving if you become upset.* When you are upset, find a place to stop. Take a short walk around the car. This would be a good time to stop for fuel or refreshments.

- *Do not drive if you are depressed.* Some emotional upsets, such as grief and anxiety, may last for several days. A person in a severely depressed state should not drive.

- *Train yourself to drive in an organized way.* If you make it a habit to use correct procedures, you will be better able to do the correct thing even when strong emotions are present.

## Temporary Illnesses

The temporary illness of a usually healthy driver can be a serious safety problem. A driver with a temporary impairment often is not able to cope as well as someone with a permanent disability. For example, a person with one eye may drive more safely than a hay fever victim whose eyes are filled with tears.

Everyone suffers minor illnesses from time to time—headaches, toothaches, colds, an upset stomach. Many of these temporary illnesses can reduce your vision, make you feel dizzy, drowsy, or nauseated, or cause you pain. They can also affect your timing and coordination. Any of these conditions make driving difficult and dangerous.

The medications you take for an illness can sometimes cause more problems than the illness itself when you try to drive. Read the labels on medicines to find out if you can drive when you use them. When in doubt, ask a doctor or a pharmacist.

**A cold or an allergic reaction may make your eyes tear or itch. Such illnesses impair vision, making driving dangerous.**

When you are sick, but not sick enough to be in bed, find out what effect the sickness will have on your driving. Then, if you can, take steps to minimize the effect. Finally, decide whether you should delay driving until you feel better. Your doctor can help you with these matters.

## Carbon Monoxide Poisoning

**Carbon monoxide** gas is a by-product of burning fuel. It is colorless, odorless, tasteless, and poisonous. If a car's exhaust system does not work right, carbon monoxide may be drawn into the passenger compartment. Have your exhaust system checked regularly to make sure that it is functioning properly. In station wagons and vans, the rear window should be kept shut to prevent fumes from being pulled inside. Keep fresh air circulating in your car by adjusting the air vents or opening a front window. This will reduce the effects of carbon monoxide.

When you are driving through a long tunnel or in heavy traffic, be aware of the danger of carbon monoxide from other vehicles being pulled into your passenger compartment. Increase the following distance between your car and the car in front of you. If you are forced to stop in a line of cars, stop well back from the vehicle ahead. Shut the air vents and turn off the air conditioner or heater if you are stopped in traffic for more than a few minutes. If you are in open spaces, open your windows for fresh air.

Of course, no car should be run in a closed garage. Even outside, avoid sitting in a parked car with the engine running for more than a few minutes.

## Aging

Our ability to see and react is reduced as we grow older. Aging can result in reduced perception, slower reactions, and impaired motor coordination. Many of these changes are due to hardening of the arteries. This process can affect the entire body, including the heart, brain, nervous system, eyes, and ears. The changes occur gradually. In early stages, their effect is minor. But they can cause a person to become an unsafe driver.

The effects of aging vary from one person to another. Some people in their late 60s are in better physical condition than other people in their early 30s. Also, experience gained from years of driving can compensate for some of the effects. Therefore, there is no specific age when a person should stop driving. Still, it is wise for older drivers to be aware of possible limitations and to consult a doctor if there is any question about continued driving ability.

# Vision and Hearing

Good driving decisions are based on accurate information. You use your eyes to gather most of the information you need to drive safely. If your vision is impaired, your ability to make predictions and decisions is also impaired.

Good hearing is also important for safe driving. However, people with hearing impairments can usually compensate for them and drive well.

**Visual Acuity**   Visual acuity is the ability to see clearly. Impaired visual acuity is the most common visual problem. If your visual acuity is impaired, you may have difficulty identifying signs, signals, and roadway markings as early as you should. You may also fail to notice objects that can influence your selection of a safe path of travel.

Most states administer tests of visual acuity before a driver's license is awarded and at the times of its renewal. Drivers are required to wear corrective lenses when their visual

Good vision is extremely important to a driver. If you need corrective lenses for driving, be sure to wear them.

acuity falls below a certain level. Some people's visual acuity, even when wearing glasses or contact lenses, cannot be made better than 20/70. That means that they can accurately identify letters or objects ⅜ inch high at a distance of no more than 20 feet when they should be able to identify them at 70 feet. Some states grant these people restricted licenses. They are allowed to drive only under certain conditions, such as during the day.

If you need corrective lenses, you are required by law to wear them any time you drive. They help you to gather the information you need to make sound driving decisions.

**Field of Vision**   The area to the left and to the right that you can see when you are looking straight ahead is called your **field of vision.** A broad field of vision is important when you drive. There is always a chance that objects may come at you from the sides. The sooner you see these

**A person with a normal field of vision can see or detect motion at right angles to either side while looking straight ahead. Would you be able to see the car coming from the right?**

objects, the easier it will be to avoid them.

Most people can see or detect motion at right angles to either side of them. They have a field of vision of almost 180 degrees. Some people, however, have a very narrow field of vision. This is called **tunnel vision**.

A field of vision that is less than 140 degrees is considered to be impaired. The fact that we all see less to the sides as our speed increases makes the problem of tunnel vision even more serious.

Drivers whose field of vision is restricted can usually compensate for this handicap by glancing to the sides frequently and by increasing the use of their side-view mirrors. However, this solution reduces the amount of attention the driver can give to the path ahead.

**Color Vision**   Color attracts attention. You can use your sense of color to organize your search of the traffic environment. For example, when applied to traffic-control devices, the color red from a traffic signal, a stop sign, or the brake lights of the car ahead should immediately tell you that you have to stop. Yellow indicates a warning sign. Blue or brown signs indicate no danger. They tell drivers about recreation areas and services available. Guide signs and "go" lights are green.

Color blindness, however, need not seriously impair a person's driving ability. In addition to the fact that few signs or signals are true red or green, few persons who have difficulty identifying colors are totally color blind. Further, on nearly all traffic signals, red is at the top and green is at the bottom. A color-blind person can tell the meaning of traffic lights by their location and the meaning of warning signs by their shapes and messages.

## Distance Judgment and Depth Perception

To drive safely, you need to be able to judge depth and the distance between objects. Distance judgments are more difficult to make when you are moving than when you are standing still. If you have difficulty judging depth or distance, you may have difficulty controlling your following distance and other space around you in traffic. Try to increase your following distance. When preparing to pass another vehicle, particularly at night, you should attempt to establish a longer clear passing zone. An accurate judgment of distance requires that both your eyes work together. Therefore, distance judgments are also more difficult if vision in one eye is impaired. Through practice and experience, depth perception can be improved. To do this, you must learn to compare the sizes and shapes of objects at different angles and distances.

**Night Vision** Humans cannot see as well in the dark as they can in light, and the ability to see in reduced light varies from person to person. Just because you can see well in the daytime does not mean that you will be able to see well at night. At night, you have to depend on the artificial lighting of street lamps and headlights to see the road. Artificial light is not as effective as daylight. Glare presents a problem for some drivers in that their eyes adjust very slowly to changes in light intensity. The most frequent cause of glare is the headlights of oncoming vehicles. This glare can temporarily blind you. Avoid looking directly at the headlights of oncoming cars. Look at the right edge of the road ahead until an approaching car passes you. Even with this precaution, glare will affect your vision. Most young people's eyes can adjust to glare and recover from it within 4 to 6 seconds. Older persons' eyes may take 20 to 30 seconds or more to adjust. If you find that night driving is difficult for you, have your eyes tested. It may be wise for you to avoid night driving whenever possible.

If you do drive at night, it is wise to travel at slower speeds, leave more space between your car and the one ahead, and make certain that your headlights, taillights, and windshield are free from dirt and grime.

**Hearing** It is not always easy to identify the source of a sound while driving a car. This is particularly true in the city. However, sounds can give you information about other vehicles and about the condition of your own car. They can alert you to hazards, such as trains or emergency vehicles using whistles or sirens. They can also alert you to motorcycles and other vehicles that may be hidden in your blind spots. You may hear these vehicles before you can see them. That is why it is dangerous to drive with your car radio blasting. In an increasing number of states, it is illegal to drive while wearing headphones.

People with hearing problems can

**Restricted driver's licenses permit people with physical disabilities to operate vehicles equipped with special controls.**

be excellent drivers by using their other senses more effectively to make up for their disability.

## Physical Handicaps

Most states issue a restricted driver's license to people with certain physical disabilities. This license permits them to operate only vehicles that have been equipped with special controls. With such vehicles, people who do not have the use of one or more limbs can still become skillful, safe drivers. A driver's license is very important for these people. It opens up job opportunities and provides them with the mobility that they otherwise would not have.

## *Projects*

1. Investigate your state's rules about driver impairments. How often are drivers examined for impairments? Report to your class. Do you and your class think these examinations are adequate? Are the examinations given often enough?

2. When you are a passenger in the front seat of someone's car, test your field of vision and your distance judgment. While you are traveling at different speeds, look from side to side without turning your head and estimate if your field of vision changes with the speed. Choose a stationary object ahead and estimate in how many seconds you will reach it, then check yourself.

## Words to Know

carbon monoxide
fatigue

field of vision
visual acuity

tunnel vision
depth perception

## Stop and Review

1. List some causes of fatigue.
2. What can a driver do to prevent or delay fatigue?
3. If you must stop along the roadway to rest, what practices should you follow?
4. Explain how strong emotions affect driving.
5. How can drivers control their emotions? Give three examples.
6. How can temporary illnesses create special hazards for drivers?
7. What can cause carbon monoxide to be drawn into the passenger compartment of a car?
8. What steps can you take to lessen the risk of carbon monoxide poisoning?
9. Should people older than a certain age be allowed to drive? Why or why not?
10. Are good hearing and good vision of equal importance to safe driving? Explain your answer.
11. Define the term "visual acuity."
12. What problems could you have if your visual acuity were poor?
13. What is the purpose of granting a restricted driver's license to people whose vision is not as good as it should be?
14. How does speed affect a driver's field of vision?
15. How can drivers whose field of vision is restricted compensate for this handicap?
16. Why does color blindness not seriously impair a person's ability to drive?
17. Why is depth perception important in enabling you to drive safely?
18. List 3 steps you should take to compensate for reduced vision when you drive at night.
19. What clues to danger do we normally receive through hearing? Which of those clues would we also be able to see, as soon as we heard them?
20. How do automobile manufacturers assist drivers who have physical handicaps?

## *What if...*

You and Chris spent the weekend visiting friends at a college 150 miles away. Now you are driving home at dusk. The first part of the trip is on a winding four-lane, two-way road. The glare from the headlights of oncoming cars is blinding you.

1. What will you do?

Now you are on a wide expressway. It will take about two more hours to get home, and you are tired and hungry. Chris is impatient and wants to snack in the car and keep on going. You want to stop, stretch, and have a regular meal.

2. What will you do?

Complete the sentences by filling in the blanks with the correct terms.

stop distance fresh air sleep
headlights delay tunnel vision depth
oncoming physical visual acuity carbon monoxide
field of vision disabilities

1. The only way to overcome fatigue is to _____ .

2. _____ circulating in the car will help you maintain alertness.

3. _____ is a poisonous by-product of burning gasoline.

4. The ability to see clearly is called _____ .

5. The area to the left and right that you can see without turning your head is called your _____ .

6. A very narrow field of vision is called _____ .

7. A restricted driver's license is issued to people with _____ .

8. When you are emotionally upset, it is best to _____ or to _____ driving.

9. You may not be able to control space in traffic if you have difficulty judging _____ or _____ .

10. At night, the most frequent cause of glare is the _____ of _____ vehicles.

Decide whether each of the following sentences is true or false.

11. Breathing large amounts of carbon monoxide can cause death.

12. As long as your car is not in a closed garage, it does not matter how long you leave your parked car running.

13. You will only take 1 test of visual acuity, and that will be when you apply for your first license.

14. Emotions influence the way people drive.

15. A headache can affect your timing and coordination, and make you an unsafe driver.

# Alcohol and Other Drugs

## Chapter Objectives:

In this chapter you will learn how to:

- explain how alcohol affects both the body and the mind.
- list reasons why drinking alcohol can be dangerous for drivers.
- define BAC and tell how law officials measure levels of intoxication.
- list alternatives to driving drunk.
- tell about ways citizens are fighting drunk driving.
- explain how other drugs affect drivers.

## Alcohol and Driving

*Drinking and driving don't mix.* That is a slogan heard more and more often in recent years. It is part of a widespread campaign to make people aware of the dangers of driving under the influence of alcohol or any other drug.

Why is there so much concern about alcohol and driving?

| Amount of beverage | Concentration of alcohol in bloodstream | Typical effects | Time required for all alcohol to leave body |
|---|---|---|---|
| 1 cocktail (1½ oz. whiskey)<br>1 glass (5½ oz.) wine<br>1 bottle (12 oz.) beer | 0.03% | Slight changes in feeling. | 2 hours |
| 2 cocktails<br>2 glasses (11 oz.) wine<br>2 bottles beer | 0.06% | Feeling of warmth, mental relaxation, slight decrease of fine skills, less concern with minor irritations and restraints. | 4 hours |
| 3 cocktails<br>3 glasses (16½ oz.) wine<br>3 bottles beer | 0.09% | Buoyancy, exaggerated emotion and behavior, talkative, noisy, or morose. | 6 hours |
| 4 cocktails<br>4 glasses (22 oz.) wine<br>4 bottles beer | 0.12% | Impairment of fine coordination, clumsiness, slight to moderate unsteadiness in standing or walking. | 8 hours |
| 5 cocktails<br>5 glasses (27½ oz.) wine<br>5 bottles beer | 0.15% | Intoxication—unmistakable abnormality of bodily functions and mental faculties. | 10 hours or more |

**Even a small amount of alcohol causes changes in the body. Your ability to reason and your coordination are impaired the moment alcohol enters the bloodstream.**

- At least half of all highway deaths are alcohol-related.

- More than three thousand teenagers are killed each year in the United States in accidents that are alcohol-related.

- Six out of every ten people from 16 to 24 years old who die in highway accidents are killed in alcohol-related crashes.

- Over one-third of those killed in alcohol-related accidents were not the people who were drinking.

Alcohol is the most used and abused drug in the world. Even one drink of alcohol causes changes in the body. It goes, undigested, directly into the bloodstream. From there, it is carried to all parts of the body.

A drinker's weight affects the amount of alcohol in the blood. A bigger, heavier person has more body fluids, and so can drink more alcohol than a lighter person and have the same percentage of alcohol in the blood. The percentage is called **BAC**, or **blood-alcohol concentration**. A

200-pound person who has had two drinks will have about the same BAC as a 100-pound person who has had one drink.

In most states, a driver with a BAC of .10 percent or higher can be charged with **driving while intoxicated** (DWI). In some places this charge is called **driving under the influence** (DUI). A person's BAC is often measured with a breath test. Law officials have an instrument that measures the percentage of alcohol in a person's breath while the person breathes into a tube. In some states, if the breath test indicates a BAC of .10 percent or higher, that by itself is enough evidence to convict a driver of driving while intoxicated. This does not mean, however, that a person's BAC must be .10 percent or greater for that person to be charged with DWI. A police officer who stops someone after having observed him or her driving in an erratic manner can charge that driver with DWI.

Such a charge would be supported by other physical evidence, such as difficulty in performing selected physical tests (i.e., touching the nose with the index finger while eyes are closed, etc.).

What happens once alcohol is in the blood? Alcohol is a **depressant** to the central nervous system. This means that it slows down the operation of your brain. From the moment it enters your bloodstream, you begin to lose your ability to:

- reason. The brain takes longer to figure out even simple things, including how the alcohol is affecting your body.

- react. After two or more drinks, a driver becomes slower—not only physically, but also mentally. A driver who is not alert has greater difficulty smoothly managing time and space and cannot make the split-second decisions drivers often are forced to make.

Alcohol impairs side vision, color vision, and night vision. Night vision, especially, is important because most alcohol-related accidents happen at night.

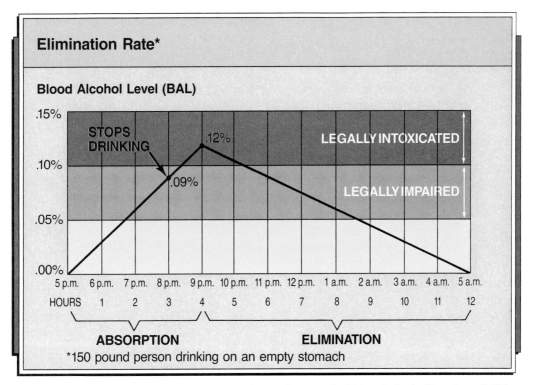

**Elimination Rate***

**Blood Alcohol Level (BAL)**

.15%

STOPS DRINKING

.12%

LEGALLY INTOXICATED

.10%

.09%

LEGALLY IMPAIRED

.05%

.00%

| 5 p.m. | 6 p.m. | 7 p.m. | 8 p.m. | 9 p.m. | 10 p.m. | 11 p.m. | 12 p.m. | 1 a.m. | 2 a.m. | 3 a.m. | 4 a.m. | 5 a.m. |

HOURS   1   2   3   4   5   6   7   8   9   10   11   12

ABSORPTION               ELIMINATION

*150 pound person drinking on an empty stomach

**Note that the blood-alcohol concentration (sometimes called blood-alcohol level, or BAL) continues to rise even after a person stops drinking.**

- see clearly. Just a few drinks impair night vision, side vision, and color vision. Side vision is especially important. Night vision is also important because most alcohol-related accidents occur at night.

- perceive. Distance, depth, and speed perception are all affected. To steer and brake smoothly, a driver needs to be well-coordinated and must know where the cars around him or her are and how fast they are going. Many alcohol-related crashes occur at high speeds because the drivers who were drinking had no sense of how fast they were going.

- hear clearly. A driver who has been drinking has greater difficulty judging where sounds around the car are coming from.

- balance. A driver who cannot walk in a steady manner because of too much to drink is not capable of operating a machine such as an automobile.

## Why Do People Drink and Drive?

Why would anyone want to drive while intoxicated? Why would anyone ride with someone who is?

People drink and drive for a variety of reasons. A recently completed survey of drivers helps answer this question. When drivers were asked why they drank and drove, they gave these reasons:

- "It's the only way to get from place to place."
- "Friends influenced my decision."
- "It was enjoyable."
- "I do it out of habit."
- "There is a low chance of being arrested."
- "It didn't seem so risky."

After reading these reasons given for drinking and driving, it is clear that these drivers are either ignorant of the facts or choose to ignore them.

## Myths vs. Facts About Alcohol

One of the best weapons against driving while intoxicated is knowing the truth about alcohol. Here are some of the myths and the facts that challenge them.

MYTH: Wine and beer are not really alcoholic beverages.

FACT: In standard servings, beer, wine, and liquor contain roughly the same amount of alcohol. Only the percentages of alcohol in each differ. Beer is generally 4 to 7 percent alcohol by volume, wine 12 to 18 percent, and

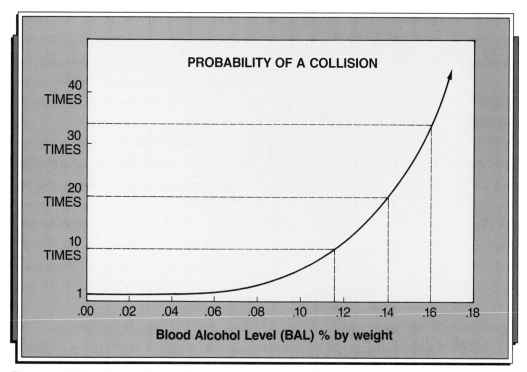

The probability of being in a collision rises sharply as the blood-alcohol level increases. After about 4 drinks, a person is 10 times as likely as a nondrinker to have an accident.

The percentage of alcohol in beer, wine, and hard liquor is not the same. However, the amount of alcohol in an average serving of each is about the same.

liquors 40 to 50 percent (100 proof liquor is 50 percent alcohol); so 1 ounce of liquor, a 3- to 4-ounce glass of wine, and a 12-ounce can of beer have almost the same alcohol content.

MYTH: Driving after drinking is the only way to get from place to place.

FACT: When drivers choose to drink, they can ask a non-drinking friend to drive for them, or leave the car behind and call a cab, or take public transportation. They do have options.

MYTH: My friends want me to drink and I have to drive.

FACT: Real friends would not want you to lose control and hurt yourself or others.

MYTH: Drinking and driving is enjoyable.

FACT: It is the single largest health risk for those under 30 years of age and the number one killer of teenagers.

MYTH: Drinking and driving is not risky.

FACT: In 1984, at least half of all motor vehicle deaths were alcohol-related.

MYTH: It is possible for a drinker to get sober quickly by drinking coffee, taking a cold shower, or exercising vigorously for a short while.

FACT: It takes a fixed period of time for alcohol to leave the body. Nothing can speed up the process. The human body burns up about ½ ounce of alcohol in 1 hour. Suppose you have had 2 glasses of wine. It will take about 2½ hours before the wine is out of your body. The BAC builds up in your body for a while even after you stop drinking. A good rule of thumb is to drink no more than one alcoholic beverage per hour.

MYTH: Alcohol makes you feel better when you are down.

Never allow a friend who has been drinking to drive. Help the person find a taxi or get a ride with someone who is sober.

FACT: Alcohol acts as a depressant, a "downer." It slows down the nervous system. For this reason, it could make you feel worse—emotionally and physically.

MYTH: You cannot get intoxicated on a full stomach.

FACT: It is possible to become intoxicated on a full stomach because though food in the stomach means that alcohol is absorbed more slowly, *all* the alcohol still gets into the blood.

**Taking Care of Yourself** Alcohol is a powerful drug. It dulls the nerve centers of the brain that control judgment, attention, memory, and self-control. It can also do long-term damage; heavy drinking over a long period of time can lead to early death from heart or liver disease. The effects of alcohol on mental health are as serious as the effects on physical health.

For all these reasons, more and more people are rejecting the use of alcohol. Teenagers have another important reason to say "no"—in many states it is illegal for anyone under the age of 21 to buy or possess alcohol.

There are a lot of different ways to say "no"; sometimes it helps to know

## BAC CHART

| Weight pounds | 1 Drink | | | | 2 Drinks | | | | 3 Drinks | | | | 4 Drinks | | | |
|---|---|---|---|---|---|---|---|---|---|---|---|---|---|---|---|---|
| After hours | 4 | 3 | 2 | 1 | 4 | 3 | 2 | 1 | 4 | 3 | 2 | 1 | 4 | 3 | 2 | 1 |
| 80 | — | — | — | .02 | — | — | .05 | .08 | .07 | .10 | .10 | .10 | .12 | .12 | .15 | .15 |
| 100 | — | — | — | .02 | — | — | .04 | .06 | .05 | .07 | .08 | .09 | .09 | .10 | .12 | .13 |
| 120 | — | — | — | .02 | — | — | .03 | .04 | .03 | .04 | .06 | .08 | .06 | .08 | .09 | .11 |
| 140 | — | — | — | .01 | — | — | .02 | .04 | .02 | .03 | .05 | .06 | .04 | .06 | .08 | .09 |
| 160 | — | — | — | .01 | — | — | .02 | .03 | .01 | .02 | .04 | .05 | .03 | .04 | .06 | .08 |
| 180 | — | — | — | .01 | — | — | .01 | .03 | — | .02 | .03 | .04 | .02 | .04 | .05 | .07 |
| 200 | — | — | — | — | — | — | .01 | .02 | — | .01 | .03 | .04 | .01 | .03 | .04 | .06 |

| Weight pounds | 5 Drinks | | | | 6 Drinks | | | | 7 Drinks | | | | 8 Drinks | | | |
|---|---|---|---|---|---|---|---|---|---|---|---|---|---|---|---|---|
| After hours | 4 | 3 | 2 | 1 | 4 | 3 | 2 | 1 | 4 | 3 | 2 | 1 | 4 | 3 | 2 | 1 |
| 80 | .17 | .17 | .19 | .20 | .19 | .22 | .22 | .25 | .25 | .27 | .27 | .30 | .29 | .30 | .32 | .33 |
| 100 | .13 | .14 | .16 | .17 | .16 | .18 | .19 | .21 | .20 | .22 | .23 | .25 | .24 | .25 | .27 | .28 |
| 120 | .09 | .11 | .13 | .14 | .13 | .14 | .16 | .17 | .15 | .17 | .19 | .20 | .19 | .20 | .22 | .23 |
| 140 | .07 | .09 | .10 | .12 | .10 | .12 | .13 | .15 | .13 | .14 | .16 | .17 | .15 | .17 | .18 | .20 |
| 160 | .06 | .07 | .09 | .10 | .08 | .09 | .11 | .13 | .10 | .12 | .13 | .15 | .13 | .14 | .16 | .17 |
| 180 | .04 | .06 | .07 | .09 | .06 | .08 | .09 | .11 | .09 | .10 | .12 | .13 | .11 | .12 | .14 | .15 |
| 200 | .03 | .04 | .06 | .08 | .05 | .07 | .08 | .09 | .07 | .09 | .10 | .12 | .09 | .10 | .12 | .13 |

☐ You are affected by the alcohol and should not drive.
Numbers equal the percentage of alcohol in the blood. Dash (—) = a trace of alcohol.

**Your weight influences the amount of alcohol you can drink before it impairs you. A person with a BAC of .05 is considered legally impaired.**

in advance what you are going to say if you are offered a drink. Here are some suggestions:

- "It's not for me."
- "Thanks, but I want to *remember* this party."
- "I don't need alcohol to have a good time."
- "No thanks. I'm driving."
- "I have a better time without it."
- "I'd just as soon have a soft drink."
- "No thanks."

## When Someone Has Been Drinking

If a person is ever in a situation where someone has been drinking, remember that there are alternatives to that person driving home after drinking:

- The person could stay overnight at a friend's house that is within walking distance.
- The person could call a friend, relative, or taxi company to arrange a ride home.
- If he or she has had only one drink, the person could wait an hour or so before driving.

## MADD and SADD

The problem of people driving while intoxicated and then causing injuries or deaths was once seen as unsolvable. But the numbers of victims and tragic stories

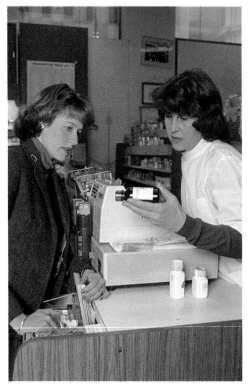

**Prescription and nonprescription drugs can affect a person's ability to drive. When in doubt, consult a pharmacist.**

than 3,000 teenagers died in 1984 because someone drank and drove.

Citizen groups are not letting up on their efforts. Among these groups are some, such as Mothers Against Drunk Driving (MADD), founded by parents whose children were killed by intoxicated drivers. After two of his students were killed in car crashes, a teacher founded Students Against Driving Drunk (SADD). It now has chapters in all 50 states.

SADD has drawn up a lifetime contract. In it, students pledge that if they drink at any gathering or party, they will call their parents to come and give them a ride home. Parents pledge "to come and get you at any hour, any place, no questions asked, and no arguments at that time."

In an increasing number of places, restaurant and bar owners and hosts of private parties can be held legally responsible for any deaths or injuries resulting from an accident caused by a person to whom they served drinks when there was evidence to indicate that that person was already intoxicated.

## Other Drugs

Some drugs can, by law, be bought only from a pharmacy after a doctor or a dentist prescribes them. Other drugs do not need a prescription. Some are against the law, but are often sold on the street illegally.

Many drugs, both legal and illegal, impair a person's ability to drive. Remember that besides their intended

of accidents kept increasing. Citizen groups, outraged by the unnecessary tragedies, started publicizing the stories. Under pressure, a number of states raised their drinking ages to 21 because the majority of alcohol-related traffic accidents involve young people. New, stricter laws against driving while intoxicated were passed by state governments. Law enforcement officials began viewing intoxicated drivers as criminals, even as murderers, rather than as nuisances.

In recent years the number of teenagers killed in alcohol-related traffic accidents has gone down. Still, more

**Many accidents are the result of a person's driving while under the influence of drugs. Drugs can affect a driver's ability to react and to make decisions quickly.**

purpose, drugs may have side effects. Some drugs may affect your ability to stay alert. Drugs can have different effects on different people. They can also have different effects on the same person at different times.

Just about everyone knows that illegal drugs have harmful effects. But it may be surprising to know that legal drugs can also be damaging. Even nicotine (found in cigarettes) and caffeine (found in coffee and many cola-flavored soft drinks) affect the heart, brain, and other parts of the body.

**Prescription Drugs**    Directions for the use of prescription drugs are usually printed on the label that the pharmacist puts on the container in which these drugs are purchased.

The directions must be followed exactly. In addition, ask your doctor or pharmacist if the prescribed drug will affect your driving ability. Prescription drugs such as amphetamines, barbiturates, and tranquilizers should not be combined with driving.

Some drivers misuse amphetamines, taking them to stay awake—especially when they are driving for long distances on straight, flat roads. Amphetamines do speed up the central nervous system. But they go just a little bit—a dangerous bit—further than making drivers feel alert. These drugs may encourage drivers to be more willing than usual to take risks—such as trying to make it across train tracks when there is a train approaching. When the effect of the drug wears off, which can happen suddenly, the user may become very tired and depressed.

Barbiturates are used by some people to calm their nerves. Like alcohol, barbiturates slow down the central nervous system, making the user less alert than one needs to be to operate a motor vehicle. When the effect of the drug wears off, depression often follows.

Tranquilizers are also called "downers," and they are depressants. Since they slow down the central nervous system, they are used by people to reduce anxiety. Tranquilizers cause drowsiness and can cause drivers to fall asleep at the wheel. People who use tranquilizers sometimes mix them with alcohol. The combination can be deadly. It can reduce blood pressure, reduces the supply of oxygen to the brain, and, in extreme cases, can stop the heart.

**Nonprescription Drugs** Nonprescription drugs, or **over-the-counter drugs**, include lozenges, capsules, tablets, and syrups. They must by law provide "adequate directions for use." Before taking any nonprescrip-

tion drug, read the label carefully. Check to see if driving after taking the drug is discouraged.

**Illegal Drugs** An increasingly common cause of highway accidents is a drug many people think is fairly harmless. It is marijuana. Marijuana is not so harmless for drivers. It may make a user drowsy. It often causes people to lose the ability to judge time and space and lose awareness of how fast they are driving. It alters mood, vision, and reaction time. After smoking marijuana, some people also tend to concentrate on one thing at a time, ignoring all else around them. A good driver must be able to take in many things at once.

Marijuana is the most frequently used illegal drug. Other street drugs are cocaine, "angel dust" (phencyclidine, or PCP), and hard drugs such as heroin. Illegal drugs are sold without identification or prescription. One obvious danger in using these drugs is not knowing their content or concentration and, therefore, what effect they could have on your system.

## Projects

1. Invite a local police officer or traffic official to talk to your class about drinking and driving. Ask what problems he or she most often encounters when trying to enforce laws relating to drinking and driving.

2. Investigate the regulations in your state concerning the purchase, sale, possession, and consumption of alcohol, tobacco, and other drugs. Report your findings to your class, and discuss whether these laws are appropriate.

blood-alcohol concentration (BAC)          depressant
driving while intoxicated (DWI)            designated

1. Are drinkers the only victims of alcohol-related accidents?
2. How is alcohol digested differently from food?
3. How does a drinker's weight affect the rate of intoxication?
4. What does BAC stand for?
5. What happens during a breath test?
6. List 5 effects of alcohol.
7. When do most alcohol-related accidents occur?
8. Why do some people choose to drive with someone who is drunk?
9. Why is the belief that alcohol makes you feel better false?
10. How is it possible to become intoxicated on a full stomach?
11. What are 2 tips for partygoers?
12. What is a "designated driver"?
13. What are MADD and SADD, and who started them?
14. Describe the SADD contract.
15. What do all drugs have in common?
16. How can you find out if you should drive while you are taking a prescription drug?
17. List 3 prescription drugs that should not be combined with driving.
18. What are tranquilizers?
19. What is an illegal drug?
20. What are some of the effects of marijuana?

## What if...

You have driven 3 friends to a party at Pat's house. You are 18 years of age. You are drinking a soda when Pat walks up, takes away your glass, and hands you a mixed drink. "Be a sport!" she laughs. "C'mon, have some fun!" You don't want the drink, but you don't want to make a scene, either.

1. What will you do?
Fred also drove a group over. He is tall and slim and is usually on the quiet side. He has clearly had too much to drink, but he insists on driving his group home, anyway.
2. Is it dangerous for Fred to drive? If so, why? Should you try to stop him? If so, how?

# CHAPTER 15 TEST

Complete the sentences by filling in the blanks with the correct terms.

nonprescription   blood-alcohol        nothing       designated driver
   drug                concentration (BAC)   marijuana   at least half
amphetamines     Mothers Against Drunk   .10 percent or
one-third           Driving (MADD)     higher

1. The percentage of alcohol in the blood is called the _____ .

2. _____ is a citizen group started by parents who had children killed by drunk drivers.

3. _____ of all highway deaths are alcohol-related.

4. A driver can be convicted of driving while intoxicated with a BAC of _____ .

5. Before taking any _____ , read the label carefully.

6. A _____ is the person in the group who does not drink at a party and makes certain the other guests get home safely.

7. _____ can speed up the time it takes for alcohol to leave the body.

8. _____ often causes people to lose the ability to judge time and space.

9. _____ are prescription drugs that speed up the central nervous system.

10. Over _____ of those killed in alcohol-related accidents were not the people who were drinking.

---

Select the one best answer to each of the following questions.

11. Which of the following is *not* true?
(a) Alcohol-related accidents kill 1,000 teens a year. (b) 50 percent of all highway deaths are related to alcohol. (c) Over ⅓ of those killed in alcohol-related accidents had not been drinking. (d) Over half of all 16-to-24-year-olds who die in highway accidents are killed in alcohol-related crashes.

12. Blood-alcohol concentration:
(a) can be measured with a breath test. (b) is also DWI. (c) is the same number for everyone. (d) stands for blood-alcohol count.

13. Which is *not* an effect of alcohol?
(a) cloudy vision (b) improved depth perception (c) dulled hearing (d) slower reaction times

14. Which of the following is a myth?
(a) Alcohol slows down the nervous system. (b) Exercising reduces the time it takes for alcohol to leave the body. (c) The BAC continues to build up in your body after you stop drinking. (d) Standard servings of beer and wine contain the same amount of alcohol.

15. Prescription drugs:
(a) are called over-the-counter drugs. (b) have no side effects. (c) can be ordered by a police officer. (d) may affect the ability to drive.

# Vehicle Failure

## Chapter Objectives:

In this chapter you will learn how to:

- effectively handle situations involving brake failure, steering failure, and engine failure.
- cope with additional vehicle failures (stuck accelerator pedal, hood fly-up, headlight failure).
- change a flat tire and jump-start a car with a dead battery.

No matter how well you maintain your car, it may break down suddenly. Vehicle breakdowns range from minor inconveniences to serious hazards. Proper vehicle maintenance can help you avoid most breakdowns. Understanding what is involved will help you know what to do when certain types of breakdowns occur.

If your car is moving when a breakdown occurs, you must control the vehicle's speed and direction and drive out of the stream of traffic. Once you are safely off the road, you can deal with the breakdown with less risk of an accident.

# Brake Failure

When driving, be alert for symptoms of brake failure, such as a squeaking, hard, or sinking brake pedal. In two cases, brake failure can be temporary. Brakes can fail temporarily after you have driven through a deep puddle. You can dry your brakes by driving with your left foot lightly on the brake pedal. Heat produced by friction will dry your brakes. **Brake fade** is the result of brakes overheating after being applied hard for a long period of time. Pull off the road and let them cool down. If the symptoms persist for more than a few minutes, the vehicle should be checked by a mechanic as soon as possible.

If you have power brakes and your engine stops running, the power assist on your brakes will fail. They will still work, but you must brake much harder to stop the car.

All new cars are equipped with a **dual-service brake system**. This means that there are separate systems for the front and rear wheels. Therefore, total failure seldom occurs. If it does occur, though, there are several things that you can do:

- Pump the brake pedal rapidly. This action may build up some pressure in the brake-fluid lines to provide some braking force.

- Shift to a lower gear. Slowing the engine and power train will provide a "drag" force. This will slow the car. In a manual-shift car, release the clutch pedal slowly after an emergency downshift. You will need a good amount of clear space ahead to slow down using low gear alone.

- Use the parking brake. You must depress the release button or hold open the brake handle while you are doing this. That way you can

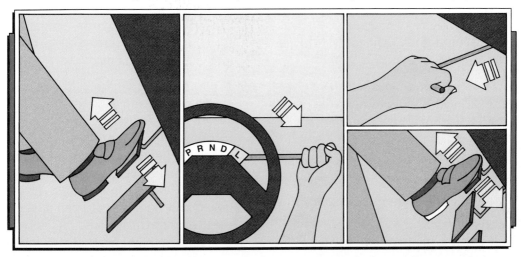

If your brakes fail, try pumping the brake pedal. If that does not work, shift to low gear. You can also hold open the brake release handle and use the parking brake as needed.

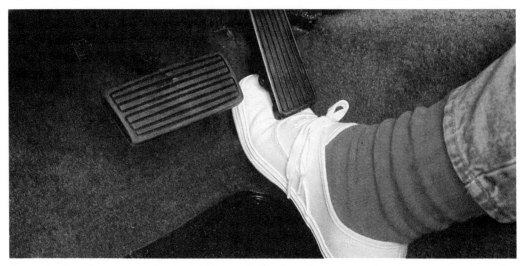

**Never try to release a stuck accelerator pedal by bending over and using your hands. If the road ahead is clear, you can try to release it with the toe of your shoe.**

control the braking action for a smooth stop rather than having the brake lock repeatedly into position (making the "clicking" sound), as it does when you are parking. With the release handle open, you can apply pressure on the brake, release it, and reapply as necessary. The parking brake works only on the rear wheels. If you apply it suddenly, the rear wheels might lock, causing a spinout.

If none of these actions slows your car and gradually brings it to a stop, sound your horn to warn other highway users. Then do one or more of the following things to try to avoid serious danger:

- Steer to the side of the street and try to rub the tires against a curb to slow the car.

- Search for an open area, such as an empty field, yard, or parking lot.

Drive into it, put the car into *neutral,* and coast around until the car slows to a stop.

- Look for an uphill road that will slow you down and take you away from other highway users.

- As a last resort, turn the ignition off and shift to low gear (*1* or *L*). This may damage your transmission, but it could help stop your car and avoid a collision.

- If you cannot avoid a collision, try to make the move with the least serious consequences. Try to steer into large bushes or small objects. Steer to the side of the road to try to slow the car by rubbing it against fences, guardrails, roadside embankments, or even parked cars. Any of these collisions is better than a head-on collision or a collision with a pedestrian or a large fixed object.

**If your car breaks down, call a garage to have it towed. Before it is towed, shift the car into neutral gear, turn off the ignition, and release the parking brake.**

- When the car's speed is reduced to about 10 mph, turn off the engine.

## Steering Failure

Abnormal shimmying or vibrations, binding when turning the wheel, and unusual free play or slack are all symptoms of possible steering or suspension failure. Have your car checked by a mechanic if you notice any of these symptoms. Total steering failure is rare. What does happen often is partial steering failure caused by a stalled engine in a car equipped with power steering. When the engine stalls, the power steering unit stops working. This makes steering hard. A broken drive belt, a faulty power-steering system, or a defective hydraulic pump also make steering difficult. If any of these parts fail, the power steering stops working and the driver must work hard to turn the steering wheel. But steering control is not lost. If a power steering failure occurs, you should keep steering.

Signal to other drivers that you are having problems by honking your horn and turning on your hazard flashers. Get your car safely off the road and brake to a stop.

An upper or lower control arm or ball joint breakdown is a more serious problem. (These parts are described on pages 228–229.) This will make one front wheel collapse. If this

**Be prepared for emergencies. Know what to do in the event that your car breaks down and needs to be towed *before* you are in that situation.**

happens, keep steering. Do not step on the brake. Even slight brake pressure can cause the car to pull sharply to one side. If you are traveling at highway speed, take the same steps you would take in case of brake failure. Shift to a lower gear (except in front-wheel-drive vehicles, where downshifting would have the same effect as braking). Use the parking brake. Because it only works on the rear wheels, using the parking brake should not affect steering in a front- or rear-wheel-drive vehicle. (Remember that the parking brake release must be held open so that the brake is not held in a locked position.)

## Engine Failure

Engine failure is the most common vehicle failure. Many things can cause it, including a broken timing gear, a problem in the fuel system, lack of fuel, electrical system failure, or a cold engine that stalls or one that overheats. As soon as you find that the engine is failing, try to steer off the road.

Turn on your hazard flashers to let other drivers know you are in trouble. Once you have pulled safely off the road, raise your hood as a signal that your car has broken down. If the engine stops completely before you can leave the road, try to coast to a safe area. Shift to *neutral*; the car will coast farther than it will in *drive*.

If you stall in an intersection, you will need to act quickly. Shift to *neutral* and restart the engine, if possible, then shift back to *drive*. (In a manual-shift car, depress the clutch to restart, shift to *second* gear, and let the clutch out.) In either case,

274

If your car stalls after going through water, turn off the ignition and check for water around the spark plugs. If the plugs are wet, dry off the porcelain part with a cloth.

keep your eyes up (except for quick glances) looking for road and traffic conditions.

Remember, power steering and power brakes do not work the same when the engine is off, so it may be harder to steer or brake. With extra effort, though, you can still control the car.

**Wet Engine** When you drive through water, even at a slow speed, the water may splash the engine and make it stall. There are two reasons why a wet engine stalls:

- Water may short out the electrical system.
- Water may be drawn into the engine combustion chamber through the air cleaner and carburetor.

If your car stalls while or after going through water, steer to the side of the road. When you are off the road, turn off the ignition. Then raise the hood and check for water around the spark plugs. If the plugs are wet, dry the porcelain part of the plug with a cloth (be careful if the engine is hot). if the car still does not start, wait until the engine dries. If it is not raining, leave the hood up. The air can speed the drying.

**Flooded Engine** The engine may be flooded if you have pumped the accelerator repeatedly when trying to start the car. You can usually smell gasoline. To start the car, first push the accelerator to the floor and hold it there to let air into the engine. While the pedal is still depressed, turn the ignition switch. If the car starts, gently release the accelerator. If it does not, wait for about 10 minutes before trying again.

275

If your car overheats, turn off the engine and let it cool. Stand back and use a cloth to remove the radiator cap.

**Overheated Engine** Engine overheating can be caused by several things: driving in slow-moving traffic during hot weather; climbing up long, steep grades; a loose or broken fan belt; a broken water pump; not enough coolant in the cooling system; a stuck or broken thermostat; or a clogged radiator.

The most common problem is not having enough antifreeze or coolant in the radiator. In the winter, lack of antifreeze can lead to ice buildup in the radiator. This blocks the flow of water and causes the engine to overheat. In the summer, lack of coolant prevents proper heat transfer. Heat builds up in the engine, the fluid in the radiator starts to boil, and steam starts to come out of the front of the car.

If the needle of the temperature gauge is going toward *hot* or if the temperature warning light starts to flash, turn off all accessories, particularly the air conditioner. If the temperature light stays on or the needle stays on *hot*, signal and pull off the road. If it is impossible to pull over, turn on the heater to draw heat from the engine. Bear in mind that this is an emergency measure that will make the passenger compartment uncomfortably hot. If this does not solve the problem, you must pull off the road and stop the car.

In most cases, you will have to call for emergency road service. Check under the hood to see if there are any problems you can identify when asking for help. There may be a broken hose or belt. Without touching the radiator, you can see if the radiator overflow tank is empty.

If you have coolant or water handy to add, check the fluid level in the radiator. Make sure you wait until the engine has fully cooled off before you open your radiator. (If you remove the radiator cap while the engine is hot, even when the radiator is operating at normal temperatures, the pressure inside the system could cause the fluid to boil over and scald you.) After the engine has cooled, slowly unscrew the radiator cap and remove it. (Protect yourself by covering the cap with a cloth.) If the fluid in the radiator is low, add coolant or water. Cold water, however, could damage an overheated engine. To prevent damage, start the engine and let it run at idle speed as you add the water or coolant. (If it is winter or if you are using an air conditioner, you must add antifreeze to the water.) After you have filled the radiator to normal level, make sure you screw the cap on it tightly. Check the engine gauge to see that the engine stays cool.

## Stuck Accelerator Pedal

Accelerator pedals sometimes stick. This means that your engine does not go back to idling speed when you take your foot off the accelerator. The cause may be a sticking linkage or a broken engine mount. It may also be the result of a floor mat that has crumpled up or, in the winter, frozen snow and ice on the floor. When the accelerator sticks, leave the car in *drive* and turn the ignition off, thus shutting off the engine. Remember, if you have power steering, it will be harder to steer. You leave the car in gear so that you do not accidentally turn the key so far that you lock the steering column and lose steering completely. If you have power brakes, do not pump them. Without the engine to operate the power brake unit, pumping the brakes will quickly exhaust the system. Instead, apply steady, moderate pressure, signal a turn, and steer off the road. Use the horn or your hazard flashers as necessary to warn other drivers of your problem. If you are slowing too quickly and you want to coast farther, shift into *neutral* gear.

There is an alternate method that allows you to continue using your power brakes and steering, which could be crucial in some instances. That is to shift into *neutral* and apply the brake while the engine is still on. Allowing the engine to continue running at full speed may cause it some damage, but control of the vehicle is the most important consideration.

Only if you have a clear road ahead should you attempt to release the accelerator pedal. To do so, slip the toe of your shoe under it and pull up. Never try to release the accelerator by bending over and using your hands. You cannot control your car or see where you are going in that position.

## Hood Fly-Up

You must have a clear view to drive safely. Therefore, a hood that flies up is a great danger. Your best defense against hood fly-up is to prevent it. Before you drive, check the hood. Make sure it is fastened. After you or anyone else checks the engine, make sure the hood is locked. You can also check the hood as you drive. If the hood and fenders do not line up properly or if the hood seems to vibrate, it may not be fastened. Stop to check it.

If the hood does fly up, you can roll the side window down and try to look around the hood. Do not lean out so far that you cannot reach the pedals. You may also be able to lean forward to see through the space between the dashboard and the hood. If you have

**If your hood flies up, put on your hazard flashers. Try to look through the space under the hood. Signal and pull over.**

no other choice, brake to a stop in your lane. You may be struck from the rear. However, if the driver behind you has a clear view, there should be time and space to avoid a rear-end collision.

## Fire

Cars seldom catch on fire, even after a crash. If yours does, though, or if you see or smell smoke, pull off the road and stop immediately. As quickly as you can, turn off the engine and get all passengers out of and away from the car. If the fire is small and only in the passenger section, you can try to put it out with a fire extinguisher (a 2-pound dry-chemical extinguisher should be carried in the trunk). If you do not have a fire extinguisher, use water, sand, dirt, or snow. If you cannot put the fire out quickly, get away from the vehicle before the fire spreads. It may cause an explosion.

If you see smoke around the hood, call the fire department. Do not try to extinguish the fire yourself.

If you are involved in a collision damaging the engine of either vehicle, you should make sure the engines are turned off, get everyone away from the cars, and call the fire department.

## Flat Tire

There may come a time when you walk out to your car and find that you have a flat tire. There are many causes of flats. Sometimes, the air leaks slowly from the tire while you are driving. When this happens, you may notice a gradual change in the way your car steers. As in a blowout, the car begins to pull toward one side if the soft tire is in the front. If a rear tire is leaking air, the car may start to fishtail. In either case, maintain steering control, signal, pull well off the road, stop, and turn on the hazard flashers.

A flat tire must be changed as soon as possible. If you are not careful, this can be dangerous. To be safe, take the following precautions before you attempt to change the tire:

- Make sure the car is parked on a level surface that is firm enough to support a jack without any sinking or shifting movement.

- With the engine off, set the parking brake, and place the selector lever in *park*. (In a manual-transmission car, put the gear-shift lever in *reverse*.)

- Get all passengers out of the car.

- As soon as you stop, set up flares or warning triangles 100 and 200 feet behind your car to alert other drivers. Keep the hazard flashers on while you are working.

- Use a rock or a piece of wood (at least 4 inches by 8 inches by 2 inches thick) to block the wheel diagonally across from the tire that is flat.

All automobile manufacturers provide a list of steps to follow for changing a tire. The list is usually found in the owner's manual or in the trunk. Here are the steps on most lists:

1. Remove the jack, jack handle, lug wrench (sometimes it is part of the jack handle), wheel block, base board, and spare tire from the trunk or storage area. Place the spare on the ground near the flat tire.

2. Remove the **hubcap** (wheel cover) from the wheel that has the flat tire. With the lug wrench, loosen the lug nuts that hold the wheel, but do not take them all the way off.

3. Following the instructions in your owner's manual, place the jack in the proper position on a solid base (the road shoulder, if it is flat; if not, on a base board about 6 inches by 12 inches by 1 inch thick). Jack the car up until the flat tire clears the ground.

**Changing a tire could be hazardous if you are not careful. The correct way to change a tire is outlined in the text.**

4. Check to make sure the wheel block is in place in front of a front tire or in back of a rear one. Do not get under the car or so near it that you would be injured if the jack failed or if the car fell off the jack.

5. Remove the lug nuts by hand and place them in the hubcap so they will not get lost.

6. Pull off the wheel.

7. Put on the wheel with the spare tire and replace the lug nuts.

8. Tighten the lug nuts, first by hand and then with the lug wrench.

9. Jack the car down to the ground and remove the jack. Make the lug nuts as tight as you can with the wrench. Replace the wheel cover.

10. Place the flat tire, the jack and

If your battery is dead, you can start your car by using jumper cables and the battery of another car.

jack handle, lug wrench, wheel block, and base board back in the trunk or storage area.

After you change the tire, have the flat repaired or replaced as soon as possible. This way, you will always have a spare tire when you need one. If you have only an undersized, temporary spare tire, it must be replaced with a full-sized tire right away. Drive no faster than 50 mph to the nearest service station.

## Dead Battery

If you turn the ignition switch to *start* and nothing happens, the battery is probably dead. Using the car's lights or radio for an extended period of time with the engine off is one cause of a depleted battery. You can usually still start the car by attach-

ing your battery to the battery of another vehicle. This is called **jump-starting**. Jump-starting is fairly easy to do if you have jumper cables. Follow these steps:

1. Place the vehicles so that the jumper cables will reach from the good battery of one car to the dead battery of the other.

2. Turn off the ignition and electrical equipment in both vehicles.

3. Shift both vehicles to *park* (*neutral* in a manual-transmission vehicle) and set the parking brakes.

4. Make sure both batteries are of the same voltage. Remove the cell caps and check the fluid level in both batteries. (If the fluid is frozen, do not try to jump-start the battery. It may explode.) Cover both batteries with a heavy cloth to protect against splashing of boiling battery fluid.

5. Attach one end of a jumper cable to the positive (P or +) post of the good battery. Attach the other end of the same cable to the positive post of the dead battery.

6. Attach one end of the other jumper cable to the negative (N or −) post of the good battery. Attach the other end of the same cable to the engine or frame of the car that has the dead battery. (This connection should be as far away from the battery as possible to protect against splashing in the event of an explosion.)

7. Start the engine that has the good battery. Hold down the accelerator pedal so that the engine runs at a high idle.

8. Start the engine of the car with the dead battery.

9. Take off the jumper cables, one at a time, in the reverse order from which you attached them—negative connections first—while both engines are still running.

## Headlight Failure

Both headlights rarely fail at the same time. But if one headlight goes out, you may not notice it until the second light fails, too. The most frequent causes of headlight failure are a blown fuse or a burned-out headlamp. No matter what the cause, you must bring the vehicle to a stop, off the road, as quickly and smoothly as possible. To do this, press the dimmer switch as you reduce speed. Headlamps seldom burn out on both high and low beams at the same time. If pressing the dimmer switch gives no light, turn on the parking lights, turn indicators on either side, or the four-way emergency flashers. These can provide enough light to help you get off the road.

If you have no lights at all, look for the center- and side-lane markers on the pavement. They usually are bright white and provide some visibility. If other cars are coming toward or following you, their lights also will help you. When you bring

**Always use a cloth or towel when handling spark plugs, the radiator cap, or any other hot part of the engine.**

your car to a stop well off the road, set up flares or reflective triangles to let other drivers know you are there.

## Waiting for Help

You may be required to pull off the road in a place where there is no telephone in safe walking distance. If the problem with your car is not one you can solve yourself, you must catch the attention of passing motorists. The way to do this is by raising the hood of your car. If possible, tie a handkerchief or scarf to the antenna

**If your car breaks down on the highway and you cannot solve the problem yourself, call for emergency road service. If there is no phone nearby, raise the hood and wait in the car.**

or wedge it into an almost-closed window. Keep your four-way emergency flashers on.

If you are far enough off the road, wait in the car with the windows closed and the doors locked. When someone stops to offer help, open your window slightly and ask the person to call for emergency road ser-

vice. If you are not far enough from the stream of traffic or you fear being struck from behind for any reason, leave the car and walk to a safe spot, climbing behind a guardrail if necessary. In no case should you stand behind your car, where it will be difficult for other drivers to see you and you could be struck by traffic.

## *Projects*

1. Check a friend's or a family member's car. Is it equipped with a good spare tire, jacking equipment, jumper cables, flares or warning triangles, a flashlight, and a fire extinguisher? If any of these items are missing, ask the car owner why. Does the owner think they are unnecessary?

2. Interview some drivers or an auto mechanic about various types of vehicle failure they have experienced or witnessed. Ask for specific descriptions of the symptoms, and the traffic conditions, if possible. Imagine yourself in these situations, and tell the class how you would react.

brake fade        dual-service brake system        jump-starting

# Stop and Review

1. Name 3 types of vehicle failure.
2. If your car is moving when a breakdown occurs, what is the first thing you must do?
3. Give 2 examples of temporary brake failure.
4. If your brakes fail, what steps should you take, using your vehicle controls? If you cannot slow and stop your car using the controls, what actions should you take?
5. List 3 symptoms of possible steering or suspension failure.
6. List 3 causes of engine failure. What steps should you take if your engine stops while you are moving in traffic?
7. What should you do if your car stalls in an intersection?
8. If your car has power brakes and power steering, what will happen if the engine stalls? What should you do?
9. What are some possible causes of a stuck accelerator pedal? What should you never attempt to do in order to fix it?
10. What should you do if your accelerator pedal gets stuck while you are driving in traffic?
11. What is your best defense against hood fly-up?
12. What should you do if your vehicle catches fire?
13. What is the best way to change a flat tire? What precautions should you take when changing the tire?
14. Describe the correct way to jump-start a car that has a dead battery.
15. List 2 reasons why a wet engine stalls.
16. What should you do if your vehicle stalls after going through water?
17. How can you dry out your brakes after you have driven through a deep puddle?
18. What should you do to start an engine you have flooded?
19. List 6 causes of an overheated engine. What should you do if your car's temperature warning light starts to flash?
20. What is the most important thing you should do if your headlights fail?

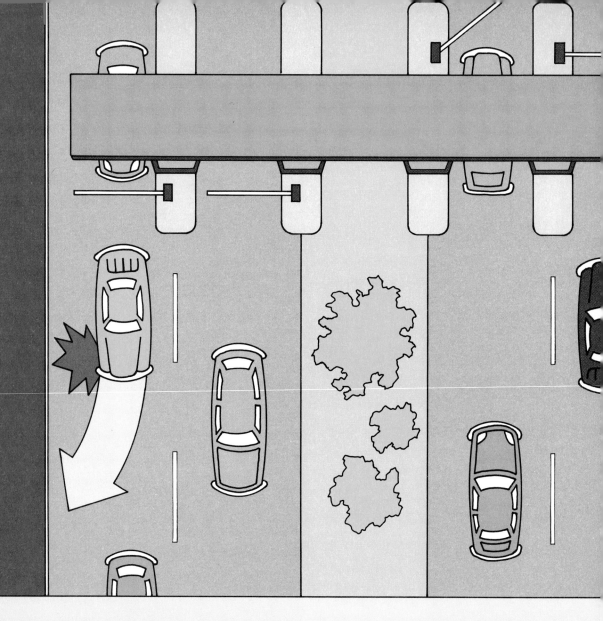

## *What if...*

You are caught in a highway traffic jam on the July 4 weekend. For almost an hour, you have been inching along, starting and stopping. Now the needle of your temperature gauge is pointing toward *hot*.

1. What should you do?

It is an hour later. You have just gone through a toll plaza. Suddenly, the front of your car starts to pull sharply toward the right. The ride feels jerky.

2. What has happened? What should you do?

Complete the sentences by filling in the blanks with the correct terms.

| | | | |
|---|---|---|---|
| coolant | warning | burned-out | engine |
| honking your horn | triangles | headlamp | jump-start |
| turning on your | blown fuse | steering | brake fade |
| hazard flashers | dual-service brake | diagonally across | suspension |
| antifreeze | system | flares | |

1. Cars equipped with separate braking systems for the front and rear wheels have what is called a _____ .

2. The most common cause of an overheated engine is not having enough _____ or _____ in the radiator.

3. _____ results from overheating after the brakes have been applied hard for a long period of time.

4. Shimmying, binding, and slack are all symptoms of _____ or _____ failure.

5. The most common vehicle failure is _____ failure.

6. The first thing you should do after you have stopped to change a tire is set up _____ or _____ .

7. Before changing a tire, block the wheel _____ from the tire that is flat.

8. If your battery is dead, you may still be able to _____ it using the battery from another vehicle.

9. The most frequent causes of headlight failure are a _____ or a _____ .

10. If you are having car problems, let other drivers know by _____ and _____ .

---

Decide whether each of the following sentences is true or false.

11. A car coasts farther in *drive* than in *neutral*.

12. A ball joint breakdown will make a wheel collapse.

13. When headlamps burn out, you usually lose both high and low beams.

14. If you have power brakes and your engine fails, the power assist on your brakes will also fail.

15. If you have power steering and your engine fails, there is no way to control the direction your car will move.

# Selecting and Insuring Your Car

## Chapter Objectives

In this chapter you will learn how to:

- purchase an appropriate new or used car.
- select financing for your car purchase.
- choose the correct insurance for your car.

A car is one of the most expensive purchases most people make. Operating expenses such as fuel, oil, maintenance, insurance, license and registration fees, and taxes all add to the expense of car ownership. These expenses may vary. The type of car you buy, where you live, and your driving record affect the cost of operating a car. Whether you use your car for work or for pleasure, the number of miles you drive each year, and the number of years you keep your car also affect the cost of operating it.

# Determining Your Transportation Needs

Before you choose a car to buy, decide what your transportation needs are. Is public transportation available to fill all or part of your needs? If not, then think about what size and type of vehicle you need. Ask yourself how many miles you will travel each day, month, or year. How many people will drive the car? How many passengers will you usually carry? If the need should arise, how heavy a load or how many large packages will you have to carry?

# Selecting a Car

Once you are ready to select your car, remember that cars are grouped by size and class (vans, station wagons, sedans). In cars of different sizes, you will find large differences in fuel mileage. You can also find large differences in fuel mileage among cars of the same class. One small car may get as few as 18 miles per gallon while another may get 28 miles per gallon.

When you buy a car, consider factors that will help your car use as little fuel as possible. Consider the following:

- *The weight of the vehicle.* In general, the less a vehicle weighs, the better mileage the vehicle will deliver. If the engine has less weight to pull, it does not have to work as hard. However, just because a car looks smaller does not mean it will weigh less than a car that appears larger.

- *The design of the vehicle.* The design of a vehicle will influence its fuel mileage. If a vehicle is streamlined, the engine will not have to work as hard to overcome air resistance. A vehicle with less air resistance will generally require less energy to move. For instance, vans usually have a large, square front. As a result, they have greater resistance to air movement. Because of their design, vans require more power to move so more fuel is burned to provide that power.

- *The type of engine.* The engine you select is very important. With the national speed limit of 55 mph, there is little need for a large V-8 (8-cylinder) engine unless you will be driving up steep hills or pulling a trailer. In fact, a 4- or 6-cylinder engine will meet the needs of most people. Between 35 and 55 mph, a compact car with a large V-8 engine will usually use more fuel than a car with a 4- or 6-cylinder engine. In fact, some standard-size cars with 6-cylinder engines get better mileage than smaller cars with 8-cylinder engines.

- *The type of transmission.* In most cases, a manual transmission will provide better fuel mileage than an automatic transmission. A manual-shift car with a 4- or 5-speed transmission provides the best mileage. Still, the greater

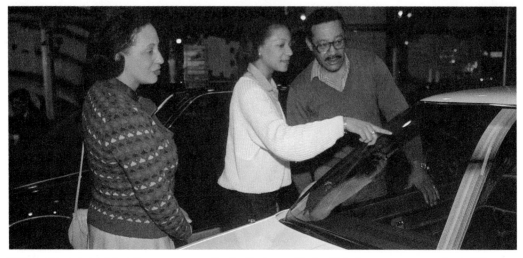

When you are looking for a new car, try to find one that will help you save on fuel. Other things you should consider before buying a car are discussed in this chapter.

ease of driving a car with an automatic transmission is a convenience many people do not want to give up. So, when choosing a car, keep in mind that some automatic transmissions are more **fuel-efficient** (use less fuel) than others. A 3-speed transmission is more efficient than one with 2 speeds. An automatic transmission with a torque converter is also usually more efficient. A **torque converter** is designed to reduce slippage in your transmission. This improves your mileage.

- *The drive train.* The axle-gear ratio is important in fuel economy. This ratio represents the number of times the drive shaft must revolve in order to turn the drive wheels once. The higher this ratio, the poorer the fuel economy. The lower the ratio, the better the fuel economy.

- *The power options.* Adding any type of power equipment to your car will generally cause it to use more fuel. It takes energy to operate power equipment. Extra equipment also adds extra weight to the vehicle.

On a medium-sized car with a medium-sized engine, power equipment will generally not cause a large drop in fuel mileage. On a small car with a small engine, extra equipment can cause a rather large drop in fuel mileage. For instance, it is true that adding an air conditioner adds weight, and weight reduces fuel mileage. However, adding an air conditioner does not always mean a big drop in miles per gallon. In some cars with low-horsepower engines, the increased wind resistance from driving with the windows open uses as much or more fuel than driving with an air conditioner on, especially at speeds above 40 mph. However, to use an air conditioner most efficiently, keep the car cool, not cold.

Other power equipment, such as power steering, may be necessary for some drivers. While it may add weight to a vehicle, the ease of steering is such that many drivers will prefer to have it. Also, keep in mind that if you buy a small car with a fuel-saving engine and drive train, you can still use less fuel and reduce operating costs.

## Shopping for a Car

Once you decide on the type and size car you need, get ready to shop. Compare different "makes" (manufacturer's brands) of cars and prices. All makes of cars within a class will not sit, feel, ride, or drive the same. Check with family and friends for their comments about various dealers. Visit different car dealers to compare their prices. Find out which dealers provide the best service. Talk with mechanics who are certified by the National Institute for Automotive Service Excellence.

**Buying a Used Car**  If you decide to buy a *used* car, your choices of where to buy are greater. You can buy from a private owner, a used-car dealer, or the used-car section of a new-car dealership. When you buy from a private owner, the purchase price is often less. However, if something goes wrong with the car, you have to pay for all repairs.

Many used-car dealers have a large selection of cars available. Some have their own repair facilities. Some offer a limited guarantee on the engine or drive train or both. Others sell their cars in the condition in which they were purchased. In such a case, the buyer takes all responsibility if anything goes wrong with the car.

You can get an idea of prices for different makes and models of used cars by looking in the *Blue Book*. Remember to put aside money to cover the cost of registration, insurance, repairs, and sales tax (if applicable in your state).

When you shop for a car, the salesperson may urge you to make your decision in a hurry. Do not allow yourself to be pressured into buying a used car without having it checked by an independent mechanic or diagnostic center. Buying impulsively

You will find a wide variety of cars for sale in a used-car lot. Some used-car dealers offer a limited guarantee.

This used car may or may not be a good choice for a buyer. What should you check when purchasing a used car?

may cost you a considerable amount of money for unanticipated repairs.

For the best selection of newer used cars, it is better to go to a new-car dealership that has its own repair facilities and trained mechanics. Cars from those dealers may cost somewhat more, but they are generally reconditioned before they are sold. Also, they usually come with a 30- to 90-day *or* 1,000- to 3,000-mile limited guarantee.

When purchasing a used car, check:

- the condition of the paint. New paint may indicate that there was collision damage.
- for rust. Examine lower edges behind bumpers, rocker panels, below the doors, door sills, floors, and inside the trunk. A car with rusted-out areas should be rejected unless you can afford repairs or know how to make them yourself.

- for worn tires, including the spare. Uneven wear on any tire may indicate front-end problems.

- the tail pipe. A light gray color indicates proper combustion. A heavy sooty appearance could mean excessive piston-ring wear.

- the radiator. Remove the radiator cap. Is the coolant clean? Does the cap have rust caked on it? Are there signs of leaks on the back of the radiator?

- the transmission. Pull out the transmission dipstick and sniff it. A burnt smell may indicate an

A car with rusted-out areas should be rejected unless you can afford repairs or know how to make them yourself.

overheated transmission and trouble. Feel the oil on the crankcase dipstick. If it is gritty, there may be dirt in the engine.

- the service stickers. These will determine the frequency of tune-ups and oil changes.
- all windows and door locks for ease of operation.
- the brake pedal. Step down on and hold the brake pedal with a steady pressure for 1 minute. If the pedal sinks down to the floor, the brake pedal needs repairing.
- the engine. Start the engine and listen for loud or unusual noises when the engine starts and while the starter is working. Make sure that all dash gauges and warning lights—oil pressure, generator, temperature gauge—go on and off when the engine starts.
- the headlights, taillights, brake lights, and turn indicators.
- the steering wheel. Take a test drive. A shaky steering wheel and wobbly ride may mean bad ball joints, misaligned front wheels, or the need for wheel balancing. Make several sharp turns at a low speed. The steering should not stiffen up. If the car has power steering, no squeaks or sudden need for increased steering effort should occur.
- for slamming sound or lurching as the car starts. An automatic transmission should take hold promptly when put in gear.
- the piston rings. On a long downhill grade or in a flat area, slow from 50 mph to about 15 mph without using the brakes. Then step hard on the accelerator. If there is blue exhaust smoke, the car may need new piston rings or an overhaul of the engine.

## Financing the Purchase of Your Car

Few people pay cash for a new or late-model used car. Most people finance their purchase with a loan.

**Shop around for auto insurance just as you shopped for your car. Discuss the types of policies with the sales agent.**

Loans are usually obtained from a bank, credit union, finance company, or a special financing arrangement with the car dealer. If you must borrow money to buy a car, use as much care in obtaining a loan as you do in selecting a car. Different loan agencies have different rules for lending money. The interest they charge you to borrow money is also different. The amount of money a loan company will allow you to borrow is based on the value of the car. The amount of time you will have to repay the loan will depend on whether you are buying a used or new car. The amount you have to pay each month will depend on:

- the amount of money you borrow to pay for the car.
- the interest on your loan.
- whether or not your car's insurance costs are included in your monthly payment.

# Buying Insurance for Your Car

The purpose of buying insurance is to protect you against a large financial loss. One type of automobile insurance protects you against damage to your car. Another type protects you financially in case you injure a person or damage the property of other persons.

There are many different types of car insurance. There are also many factors that help determine how much your car insurance will cost. These include:

- the type of policy you buy (what is covered).
- your age. (Young drivers pay more.)
- your driving record. (Convictions and collisions increase your insurance cost.)
- how far you drive each year. (The farther you drive, the more the insurance costs.)
- whether or not you drive to work, how far you drive to work, and whether you drive yourself or go in a carpool. (Carpooling reduces the cost.)
- where you live. (Rural areas cost less than cities.)
- your sex. (Males pay more because statistics show that they drive more, and have more accidents.)
- your marital status, if you are a young male. (Young married males pay less than young men who have

never been married, since statistics show they are involved in fewer accidents.)

- the cost of your car. (It costs more to insure an expensive car.)
- the number of cars insured under the policy. (Some companies offer multi-car discounts.)

Many insurance companies offer a reduction in insurance rates to students who have satisfactorily completed a driver's education program or maintain a grade-point average of B or better.

The following are the most common types of automobile insurance.

**Liability Insurance** The purpose of **liability insurance** is to protect you against claims if you are in a collision and are found to be at fault. It provides protection in case you are sued for accident damage. This type of insurance helps you to pay if people have suffered injury or loss in an accident caused by your actions.

Liability insurance is the most important car insurance you can buy. It protects you and anyone else who has your permission to drive your car. If you were found at fault in a collision and could not pay, the court could force you to sell your property. Your driver's license could be suspended until the money was paid.

In many states, drivers *must prove* that they are insured. This is called **compulsory insurance**. Where there are such laws, drivers have to carry a fixed minimum amount of liability insurance before they can have their cars registered.

Liability insurance is very important. It protects you if you are sued for damages resulting from an accident.

There are two types of automobile liability insurance:

- **Bodily injury insurance.** This insurance provides financial protection in case you cause the injury or death of another person or persons. It also covers legal fees, court costs, and loss of wages. You can usually buy this insurance in amounts of $10,000 to $300,000 or more.

- **Property damage liability.** This insurance provides you protection in case you damage the property of other persons. This includes their car as well as property in it, and damage to buildings, telephone poles, and traffic lights. The amount of protection which you can buy again generally ranges from $10,000 to $300,000.

**No-Fault Insurance** No-fault insurance is a system in which your own insurance company pays your medical bills, lost wages, and other expenses arising from injury sustained in an automobile accident, up to a certain amount. Payment is made upon submission of these bills and without regard to who caused the accident. No-fault insurance provides quick settlement of small claims and does away with the need for finding out who is at fault. In very serious accidents, the injured can still go to court to collect damages from the person who caused the accident. At the present time, fifteen states and the District of Columbia have no-fault laws.

### Medical Payment Insurance

Medical, hospital, or funeral expenses are included in **medical payment insurance**. This insurance pays a fixed amount if you or passengers in your car are injured or killed in a collision. It also pays if you or a member of your family is killed or injured while riding in someone else's car. It would usually pay if you or members of your family are struck as pedestrians or while riding on a bike, in a bus, or in a taxicab. Medical payment insurance pays regardless of who causes the accident. The amount of payment is determined by the limits of the policy, usually ranging from $1,000 to $5,000 per person.

### Collision Insurance

Damage to your car caused by a collision is covered by **collision insurance**. Collision insurance covers repairs to your car regardless of who is at fault. It pays for damage even if no one else is involved. If your car is parked and damaged in a parking lot, for instance, collision coverage would pay for the repairs.

Full-coverage collision insurance (a policy which pays the entire amount of the damage) is very expensive. As a result, most persons buy what is called a **deductible policy** (a policy in which you pay a fixed amount and the insurance company pays the rest). With most such policies, you agree to pay the first $50, $100, $250, or $500.

The cost of collision insurance is based on the value of your car. As your car gets older, it becomes worth less money. At some point you may want to drop collision insurance, but this decision should be based on your ability to repair or replace your car if it is in a collision. Many people consider dropping collision insurance when their car is 5 to 7 years old. However, if you are financing the purchase of a car, the finance company may require that you buy collision insurance until the car has been paid for.

### Comprehensive Insurance Coverage

Damage to your car caused by something other than a collision is covered by **comprehensive insurance**. This coverage is important if your car is new or expensive, and it may be dropped after you have owned the car more than 7 years. It covers damage caused by fire, theft, flying or falling objects, explosions, natural disasters, riots, or collisions with

**Collision insurance covers the cost of repairing your car if it is damaged in a collision. Most people choose a deductible policy rather than a full-coverage policy.**

wild animals. Like collision insurance, comprehensive insurance is available with a deductible. Many insurance policies require a $100 deductible on glass breakage. In such cases, the only way that you can receive full coverage on glass breakage is to agree to pay a higher insurance premium.

## Uninsured Motorist Insurance

This insurance protects you in case you are injured by a hit-and-run driver or by a driver who does not have liability insurance. Uninsured motorist insurance coverage does for you what bodily injury insurance would do if you hurt someone else. It is important for drivers to have this coverage. Many states require it.

Damage to your property is not generally covered by uninsured motorist coverage. If your car is damaged, it would be covered by your own collision insurance.

**Towing Insurance** This type of insurance covers the cost of on-road repairs as well as the cost of having your car towed.

## Projects

1. Using the checklist on pages 290–291, check your family's car or that of a friend. Would you buy this car?
2. Interview a local insurance agent.

Ask why insurance rates are so much higher for new drivers under 25 years of age. What are some steps a new driver can take to reduce insurance costs?

# Words to Know

torque converter
liability insurance
compulsory insurance
bodily injury
  insurance

property damage
  liability
no-fault insurance
medical payment
  insurance

collision insurance
deductible policy
comprehensive
  insurance

# Stop and Review

1. Name the various expenses you must pay to own and operate a car.
2. Car-operating expenses vary. List 3 factors that affect operating expenses.
3. What factors should you consider if you are planning to buy a new car?
4. How does the design of a vehicle affect its fuel mileage?
5. When might you need a large V-8 engine?
6. What factors should you consider before ordering power equipment for your car?
7. List 3 places where you can purchase a used car.
8. List 5 items you should check when buying a used car. Why should you check these items?
9. List 4 places where you can go to get a loan to buy a car.
10. What information should you check and compare before borrowing money to pay for a car?
11. Your monthly car-loan payment will depend on 3 factors. What are they?
12. List 5 factors that help determine how much your car insurance will cost.
13. What is liability insurance? Why is it important?
14. What are the 2 types of automobile liability insurance?
15. Explain the no-fault insurance system.
16. What does medical payment insurance cover?
17. What is a deductible policy?
18. When should you consider dropping collision insurance?
19. What is covered by comprehensive insurance?
20. Why should you have uninsured motorist insurance?

You have worked 2 years, saved your money, and established your credit. Now you are going to buy your first car. You will be financing the purchase. You have decided on a 6-cylinder car with a manual transmission. You need to save on fuel.

1. After the down payment, what other costs must you plan for? Suppose your area has hot temperatures in the summer.

2. Should you consider air condi-tioning? What factors influence the effect of an air conditioner on fuel economy?

Suppose you will do most of your driving in the city, and it will involve a lot of turning and parallel parking.

3. Is power steering a realistic option?

Now you need insurance.

4. What kinds of coverage are re-quired in your state, and what are the dollar limits?

Complete the sentences by filling in the blanks with the correct terms.

| | | | |
|---|---|---|---|
| comprehensive | property damage | fuel mileage | no-fault |
| insurance | liability | bodily injury | size |
| value | deductible policy | insurance | |
| liability insurance | torque converter | less | |

1. A car's _____ is the average number of miles it can travel on a gallon of fuel.

2. Cars are grouped by _____ and class.

3. The _____ a vehicle weighs, the better the fuel mileage it will deliver.

4. A _____ is designed to reduce slippage in your transmission.

5. The amount of money a loan company will allow you to borrow is based on the _____ of the car.

6. The two types of automobile liability insurance are: _____ and _____.

7. _____ protects you against claims if you are at fault in a collision.

8. The _____ insurance system does away with the need to find out who is at fault in a minor accident.

9. An insurance policy in which you pay a fixed amount and the insurance company pays the rest is called a _____.

10. Damage to your car caused by natural disasters or explosions is covered by _____.

---

Decide whether each of the following sentences is true or false.

11. Usually, the less a vehicle weighs, the better the fuel mileage it will deliver.

12. A car with a 4- or 6-cylinder engine is adequate for most people.

13. The National Institute for Automotive Service sets standard car prices for all makes of a car within a class.

14. All loan agencies have essentially the same rules for lending money, and, by law, must charge the same rate of interest.

15. One way to reduce your insurance costs is to increase the deductible amount.

# Planning a Trip

## Chapter Objectives

In this chapter you will learn how to:

- plan ahead for short and long trips.
- equip your car with necessary emergency equipment.
- read a map, compute distances, and plan a route.
- correctly pack a trailer.
- compensate for some of the special problems presented by pulling a trailer or driving a large recreational vehicle.

You can make any car trip easier, safer, and more enjoyable if you remember one key word: *preparation*. You should prepare your route, prepare your vehicle, and prepare yourself for emergencies.

## The Short Haul

Shorter trips may require fewer preparations, but you must be as alert, and your car must be in good

299

condition, whether you plan to drive 5 miles or to drive 500. It is interesting to note that most traffic fatalities happen within 25 miles of the driver's home.

Make sure you have specific directions to follow. If you are traveling to an unknown area, get a map and go over your route in advance. Listen to a local radio station for weather conditions and traffic reports. If there are delays along the route you planned to follow, select another. If possible, avoid traveling through urban areas during rush hours. And keep in mind that roads leading *into* a town or city will tend to be busiest during the morning rush hour, while exit roads will be most crowded during the evening rush hour.

Allow yourself enough time to get to your destination. Include a margin for unexpected delays in your plans. Hurrying can make you nervous and careless.

Preparing your vehicle for a short trip involves nothing more than simple maintenance. It is best to begin a trip with a full fuel tank. Have your oil checked if you have not done so recently.

## In Case of Emergency

As a matter of course, you should have certain emergency equipment in your car. These items should include a flashlight, extra fuses, a road-worthy spare tire, a working jack and lug wrench, a tire gauge, a fire extinguisher, a first aid kit, flares, a tool kit, and tire chains (if driving in bad weather).

## The Long Haul

If you will be on the road for several days or more, you should follow the same guidelines as those for a short trip, but be even more thorough. A mechanic should check your vehicle no more than a few weeks before your trip.

Just before you leave, you should take inventory of your emergency equipment. Make sure your flashlight batteries are fresh. Replace windshield-washing fluid and worn wiper blades.

If you will be traveling through several changes of climate, for example going from sea level to the high mountains, add any needed items to your emergency supplies. These might include blankets, a shovel, and snow chains. For any long trip, keep a small supply of food and water in your car.

**Packing the Vehicle** A long trip usually requires packing a lot of luggage. Before you begin to pack, make a list of what you would like to take along. Go over the list to be sure you are not taking more than you need and that you have not forgotten anything important. Keep the list handy as you pack.

When you load the vehicle, place heavy items on the bottom of the trunk. Set aside those things you will want along the way or at your first stop and put those in your trunk last or keep them in the passenger compartment with you.

Remember that the additional weight will affect the way your vehicle handles. A heavy load on the roof will make your vehicle less stable and more likely to sway in the wind or on turns. If your trunk is overloaded, the rear of the car may swing out on turns or sudden stops, and your headlights are more apt to shine into the eyes of oncoming drivers or be reflected in the mirror of the driver ahead of you. Remember, heavy loads also increase your stopping distance.

The extra weight will also affect your ability to accelerate, making it harder to go uphill and increasing your tendency to accelerate going downhill. Also, it will probably reduce the number of miles you travel on each gallon of fuel. In general, each 100 pounds of added weight will reduce your car's mileage by a mile per gallon.

With the extra load, you may have to increase the air pressure in your tires. It is a good idea to have tires inflated to the maximum amount for high-speed travel. Check your owner's manual to find out what changes to make.

**Planning Your Route** The best route to your destination is not necessarily the shortest one. You may want to travel through scenic country or stop at a national park or some

Remember that your car will handle differently when it is carrying a heavy load on the roof or in the trunk. It will accelerate, brake, and steer differently.

# Legend

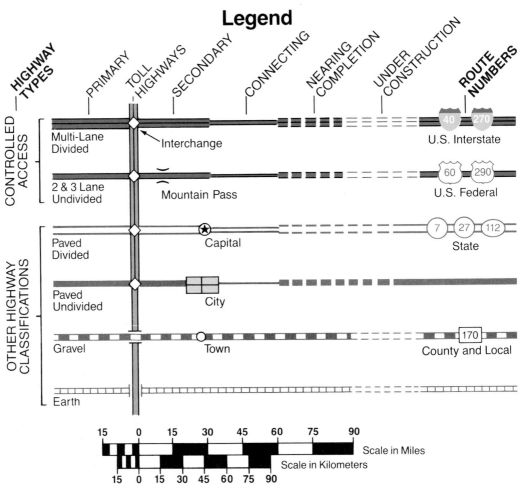

**HIGHWAY TYPES:** PRIMARY, TOLL HIGHWAYS, SECONDARY, CONNECTING, NEARING COMPLETION, UNDER CONSTRUCTION, ROUTE NUMBERS

## CONTROLLED ACCESS

Multi-Lane Divided — Interchange — U.S. Interstate (40) (270)

2 & 3 Lane Undivided — Mountain Pass — U.S. Federal (60) (290)

## OTHER HIGHWAY CLASSIFICATIONS

Paved Divided — ★ Capital — State (7) (27) (112)

Paved Undivided — City

Gravel — ○ Town — County and Local (170)

Earth

Scale in Miles: 15 0 15 30 45 60 75 90
Scale in Kilometers: 15 0 15 30 45 60 75 90

**Three-quarters of an inch equals approximately 30 miles or 48.2 kilometers.**

# Texas Index

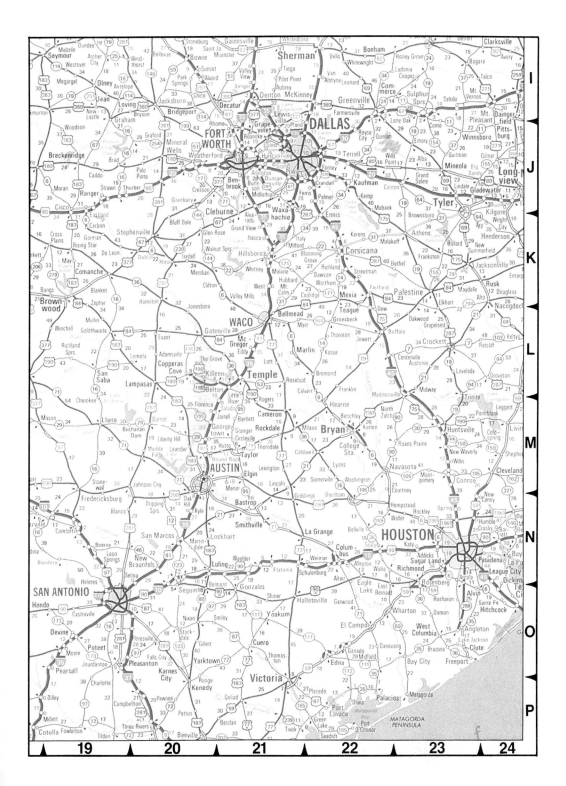

historic monuments along your way. Limited-access highways are best for making good time, but they will not give you a view of most towns. A map can help you decide the best route to serve your needs.

It is best when planning your trip to decide how far you will travel each day and make overnight reservations in advance. That way you will not be driving too much in one day, and you will be sure that you have a place to stay. Your local travel agency or auto club can help you plan your route and can provide you with maps and information.

**Reading a Map** Maps are available at service stations, bookstores, chambers of commerce, tourist information boards, and auto clubs. For a trip that will take you through several states, and through countryside as well as towns and cities, you may want to get a road atlas that contains state and city maps of an entire region or of the whole country.

In addition to federal, state, and local roads, maps show the locations of monuments, airports, parks, and other points of interest. City maps may include such details as tourist information centers and museums. All these items will be shown on the map as symbols. To find out what the symbols mean, consult the map **legend**. To compute distances, use the distance scale, the mileage chart, or mileage symbols that appear on the map.

Many maps have an alphabetical index of place names. Next to each name is a set of **coordinates**, usually a number and a letter.

Turn to the map on page 303. Notice the letters that run down the right side and the numbers that run along the bottom. The map is divided into squares by an imaginary **grid**. Some maps show this grid. Each square is defined by two coordinates.

Put your finger on any square on the map. To the right you will see which letter defines the horizontal row that square is in. At the bottom, you will see which number defines that vertical row. The letter and number together give the coordinates of that square.

To find a place on a map, find the coordinates of the place in the index. Search through the square that fits the coordinates. The place you are looking for will be in that square.

**Tricks for the Long Haul** Long hours of driving can be very tiring. Be sure to allow time for breaks. A snack and a quick stretch is often enough to make you feel refreshed. Fresh air and radio music or talk shows can keep you alert when you are driving alone. If you are traveling during the vacation season and you have not made overnight reservations in advance, plan to stop early. Motel rooms may be very difficult to find. Though it is not wise to make a habit of sleeping in a car parked along the roadside, if you become too drowsy, you may have to take a short nap. If this should occur, pull over to a safe place well off the road or at a rest stop. Turn off your car, lock your doors, and close the windows. If there is more than one driver in your car, you should share the driving.

Never try to read a map while you are driving. Plan your route in advance. Once you are on the road, have a passenger direct you, or pull over when it is safe to do so and check the map yourself.

# Trailers

Before you consider hitching a trailer to your car, make sure that your vehicle is properly designed to handle the load. Many cars do not have the necessary vertical support. Even if your car is designed for it, pulling a trailer will put extra strain on the vehicle's radiator, springs, shock absorbers, tires, and transmission. Your owner's manual may explain the requirements for the job.

You will need the proper hitch and safety chains so the trailer does not break free as you drive. The trailer must have working taillights, signal lights, and brake lights. Oversized outside mirrors placed on either side of your car will increase your visibility.

Find out in advance about state laws on trailer operation for any state you might be passing through. Some states require separate brakes and a breakaway switch.

Practice driving the trailer in a parking lot or low-traffic area before taking it out into heavy traffic. It

Visibility to the rear is limited in vans, trailers, and motor homes. These vehicles should have big outside mirrors.

takes about twice as long to pull into traffic, pass, or stop while pulling a trailer. Signal in advance and allow twice the usual space before attempting any of these maneuvers.

**Packing a Trailer** The way a trailer is packed will affect how it handles. Uneven loading may cause fishtailing.

The heaviest items should go over the trailer wheels at the bottom of the load. Place approximately 60 percent of the load in the front half of the trailer. Follow guidelines for the trailer's weight capacity.

Too much weight on the back of the towing vehicle will cause the front of the car to rise, affecting steering, braking, and headlight illumination. To ease the problem, do not carry a heavy load in the trunk or back seat of the towing vehicle.

Always pack the trailer load tightly and tie down any items that

If you are pulling a trailer, remember that you will need twice the distance to merge, pass, or stop.

When backing a trailer, be careful not to turn the wheel too far. If you do, the trailer may jackknife.

might shift. As you drive, check frequently to see that the load and hitch are secure.

**Backing a Trailer**  Backing is particularly hard to master. Always back up *slowly*. To go left, turn the steering wheel to the right and then straighten it. To go right, turn left and then straighten. Turn and straighten again and again, until you are in position. If you move too quickly or turn the wheel too far, the trailer may **jackknife** (swing out at a right angle to the car).

When backing, particularly into a parking spot, it is best to have someone guide you from outside the car.

## Recreational Vehicles

Like trailers, **recreational vehicles** (vehicles which are usually larger than a passenger car and are used mostly for pleasure, such as motor homes) can present handling problems if they are not carefully packed. Loads should be kept as low as possible and spread evenly inside the vehicle. Remember that a loaded vehicle takes a greater distance to stop and to accelerate.

The added size and height of recreational vehicles creates special problems. Such vehicles may sway in a strong crosswind. Visibility to the

**Because of their added size and height, vans and recreational vehicles are more likely to sway in a strong crosswind than a smaller vehicle would be.**

rear and the sides may be greatly reduced. Keep this in mind before backing up.

An inexperienced driver may forget just how high the vehicle is. Be sure you can clear overhead obstructions, such as the overhang at a gas station or motel, before attempting to drive under them.

A recreational vehicle may also block the view of other drivers on the road. Take this into account when you spot possible hazards ahead that they may not see.

## Projects

1. Plan an imaginary trip with a friend. Borrow a map from a relative or the library. Take turns selecting a destination alone and letting the other one of you locate that destination using the map's index and coordinates. When you have decided on a final destination, use the map's distance scale to calculate the distance to there from a starting point that is also on the map. Try different routes.

   Check to see if the map lists any points of interest along the way.
2. Make a list of items you would like to take along on an imaginary road trip. Include clothing, food, and camping or sports equipment. Maybe you will want to take a boat along. When your list is complete, choose a type of car you know well and decide what you will pack where and in what order for a safe and comfortable trip.

## Words to Know

legend                 grid                            recreational vehicles
coordinates       jackknife

## Stop and Review

1. How can you make a car trip easier, safer, and more enjoyable?
2. What effect should rush hour have on the way you plan your route?
3. List 8 pieces of emergency equipment that you should have in your car.
4. How should you pack your trunk?
5. How does a heavy load on the roof affect the way your car handles?
6. Where can you obtain maps to help you plan a trip?
7. When is a road atlas useful?
8. List 3 things that maps may show in addition to roads.
9. How do you find out what the symbols on a map mean?
10. What can you use to compute distances from a map?
11. What is a map index?
12. How do you locate places using a set of coordinates?
13. List 3 things you can do to keep alert during a long trip.
14. Driving with a trailer puts extra strain on your car. Which parts does the strain affect the most?
15. A trailer must have 3 sets of working lights. List them.
16. How does pulling a trailer affect your driving maneuvers?
17. How do you correctly distribute the load on a trailer?
18. Describe how you back up a trailer.
19. How would you adjust your driving in order to handle a recreational vehicle properly?
20. How does visibility in a recreational vehicle compare with visibility in a car?

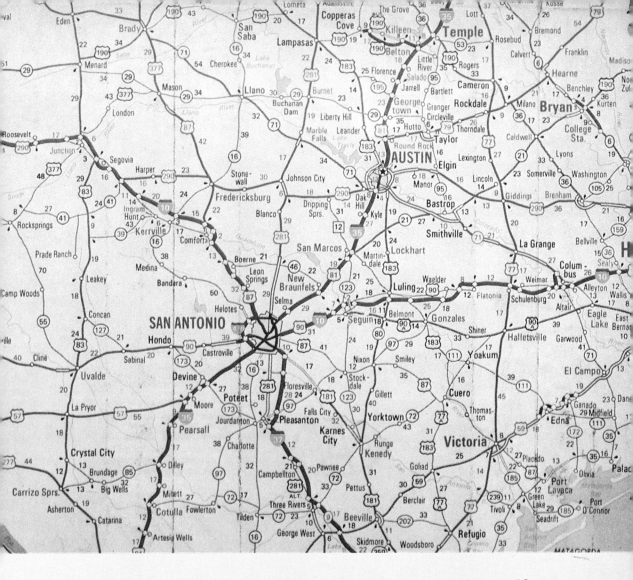

## What if...

You are going to drive from Austin to San Antonio, Texas. (Look at the map above and at the map legend on page 302.)

1. What things should you do before you leave on this trip?

2. What is the most direct route? What type of road is this?

3. What is the mileage between Austin and San Antonio on this road?

4. About how long would it take to drive this distance at an average rate of 50 miles per hour?

5. Suppose you wanted to stop by Blanco on the way. What routes would you take? What would your total mileage to San Antonio be?

6. What routes would you take to return from San Antonio to Austin by way of Fredericksburg?

**309**

# CHAPTER 18 TEST

Complete the sentences by filling in the blanks with the correct terms.

greater    fishtail    legend    jackknife    safety chains    road atlas
handles    rear    grid    proper hitch    map

1. If you are traveling to an area you do not know well, be certain to get a _____ and go over your route in advance.

2. Additional weight will affect the way your car _____ .

3. If your trunk is overloaded, the _____ of your car may swing out on turns.

4. A _____ contains state and city maps of an entire region.

5. The symbols on a map are explained in the _____ .

6. Many maps are divided into squares by a _____ .

7. Towing a trailer requires the _____ and _____ to keep the trailer from breaking free as you drive.

8. A trailer that is unevenly loaded may _____ .

9. A _____ takes place when a trailer swings out at a right angle to the car towing it.

10. A loaded vehicle takes _____ distances to stop and accelerate than one that is not loaded.

---

Select the one best answer to each of the following questions.

11. Which of the following is *not* a piece of emergency equipment that you should have in your car?
    (a) fire extinguisher  (b) tool kit
    (c) oversized mirror  (d) flashlight

12. Additional weight in your vehicle:
    (a) will affect the way it handles.
    (b) will affect your acceleration.
    (c) may require increased air pressure in your tires.  (d) all of these

13. Pulling a trailer:
    (a) takes no special equipment.
    (b) strains your car's transmission.
    (c) decreases the time it takes to stop.  (d) is illegal in some states.

14. Which of the following is *not* true of recreational vehicles?
    (a) They sometimes block the view of other drivers on the road.
    (b) Visibility to the rear in a recreational vehicle is better than that in a car.  (c) They can present handling problems.  (d) You must be aware of overhead obstructions when driving recreational vehicles.

15. Map legends:
    (a) are found only on city maps.
    (b) give the history of the city or state pictured.  (c) explain symbols used on the map.  (d) explain the grid coordinates shown on the map.

# Careers in the Highway System

Do you enjoy driving? Do you have an interest in cars? If so, then you might be heading for a career in the highway system. The number and variety of car- and truck-related jobs is wide ranging. Most are in the following categories.

**Driving** Most driving jobs involve a lot of contact with people. Taxicab, limousine, and bus drivers spend almost all their working hours with the public. So, in addition to excellent driving skills, they also need patience and an ability to cope with many different situations.

Truck driving may be a more solitary occupation. Some truck drivers start their careers by driving vans and small delivery trucks. These jobs also involve public contact. Long-haul truckers, though, spend much of their time on the road alone.

Long-haul trucking usually means driving across state lines, so truckers must meet standards set by the federal government. Long-distance truckers must be at least 21 years old. They must be healthy and have excellent driving records. They must pass several tests, including tests on safety regulations and road tests to show knowledge of the truck they will be driving.

Long-haul truckers earn higher salaries than those who drive short haul. Some own their rigs, which allows them more freedom in choosing routes and working times.

**Maintenance** One of the first things drivers discover on owning a car is that it requires a lot of care and upkeep. Maintaining cars can be a busy and lucrative job. It is perfect for people who like to work with their hands and are interested in and curious about how things work.

Some car maintenance jobs are in garages. There, depending on the size of the garage, a maintenance worker can either do general repairs or specialize. Some people specialize in working on brakes, transmissions, body work, or mufflers, for example.

Repairing a car damaged in an accident requires patience, imagination, and knowledge of heavy tools. People who work in body repair shops, like those who work in garages, must keep up to date on what is new about cars and how models differ.

Though some maintenance and repair workers have few dealings with car owners, others who work in

**Engineers use computer technology to create the designs for new car styles.**

garages and repair shops often deal directly with the public. Car owners who have been involved in accidents or who need repairs on their cars (repairs that are often costly) must be handled with care.

## Manufacturing and Engineering

Years of thought, planning, and work have gone into every part of every car.

Teams of engineers, designers, trend forecasters, and auto industry officials have pooled their knowledge of what the public wants and what they think it needs. The result: the development and manufacture of every car you see on the road.

Jobs in manufacturing, design, and engineering require brain power rather than muscle power, though anyone who wants to be a success in the auto-manufacturing field needs hands-on experience with what makes a car work.

Cars are designed by **automotive engineers**. Many automotive engineers have advanced college degrees. If you hope to make auto design your career, you must be prepared to go beyond high school and college for a higher education.

The auto industry in the United States produces products that are strictly regulated by the federal government. Cars coming off the assembly line must meet safety and environmental regulations. A car's fuel use, for example, must be economical so fuel is conserved and must be clean so that the air is not further polluted. Those are factors that auto-motive engineers and others involved in car design must take into account as they do their jobs.

**Education** Instructors of driver education must be more than skilled drivers. They must be skilled drivers who can communicate their feelings and knowledge about safe driving in a way that is clear and understandable to others.

Driving instructors may work for a school system, a commercial driving school, a municipal safety council, a local government, or a private company. Instructors not only teach about traffic regulations and the basics of driving safely, but also about driving strategies and coping with road emergencies. Some also handle the reeducation of incompetent drivers.

Driver education instructors may write pamphlets and manuals. They

A car-dealership owner must check the options ordered for a new car.

**Traffic-control officers aid the safe flow of traffic in large cities.**

may teach children as well as adults about traffic safety.

Most driving teachers in schools must have teaching certificates. Some teachers who are not certified in this area may do classroom driving instruction. In some states, commercial driving schools and their instructors must be specially licensed.

All driving teachers spend a lot of time in their careers working with the public. So the ability to work well with small and large groups of students is essential.

**Support Services** When you leave school today or the next time you leave your house, take a look around you. How many people on the street are doing jobs that are connected in some way with driving a vehicle? A huge number of people do work that could not be done if a vehicle were not used. One of those jobs may appeal to you. Here are a few.

- **Driving license instructor.** People who administer driving license tests must be diplomats as well as excellent drivers. They have the pleasure of testing good drivers. But they must also use their judgment and knowledge of driving regulations to weed out people who are not yet ready to be given a license.

- **Law enforcement officials.** In many areas, police officers work from patrol cars. So, of course, they must be able to drive well under normal as well as extraordinary conditions. Some law officers specialize in traffic control or work in traffic courts.

- **Salespeople.** A way with words and the ability to sell an idea as well as a product are skills needed by those who sell cars, car parts, fuel, and car-related services.

- **Industrial vehicle drivers.** Roads must be maintained and repaired. Highways must be built and kept up. Many workers are needed to do those jobs. And most of those workers, especially those who drive construction rigs, need good driving skills.

- **Emergency vehicle drivers.** People who work well under stress, can drive well in all circumstances, and want to help others can become paramedics or ambulance drivers.

- **Assembly line workers.** The bottom line for any car-related career is that there must first be a car. Assembly line workers are the first to suffer when the car industry is in a slump. But, when times are good, they are the backbone of the industry.

# First Aid

First aid is emergency treatment given to a person who is injured or ill. First aid takes place before medical or surgical care arrives. Fire and police departments in many communities have first-aid equipment and trained personnel to help in emergencies. However, everyone who drives should have some knowledge of first aid. Both training and practice are important. The American Red Cross gives free first aid courses in many communities.

Some general guidelines:

- If there is more than one injured person, care for the most seriously injured first.

- Keep calm and act quickly and quietly. Speak in a normal tone of voice. Try not to worry the victim.

- Find out if the injured person is bleeding. Serious bleeding must be stopped as quickly as possible.

- Check for breathing. Make sure that the victim has an open air passage. If the victim is not breathing, start artificial respiration at once.

- Do not move an injured person unless you must do so for his or her safety. Moving an injured person the wrong way may harm the person even more. Do not let the person move until help arrives.

- Get trained medical help fast. However, do not leave the victim in order to get help unless you have no other choice.

**How to Control Bleeding** Controlled bleeding can be helpful. It is a way a wound cleans itself. But bleeding that is out of control can kill the victim.

Heavy bleeding, or a **hemorrhage**, must be stopped at once. Place a clean cloth—such as a clean handkerchief or a piece of a shirt—over the wound and press down firmly. If there is no clean cloth around, press your hand directly on the wound and keep it there. It is the firm, constant pressure that will stop the bleeding. Keep pressing, without lifting your hand, until medical help arrives. In addition to applying pressure to the wound, raise the injured part of the body if you are sure that no bones are broken. This will help slow the loss of blood from the wound.

Suppose even firm pressure does not stop the bleeding and no emergency help has arrived. Then, as a last resort, use a **tourniquet**. A tourniquet is a band of cloth, usually about 2 inches wide, that is pulled tightly around an arm or leg. It is placed above the wound so that it is between the injury and the heart. A tourniquet can be very dangerous, since it cuts off the supply of blood to the tissues of the arm or leg being treated. The decision to apply a tourniquet is really a decision to risk a limb in order to save a life. It should only be used in a life or death situation and should be released only by a doctor.

**How to Treat Shock** Shock in this case means that a person's blood is not circulating as it should. A very serious injury, bleeding, or burns can cause shock. A shock victim usually feels faint, weak, cold, and often nauseated. The victim's skin will feel cold and clammy and may look pale, even blue. Breathing is irregular and the pulse is weak and fast.

Keeping the victim warm is important in treating shock. But he or she should be covered only enough to keep the body temperature near normal. The victim should be placed flat on the back, with the feet slightly raised. If the victim is bleeding, try to control it. Also make sure that the person in shock can breathe easily. Loosen tight clothing. Do not give the person anything to eat or drink.

**How to Restore Breathing** Any victim whose breathing has stopped needs help immediately. After two or three minutes of not breathing, a person can suffer permanent brain damage. Six minutes without breathing can be fatal.

The best way to restore breathing in most circumstances is with mouth-to-mouth resuscitation. First, clear the victim's mouth with your fingers. This gets rid of anything that may be blocking breathing. Put one hand under the victim's neck. Put your other hand on the forehead. Gently tilt the victim's head backward. Using your thumb and index finger, pinch the victim's nostrils shut.

Now take a deep breath. Place your mouth right over the victim's

First aid classes will help you handle unexpected emergencies.

mouth. Blow into the victim's mouth until you can see his or her chest rise. Stop your treatment and listen for air being let out of the victim's lungs. Keep repeating, checking after each breath, until the victim resumes breathing independently or health care professionals have arrived.

**General Information** Remember, first aid is only the care given directly after an accident. It should not take the place of trained professional help. That means you should call for the police or an ambulance as fast as you can. If there is no one else around to go for help, give first aid, make the victim comfortable and safe, and then go yourself.

Sometimes a person may look uninjured, but be unable to move. That could mean there is some sort of injury to the spine. Do not try to move the person. Cover the victim and then go for help.

# Metric Measures

The United States uses the English System of measurement. Most other countries use the metric system, which is based on units of 10.

Conversion formulas are listed below for some units of measurement you might use while driving.

## Distance:

To translate miles to kilometers, multiply by 1.6

| | |
|---|---|
| 10 miles | = 16 kilometers |
| 20 miles | = 32 kilometers |
| 40 miles | = 64 kilometers |
| 60 miles | = 96 kilometers |
| 80 miles | = 128 kilometers |
| 100 miles | = 160 kilometers |

To translate kilometers to miles, multiply by .62

| | |
|---|---|
| 10 kilometers | = 6.2 miles |
| 20 kilometers | = 12 miles |
| 40 kilometers | = 25 miles |
| 60 kilometers | = 37 miles |
| 80 kilometers | = 50 miles |
| 100 kilometers | = 62 miles |

## Speed:

To translate miles per hour to kilometers per hour, multiply by 1.6

| | |
|---|---|
| 10 mph | = 16 km/h |
| 20 mph | = 32 km/h |
| 30 mph | = 48 km/h |
| 40 mph | = 64 km/h |
| 50 mph | = 80 km/h |
| 55 mph | = 88 km/h |

To translate kilometers per hour to miles per hour, multiply by .62

| | |
|---|---|
| 10 km/h | = 6.2 mph |
| 20 km/h | = 12 mph |
| 40 km/h | = 25 mph |
| 60 km/h | = 37 mph |
| 80 km/h | = 50 mph |
| 90 km/h | = 56 mph |

## Volume:

Some pumps now dispense fuel in liters.

To translate gallons to liters, multiply by 3.8

| | |
|---|---|
| 5 gallons | = 19 liters |
| 10 gallons | = 38 liters |
| 15 gallons | = 57 liters |
| 20 gallons | = 76 liters |
| 25 gallons | = 95 liters |

To translate liters to gallons, multiply by .26

| | |
|---|---|
| 5 liters | = 1.3 gallons |
| 10 liters | = 2.6 gallons |
| 15 liters | = 3.9 gallons |
| 20 liters | = 5.2 gallons |
| 25 liters | = 6.5 gallons |

# Checking Your Car

| The Car Part | Why Check | What to Check | When to Check |
|---|---|---|---|
| **Headlights** | • Dirty lenses can cut your night vision by more than half.<br>• Even with good lights, at 50 mph, you can see only about 4 seconds ahead.<br>• A dead headlight may keep you from seeing a stalled car or a sharp curve in time.<br>• An out-of-line light can shine where it does not help you and may blind other drivers. | *Driver checks*<br>• Burned out bulbs.<br>• Dirty lenses.<br>*Mechanic checks*<br>• Where lights shine. | *Driver checks*<br>• When you fill up with gas.<br>• After driving on wet or muddy roads.<br>• Shine the lights on a wall before driving at night. Make sure that both high and low beams are working.<br>*Mechanic checks*<br>• Twice a year. |
| **Brake and Signal Lights** | • Brake lights tell others that you are stopping.<br>• Signals tell others what you are about to do. | *Driver checks*<br>• Burned out bulbs.<br>*Mechanic checks*<br>• Wiring and sockets. | *Driver checks*<br>• When you fill up with gas.<br>*Mechanic checks*<br>• Twice a year. |
| **Windows and Windshields** | • Dirty windows make it hard to see.<br>• Scratched, cracked or dirty glass can increase glare and make it hard to see.<br>• Damaged glass can break even in a minor collision. You can get pieces in your face. | *Driver checks*<br>• All glass inside and out to make sure it is clean.<br>• Scratches and cracks to see if glass needs to be changed.<br>• Windshield wiper fluid level to make sure there is a sufficient amount. | *Driver checks*<br>• When you fill up with gas.<br>• Every time you drive.<br>• Whenever you check under the hood. |
| **Tires** | • Worn or bald tires increase your stopping distance.<br>• Worn or bald tires lessen overall control.<br>• Unbalanced tires and low pressure can cause tread wear.<br>• Unbalanced tires cause the steering wheel to shake.<br>• Low air pressure cuts down on gas mileage.<br>• Worn tread is also one of the causes of "hydroplaning."<br>• You may have a blowout. | *Driver checks*<br>• Tire air pressure when tires are cold (24-32 lbs., check owner's manual).<br>• Tread wear (stick a Lincoln penny into the tread "head" first. If the tread does not come at least to Abe's head, the tire is unsafe).<br>*Mechanic checks*<br>• Tire balance and damage. | *Driver checks*<br>• Once a week.<br>*Mechanic checks*<br>• Once a month. |

# Checking Your Car — *CONTINUED* —

| The Car Part | Why Check | What to Check | When to Check |
|---|---|---|---|
| **Brakes** | • They may not stop you fast enough to avoid a collision.<br>• They may pull the car to the side when stopping.<br>• Failure to fix brakes is unsafe and can lead to more costly repairs.<br>• If you repair brakes when a problem first appears, it saves costly repairs later. | *Driver checks*<br>• Pedal pressure (pedal when pushed should stay well above the floor).<br>• Car pulling to the side when brakes are used.<br>• Scraping and squealing noise.<br>*Mechanic checks*<br>• Brake lining wear and fluid leaks. | *Driver checks*<br>• Every time you start the engine.<br>• Every time you drive.<br>*Mechanic checks*<br>• Twice a year.<br>• When driver thinks something is wrong. |
| **Steering** | • Car may be hard to turn.<br>• Car may not turn when the steering wheel is first turned.<br>• It can take more time to avoid an emergency. | *Driver checks*<br>• If the steering wheel moves 2 inches or more without moving the car, it has too much play. | *Driver checks*<br>• Every time you drive.<br>*Mechanic checks*<br>• Twice a year. |
| **Suspension** | • Car may not hold the road on turns.<br>• Ride will be uncomfortable over bumps.<br>• It can cause tires and other parts to wear out. | *Driver checks*<br>• Push down hard on the front and rear of the car. If the car bounces more than twice before stopping, you need new shocks.<br>*Mechanic checks*<br>• Shocks.<br>• Springs. | *Driver checks*<br>• When car seems to bounce too much, or you have trouble controlling the car.<br>• After the winter season.<br>*Mechanic checks*<br>• Every 20,000 miles. |
| **Exhaust** | • Fumes from a leaky exhaust can cause death in a very short time. Never run the engine in your garage, or sit in the car with the engine running without opening a window.<br>• Worn-out exhaust parts increase the chance of the car catching on fire. | *Driver checks*<br>• For loud noise or rattles.<br>• Signs of rust or holes in the muffler and tailpipe.<br>*Mechanic checks*<br>• Leakage, wear and loose mountings. | *Driver checks*<br>• Every time you drive.<br>• Before and after the winter season.<br>*Mechanic checks*<br>• Twice a year. |

| | Why it matters | What to check | How often |
|---|---|---|---|
| **Windshield Wipers** | • Poor wiper blades will not clean the water off. They also skip places and leave streaks.<br>• A dirty windshield makes it harder to see.<br>• Poor wiper blades can scratch the windshield, causing glare. | *Driver checks*<br>• Wiper blades for wear and tension on the glass. Rubber on the blades can pull off in cold weather.<br>• Windshield wiper fluid for cleaning windshield. | *Driver checks*<br>• Several times a year.<br>• Frequently in cold weather. |
| **Engine/Tune-Up** | • Car may lose power that is needed for normal driving and emergencies.<br>• Poorly tuned engines do not get good gas mileage.<br>• Engine may not start. | *Driver checks*<br>• Signs of less power.<br>• Hard starting.<br>• Fuel mileage should not be allowed to drop more than two miles per gallon.<br>*Mechanic checks*<br>• Points, plugs, condenser.<br>• Wiring and timing.<br>• Fuel system. | *Driver checks*<br>• Every time you drive.<br>• Every few fill-ups.<br>*Mechanic checks*<br>• Every 10,000 miles, or<br>• Every 12 months (if possible, before winter). |
| **Cooling System** | • Car engine may overheat or freeze.<br>• To prevent unnecessary engine wear and serious engine damage. | *Driver checks*<br>• Cracked or broken hoses.<br>• Loose belts.<br>• Insufficient levels of antifreeze coolant.<br>*Mechanic checks*<br>• Radiator rust, clogs and leaks. | *Driver checks*<br>• Several times a year.<br>• Before and after the winter season.<br>*Mechanic checks*<br>• Every 12 to 24 months, or<br>• Every 15,000 to 30,000 miles. |
| **Oil and Oil Filter** | • To prevent excessive heat, engine wear and serious engine damage. | *Driver checks*<br>• Oil level and miles driven since last checked.<br>*Mechanic checks*<br>• Oil and oil filter for cleanliness. | *Driver checks*<br>• Every time you fill up, or per your owner's manual.<br>*Mechanic checks*<br>• Every 5,000 to 10,000 miles (gasoline engine), or every 3,000 to 5,000 miles (diesel engine), or<br>• Every 12 months. |

# Glossary

**acceleration**  Gaining speed. Going from a slower rate of motion to a steadily increasing one.

**accelerator**  The gas pedal. This pedal is used to control the amount of fuel fed into the engine cylinders. It controls speed.

**adhesion**  Sticking together. In automotive terms, traction.

**administrative law**  A law regulating driver licensing, vehicle registration, financial responsibility of drivers and vehicle owners, or minimum equipment and care standards for vehicles.

**air bag**  A safety bag that becomes filled with air automatically upon impact in a collision. The inflated bag is a cushion that keeps occupants of the car from striking the interior parts of the automobile.

**alternate path of travel**  An emergency route to be taken if the intended (immediate) path of a vehicle is suddenly blocked. This escape route should be planned 4 seconds ahead at any given time.

**alternator**  A device that is driven by the engine and that produces electric current.

**alternator gauge or light**  An instrument that tells whether the car battery is being charged or discharged, by means of a gauge or a light.

**ammeter**  An alternator gauge or light.

**angle parking**  Parking so that cars are arranged side by side, at an angle with a curb or other boundary.

**antifreeze**  A chemical preparation used in a motor vehicle's cooling system to reduce the possibility that the coolant will freeze.

**automatic transmission**  A system in which gears are changed automatically.

**axle**  The shaft upon which the wheels revolve.

**banked**  Sloping up toward the outside. A well-designed road is banked at curves.

**battery**  A group of electric cells connected as a unit to furnish current by means of chemical reaction.

**blind spot**  An area outside a vehicle that is not visible to the driver, even in the mirrors.

**blind turn**  A turn along which the driver's vision is blocked. Only the section of the road immediately ahead is in sight.

**blood-alcohol concentration (BAC)**  The amount of alcohol in the blood. (Usually a BAC report is made on a driver charged with drunk driving.)

**blowout**  The sudden bursting of a tire.

**bodily injury insurance**  A type of liability insurance to provide financial protection in case you cause the death or injury of another person.

**brake fade**  A type of temporary brake failure; the result of brakes overheating after being applied hard for a long period of time.

**brake lights**  Part of the taillight assembly. They light up when the brakes are applied.

**braking skid**  A skidding movement caused when the brakes are applied so hard that one or more wheels lock.

**broken white line**  Roadway marking to divide traffic going in the same direction.

**broken yellow line**  Roadway marking to divide traffic going in opposite directions.

**carbon monoxide**  A colorless, odorless, poisonous gas; a byproduct of burning fuel.

**carburetor**  The part of an engine that combines fuel with air so the mixture will burn properly.

**catalytic converter**  A device that reduces the harmful gases carried off by the exhaust system.

**center of gravity**  The point around which all the weight of an object is distributed evenly.

**centrifugal force**  The force that pushes a moving object out of a curve into a straight path.

**centripetal force**  The force that pushes a moving object, such as a car, from a straight line into a curved path.

**chassis**  The steel frame that holds together a vehicle's major operating parts (the engine, transmission, brakes, wheels, etc.).

**citation**  A ticket or summons to appear in court to answer a charge of breaking a law.

**closing movements**  Actions by other highway users that may lead them into a driver's path and cause a collision.

**clutch**  A pedal or lever that controls the coupling and uncoupling of two sections of a rotating shaft. One section is connected to the engine, the other to the drive shaft.

**collision insurance**  Insurance that covers the cost of repairs to your car due to damage caused by a collision, even if no other car is involved.

**comprehensive insurance**  Insurance that covers damage to your car caused by something other than a collision.

**construction sign**  Warning sign to advise drivers that road crews are working on or near the road. Unlike other warning signs which are yellow, construction signs are orange.

**controlled slipping**  A method of returning the steering wheel to a straight position after making a turn.

**coolant**  A liquid added to a motor vehicle's radiator to reduce heat.

**cooling system**  System to keep engine cool by forcing air over metal cooling vanes that surround the cylinders.

**cornering skid**  A skidding movement on a turn, caused by a driver's turning too fast, poor tires, or a slippery road surface.

**counterskid**  The result of oversteering to correct a skid, when the car begins to slide in the opposite direction of the original skid.

**countersteer**  To turn the steering wheel back in the opposite direction in order to straighten the car.

**crankshaft**  The shaft that is turned as the pistons move up and down in the cylinders of the engine.

**crossbuck**  A sign with a large, white X placed a few feet from railroad tracks as a warning.

**crosswalk**  A pathway marked off for use by pedestrians when they cross a street.

**crowned**  Higher in the center than at the edges. A road that is crowned at curves is good for right turns but dangerous for left turns.

**decelerate**  To slow down.

**deceleration lane**  A lane used for slowing down as you exit from an expressway.

**deductible policy**  An insurance policy providing that the driver pay a given amount of the damage (the first $100, for example) and the insurance company the rest.

**defroster**  A heating unit that clears moisture from the inside of the front and rear windows and ice from the outside surfaces.

**differential**  An arrangement of gears that connects two shafts and permits them to rotate at different speeds. On the drive axle, it allows it each of the drive wheels to turn at a different speed when going around a curve.

**directional control**  The ability of a motor vehicle to hold to a straight line.

**directional, or turn, signal**  A signal that tells other drivers that a motor vehicle plans to turn or move to the right or left. It may be given by blinking a light on the right or left side on the front and rear of the vehicle, or as a hand signal given by putting the left arm out the window.

**distributor**  The engine switch that sends electric current to each spark plug in proper order and at the proper time.

**downshift**  To shift down to a lower gear.

**drive shaft**  A rotating shaft that sends mechanical power to the place in a vehicle where the power is being demanded.

**drive train**  The engine, transmission, and clutch.

**drive wheels**  The wheels to which power is sent by the engine to pull the vehicle.

**driving under the influence (DUI)**  An offense a driver may be charged with if the BAC at the time of arrest falls between 0.05 and 0.10 percent.

**driving while intoxicated (DWI)**  An offense a driver may be charged with if the BAC at the time of arrest is 0.10 percent or higher or if a police officer can support the charge with evidence that the driver had difficulty in performing selected physical tests.

**dual-service brake system**  An arrangement of separate braking systems for front and rear wheels.

**edge line**  Solid white line to mark the outside edge of the outermost lane of traffic.

**electrical system**  In a car, consists of the battery, the alternator or generator, the voltage regulator, and wires to carry electricity throughout the car.

**emergency brake**  The parking brake.

**emission-control device**  A device that prevents or controls pollution by regulating exhaust gases.

**engine**  Part of car that produces the car's power by exploding an air-fuel mixture within its cylinders.

**engine braking**  Releasing the amount of pressure placed on the accelerator.

**escape route**  A path or route that permits a driver to stay out of a collision. This route is made available by identifying an alternate path of travel to steer to in case of an emergency.

**evasive action**  A quick change in speed or direction to avoid a collision.

**exhaust manifold**  A collecting system for unburned gases as they exit from the cylinder.

**exhaust system**  The parts of a motor vehicle that, working together, get rid of waste gases and vapors from the engine and reduce the noise of the explosions within the engine cylinders.

**expressway**  A divided highway with limited access that has more than one lane running in each direction. It is designed for high-speed travel.

**field of vision**  The area to the left and right that you can see when looking straight ahead.

**fixed, or absolute, speed limit**  A speed limit that may not be exceeded for any reason.

**flashing red light**  Light to indicate that a driver must come to a full stop before proceeding.

**flashing yellow light**  Light to indicate a possible hazard. It means slow down, check traffic, and proceed with caution.

**flashing yellow X**  A special lane-control light to indicate that a particular lane is for left-turning vehicles only.

**flexible, or prima facie, speed limit**  A limit that varies according to existing conditions.

**following distance**  The time-and-space gap between vehicles traveling in the same lane of traffic.

**force of impact**  The force with which a moving vehicle hits another object.

**four-speed transmission**  A manual transmission with 4 forward gears and a reverse gear.

**friction**  Resistance between 2 objects when they rub against each other.

**friction point**  While the clutch pedal is being released, the point at which the clutch and other power-train parts begin to work together.

**fuel gauge**  An indicator that shows the amount of fuel in the fuel tank.

**fuel system**  Consists of the fuel tank, the fuel pump, the carburetor, and the intake manifold.

**gas pedal**  The accelerator.

**gear**  A wheel with teeth that interlocks (meshes) with another toothed part and, in doing so, transmits motion or changes speed or direction. The choice of gears determines a car's direction (forward or reverse), power, and speed.

**gear-indicator quadrant**  Tells you which gear the car is in.

**gear-selector lever**  The lever that allows the driver to select a gear.

**gearshift**  An assembly of parts that permits changing from one gear to another by engaging and disengaging the transmission gears.

**gearshift lever**  A lever with which a driver changes gears (shifts).

**generator**  A machine that is driven by the engine and that converts mechanical energy into electrical energy.

**gravity**  The invisible force that pulls objects toward the ground.

**green arrow**  Used on a traffic signal to permit drivers to move only in the direction shown by the arrow. Used also as a special lane-control light if the lane is open to traffic facing the signal.

**green X**  A signal light hung over a lane of traffic to indicate that the lane is open to traffic facing the signal.

**ground search**  A low-level search by a driver for objects in or near the vehicle's path that may be hidden by shrubs or parked cars.

**guide sign**  Route marker or destination sign showing directions or distances. May also show points of interest or scenic areas and campgrounds.

**hand brake**  The parking brake.

**hand-over-hand steering**  A method of steering on turns that ensures the greatest control of the steering wheel through use of separate movements of both hands.

**hazard flasher**  A signaling device that makes all four turn signal lights flash at once. It is used to warn other drivers that a vehicle ahead has stopped or is moving very slowly.

**head restraint**  A fixed or adjustable safety device designed to prevent injury to the head and neck in the event of a sudden stop or rear-end collision.

**high-beam**  Bright: said about headlights.

**highway** A main public roadway, especially one that runs between cities. It includes roads, streets, bridges, and tunnels.

**hydraulic brake system** A system of brakes that works on the principle that fluid cannot be compressed. The fluid in the master brake cylinder is pushed, under pressure, through brake-fluid lines. The resistance to this forcing activates brake cylinders in each wheel.

**hydroplane** To ride on top of a film of water instead of with tires maintaining firm contact with the road.

**idle** To run at a slow speed with little or no pressure on the accelerator: said about an engine. Generally, the transmission is in neutral gear.

**ignition** A system, controlled by a switch, which provides the spark that causes the fuel and air mixture in the engine to burn.

**ignition interlock** A system that automatically keeps a car's engine from starting when certain safety conditions are not met, as when safety belts are not properly buckled.

**immediate path of travel** The route to the point where a driver hopes to be, in normal traffic, 4 seconds from a given time.

**impact-resistant** Especially made to absorb the force resulting from striking an object: said about a bumper.

**implied consent law** A law that requires a driver charged with being under the influence to take a chemical test that measures the amount of alcohol in the blood.

**inertia** The tendency of an object in motion to resist any change in direction and of an object at rest to resist motion.

**inertia reel system** The system that safety belts operate on which allows the belt to unreel freely (for greater comfort) unless there is a sudden deceleration.

**information sign** Sign to guide and direct drivers. All have symbols that can be easily recognized.

**internal-combustion engine** The kind of engine (used in automobiles) in which a fuel mixture is burned within the engine. The energy that produces the car's motion comes from burning within the engine cylinders, not from burning outside, as in a steam engine.

**international traffic sign** A road sign with pictures or symbols instead of words so it can be understood in any country.

**intersection** A place where two or more streets cross.

**interstate** Involving, or connecting, two or more states.

**jackknife** To form the shape of a letter L— a 90-degree angle (the action of a vehicle and its trailer in making a turn improperly).

**jump-starting** Starting a car by attaching its battery (which is dead) to the charged battery of another vehicle by means of cables.

**kinetic energy** Energy of motion. Also called **momentum.**

**lap belt** See **safety belt.**

**lateral** On, toward, or from the side or sides.

**lateral evasive maneuver** A turning of the steering wheel quickly and accurately, swerving sharply to avoid a collision.

**lateral maneuver** A sideways motion, either to the front or to the rear.

**law of inertia** Law stating that an object in motion will continue in a straight line unless some force acts against it.

**legend** Description of symbols on a map.

**liability insurance** Insurance to protect you against claims if you are in a collision and are found to be at fault.

**liable** Responsible according to the law.

**limited access (road)** A road that only certain vehicles may use and one which has limited points of entry and exit.

**low-beam** Of low-degree brightness: said about headlights.

**lubricating system** A system that reduces heat by coating the engine parts with oil.

**maintenance** Upkeep.

**maintenance sign** A warning sign to advise drivers that road crews are working on or near the road. Unlike other warning signs which are yellow, these are orange.

**manually** By hand.

**manual shift** Hand-operated gearshift.

**mass** Weight.

**medical payment insurance** Insurance that pays a fixed amount if you or passengers in your car are injured or killed in a collision.

**momentum** Energy of motion. Also called **kinetic energy.**

**moped**  A bicycle that runs on power from a small engine.

**muffler**  An attachment that reduces engine noise caused by the explosion of the air and fuel mixture.

**multiple-hazard condition**  A situation having several hazards at once.

**multiple-lane highway**  A highway having more than one lane running in each direction.

**neutral**  The position in which the car gears are not engaged and no power can be transmitted.

**no-fault insurance**  System in which your insurance company pays your expenses, up to a certain amount, arising from injuries sustained in an auto accident. Payment is made without regard to who caused the accident.

**octagon**  Eight-sided figure. The stop sign is always a red octagon with white lettering.

**odometer**  A gauge that shows the total distance that a car has been driven.

**off-road recovery**  Returning to the road from a shoulder.

**oil-pressure gauge**  A gauge that shows the pressure at which oil is being pumped to the engine's moving parts.

**optional equipment**  One or more extra features that a car buyer is not required to take.

**overcorrect**  Oversteer.

**oversteering**  Too much movement of the front of a car to the inside of a turn.

**overtaking**  Passing a vehicle on a one-lane road.

**parallel parking**  Parking so that a given car is in line with a group of cars arranged one behind the other, parallel to and close to a road edge.

**park**  The reading on the selector quadrant which shows that the transmission is locked.

**parking brake**  The brake, separate from the hydraulic brakes, that holds the rear wheels. It is used to keep a parked car from moving.

**passive safety belt (passive restraint belt)**  A shoulder strap that connects from the center of the seat to the car door. It is used with a regular lap belt.

**pedestrian**  A person traveling on foot rather than in an automobile or on a motorcycle, bicycle, or other vehicle.

**perpendicular parking**  Parking so that a car forms a 90-degree angle with a curb or boundary.

**piston**  A steel cylinder that is enclosed in a cylinder within the engine. As the piston moves up, it compresses a fuel and air mixture. The piston is forced down by the explosion of this mixture. This up-and-down movement turns the crankshaft.

**play**  The amount of free movement in a lever, foot pedal, or steering wheel that is possible without affecting the device being controlled.

**points**  The electrical contacts in the distributor of a car engine which make and break the connection, permitting a flow of current.

**positive crankcase ventilation (PCV) system**  A system that recycles gases in the crankcase so that they can be burned again in the cylinders.

**power-assisted brakes (power brakes)**  Brakes that make it easier to slow or stop by increasing the pressure beyond that exerted by the foot.

**power skid**  A skidding movement caused when the gas pedal is pressed suddenly, too hard.

**power steering**  A system of steering in which the front wheels are turned by a force supplied by an extra (auxiliary) source of power, together with the regular force provided by the driver.

**property damage liability**  Insurance that provides financial protection in case you damage the property of other persons.

**race**  To run at high speed: said about an engine.

**radiator**  A cooling device in a car which, by a fan, air-cools liquid pumped from the engine.

**rate of acceleration**  The time it takes to accelerate from a stop or from one speed to another.

**recreational vehicle**  A large vehicle, such as a motor home, used mainly for pleasure.

**red brake lights**  Taillights that go on when you press the brake pedal. They alert drivers behind you that you are slowing down or stopping.

**red taillights**  Lights that go on when you turn on your parking lights or headlights.

**red X**  A signal light hung over a lane of traffic to indicate that the lane is closed to traffic facing the signal.

**regulatory sign**  A roadway sign that indicates certain legal controls over a driver's actions.

**restraint**  Any device, such as a safety belt, that checks the movement of a car occupant at the time of a sudden stop or a collision.

**reverse**  The gear used for backward movement.

**revoke**  To take away (a driver's license, for example) permanently.

**right-of-way**  The right of a vehicle or pedestrian to go first, before other traffic moves, when there is a conflict. It is granted by law or custom.

**rotary motion**  Rotating movement.

**safety belt**  A restraining belt designed to protect the driver and riders. Lap belts are fastened across the hips; shoulder belts, across the shoulder and chest.

**scan**  To move the eyes over a wide area (of a road), rather than looking at one fixed point.

**service sign**  A sign to tell drivers where to find food, gas, and rest areas.

**shift**  To change (gears) by means of a mechanism.

**shared left-turn lane**  A lane sometimes shared by drivers moving in either direction to make a left turn.

**shock absorbers**  Devices that act as cushions for a car's frame against the impact of bumps in the road. They also act to control bouncing.

**shoulder**  The off-road area running along the edge on either side of a road.

**shoulder belt**  See **safety belt.**

**side-marker lights**  Lights that mark the sides of a car. They are operated by turning on the headlight switch.

**sideswipe**  To strike (another vehicle) along the side while trying to pass it.

**skidding**  Loss of control over the direction in which your car is moving.

**solid white line**  Roadway marking to separate traffic going in same direction.

**solid yellow line**  Roadway marking to divide traffic going in opposite directions.

**space margin**  The amount of space around a vehicle, separating it from possible sources of danger in traffic.

**spark plug**  A device in a cylinder head of an engine that ignites the mixture of fuel and air by means of an electric spark.

**speed zoning**  Surveying roads to determine the speed that is appropriate for the road under normal conditions. Since one speed limit may not meet the conditions on all sections of a road, the road may have varying speeds posted along the different sections.

**speedometer**  A gauge that shows how fast a vehicle is moving, in miles per hour or in kilometers per hour.

**spinout**  A spinning movement by a car, resulting from lack of traction of the rear wheels.

**square**  A number times itself.

**stale green light**  A green light on a traffic signal that has been on for some time and will turn yellow soon.

**standard equipment**  Those parts of an automobile that the owner must take, and pay for, when buying a car.

**start**  The position to which the ignition switch is turned in getting the engine to begin running.

**starter**  An electric motor that starts the engine.

**steering-column lock**  The locked condition of the steering wheel when the ignition switch is in the *lock* position.

**stop sign**  An 8-sided sign, with white letters on red. It means: "Come to a full stop and do not move until it is safe to do so."

**suspend**  To take away (a driver's license) for a time.

**suspension system**  The assembly of springs, shock absorbers, and related parts that insulate (protect) the chassis of a vehicle against road shocks coming through the wheels.

**tailgate**  To drive behind another vehicle too closely to permit stopping or swerving quickly.

**tailpipe**  The part of the exhaust system that carries exhaust gases out from under a vehicle.

**temperature gauge**  A gauge that shows whether the engine is running at a proper temperature. Sometimes in the form of a warning light.

**The Highway Safety Act**  Law establishing standards which are specific requirements for state highway safety programs.

**The National Traffic and Motor Vehicle Safety Act**  Law requiring that motor vehicles be constructed with certain safety features and providing for correction by automobile manufacturers of any vehicle defects recognized after car models are sold.

**three-point turn**  A turnabout made in the street by turning left, backing to the right, then moving forward.

**time-and-space gap**  The distance separating a vehicle from the vehicle directly ahead of or behind it.

**torque converter**  Device designed to reduce slippage in a transmission, thus improving fuel mileage.

**tracking**  Keeping a vehicle steadily and smoothly on a desired course by making the necessary steering corrections.

**traction**  The friction (between a vehicle's tires and the road surface) that keeps the wheels from slipping or skidding.

**transmission**  The gears and related parts by means of which power is carried from the engine to a driving axle.

**tread**  The outer surface of a tire, with its pattern of grooves and ridges.

**tunnel vision**  A narrow field of vision.

**turnabout**  A turning maneuver in which a driver moves a vehicle so that it faces in the opposite direction.

**turn signal**  A directional signal.

**two-point turn**  A turnabout made by first backing into a driveway or alley. It can also be made by heading into an alley or driveway and then backing into the street.

**underinflated**  Having too little air pressure: said about tires.

**understeering**  Failure of the front of a car to respond satisfactorily to a turn of the steering wheel.

**universal joints**  Joints that connect the drive shaft to the transmission and differential and allow the drive shaft to move up and down or sideways.

**U-turn**  A turnabout carried out by a full, U-shaped, left turn.

**V-8 engine**  An eight-cylinder engine.

**velocity**  Speed.

**violation**  A breaking of a law.

**visibility**  1 The distance and area a driver can see. 2 The ability of a vehicle or pedestrian to be seen.

**visual acuity**  Sharpness of eyesight.

**visual lead time**  The distance ahead to which a driver should be scanning and which the vehicle will reach in a given time.

**voltage regulator**  The device which controls the amount of electricity generated and the rate at which the battery is recharged.

**warning sign**  Yellow sign, either diamond-shaped or round, with black letters or symbols that warns drivers of potential hazards ahead.

**water jacket**  The passageway that surrounds an engine cylinder, through which coolant flows to cool the engine.

**weaving lane**  A lane near the entrance or exit of an expressway to be used by cars preparing either to enter (speeding up) or exit (slowing down).

**yellow arrow**  Used on a traffic signal to indicate that movement in that lane is about to end.

**yellow X**  Used as a special lane-control light to indicate that traffic flowing in that lane is about to end.

**yield**  To let another road user go first or have the right-of-way.

**yield sign**  A red and white triangular sign that tells a driver to be ready to give the right-of-way to another highway user. It means: "Be prepared to stop or slow down."

# Index

Muffler, 223

Narcotics, *see* Drugs
National Driver Register Service, 11–12
National Institute for Automotive Service
    Excellence, 289
National Traffic and Motor Vehicle Safety
    Act (1966), 9
Natural laws, 133–147
Neutral gear, 24, 76, 209
Nicotine, 265
Night driving, 189
Night vision, 251
No-fault insurance, 293–294
Nonmotorized highway vehicles, 154
Nonprescription drugs, 266
No-passing zone, 59–60

Obstructions, *see* Hazards; Visibility
Odometer, 26
Off-road recovery, 205–207
Oil change, 220
Oil-pressure gauge, 26
Overheated engine, 225–227, 276–277
Oversteering, 143, 144

Parallel parking, 108–111
Park gear, 24, 36
Parking
    angle, 119–121
    brake, 26, 231, 271
    brake light, 27
    downgrade, 82–83
    lights, 30, 232
    near intersection, 102–103
    parallel, 108–111
    perpendicular, 122–123
    signs, 48
Passing vehicles, 42, 92–93, 105–106
Pavement markings, 59–61
Pedestrians
    and accidents, 177–181
    blind, 181
    in business districts, 178
    children, 178, 180
    elderly, 178, 180
    and ground search, 179–180
    and strollers and carriages, 181
Perception, 152–158
Perpendicular parking, 122–123
Physical handicaps, and driving, 252
Piston, 219–220
Planning a trip, 299–307
    and emergency equipment in car, 300

long trip, 300–305
maps for, 302–303, 304, 305
with recreational vehicle, 306–307
short trip, 237, 299–300
with trailer, 305–306
Point system, 10–11
Pollution-control devices, 221
Positive crankcase ventilation (PCV) system,
    223
Power brakes, 231
Power skid, 211–212
Power steering, 230
    failure, 273
Power train, 221–222
    *see also* Transmission
Predriving procedures, 33–37
Preparing to drive, 19–37
Prescription drugs, 265–266
Protective system, 20–21

Quadrant, 24–25

Radiator, 221, 226
Railroad crossings, 48, 197
Rain, and driving, 138–139, 188
    effects on traction, 138–139
Rear-view mirror, 29, 35, 155
Recreational vehicles, 306–307
Red light, 55–56
Registration of vehicle, 12
Regulatory signs, 47–49
Reverse gear, 24, 76
Right-hand turns, 56, 94, 117–118
Right-of-way, 43–44
Roadway markings, 153
Rules of the road, 41–42

SADD (Students Against Driving Drunk),
    264
Safety belts, 20–21, 35, 141
Safety restraints, 146
School bus, 44
Seat adjustments, 22
Selecting a car, 286–292
    and car insurance, 292–295
    equipment for, 287–288
    and financing, 291–292
    for fuel efficiency, 287–288
    used, 289–291
Selector lever, 24–25
Service signs, 54
Shifting gears, *see* Transmission
Shock absorbers, 227–228, 229
Shoulder belts, *see* Safety belts

# Photo Credits

(All photographs are listed in clockwise order, starting with the photo on the upper left-hand side.)

2: Charles Steiner/Int'l Stock Photo, Ltd.; 3: Jeorge Hall/Woodfin Camp & Associates; 4: John Yates/Shostal Associates; 6: Dr. Francis C. Kenel/AAA; 7: Ted Horowitz/The Stock Market; 8: Dan Brody/Stock, Boston; 9: Robert J. Capece/McGraw-Hill; 10: Dr. Francis C. Kenel/AAA; 12: P. F. Bentley/Photoreporter; 13: Whitney Lane/The Image Bank; 14: Michael Monheim/Photo Researchers; 19, 21, 22, 26, 27, 28, 29, 30, 32, 34, 37: Robert J. Capece/McGraw-Hill; 39: Peter Vadnai/McGraw-Hill; 41, 45: Robert J. Capece/McGraw-Hill; 44: Kay Chernush/The Image Bank; 46: Courtesy, General Motors; 47: Steve Wilson/DPI; 50: Nancy Grimes/McGraw-Hill; 56: Elliott Erwitt/Magnum Photos; 59: Bill Binzen/The Image Bank; 65: Shostal Associates; 68, 74, 75: Robert J. Capece/McGraw-Hill; 74: Courtesy, Chrysler Corporation; 85: Peter Vadnai/McGraw-Hill; 87: Bill Stanton/Int'l Stock Photo, Ltd.; 88: Nancy Grimes/McGraw-Hill; 89, 92: Robert J. Capece/McGraw-Hill; 95: M. Montfort/Peter Arnold; 97: Gary Gladstone/The Image Bank; 101: Joe Azzara/The Image Bank; 103: Robert J. Capece/McGraw-Hill; 104: David Pollach/The Stock Market; 115: White & Pite/Int'l Stock Photo, Ltd.; 129: Robert J. Capece/McGraw-Hill; 133: Endress/Int'l Stock Photo, Ltd.; 134: Robert J. Witkowski/The Image Bank; 136, 137, 138, 144: Robert J. Capece/McGraw-Hill; 135: Weinbert-Clark/The Image Bank; 139: R. Tesa/Int'l Stock Photo, Ltd.; 140: E. Sparks/The Stock Market; 142: Mike J. Howell/Int'l Stock Photo, Ltd.; 145: Roy Morsch/The Stock Market; 146: Tony Howarth/Woodfin Camp & Associates; 151: Elliott Varner Smith/Int'l Stock Photo, Ltd.; 152: Richard Reynolds/Texas Tourist Development Agency; 153 (top, bottom): Robert J. Capece/McGraw-Hill; 153 (middle): Dr. Francis C. Kenel/AAA; 154, 158: Nancy Grimes/McGraw-Hill; 155: Luis Villota/The Stock Market; 157: Hugh Rogers/Monkmeyer Press; 162: Bill Stanton/Int'l Stock Photo, Ltd.; 163, 167: Robert J. Capece/McGraw-Hill; 169: Tim Davis/Photo Researchers; 170: Loweil Georgia/Photo Researchers; 171: Farrell Grehan/Photo Researchers; 172: David Hamilton/The Image Bank; 173: Nancy Grimes/McGraw-Hill; 173: Mimi Forsyth/Monkmeyer Press; 174: Dean Abramson/F-Stop Pictures; 175: Rene Pauli/Shostal Associates; 176: Billy Barnes; 177: Mark Antman/The Image Works; 178: CEZUS/Click, Chicago; 179: Robert J. Capece/McGraw-Hill; 180: Craig Blouin/F-Stop Pictures; 181: Yoav Levy/Phototake; 182: D. J. Forbert/Shostal Associates; 186: Alvis Upitis/The Image Bank; 188: D. Smiley/Peter Arnold; 189: Alec Duncan/Taurus Photos; 190, 192: Robert J. Capece/McGraw-Hill; 190: Dagmar Fabricius; 193: Nancy Grimes/McGraw-Hill; 194: CEZUS/Click, Chicago; 195: Mike Kagan/Monkmeyer Press; 196: Yoav Levy/Phototake; 197: Dan McCoy/Rainbow; 198: Murray Greenberg/Monkmeyer Press; 202: Peter Vadnai/McGraw-Hill; 203, 204, 206: Robert J. Capece/McGraw-Hill; 205: Nancy Grimes/McGraw-Hill; 209: Sepp Seitz/Woodfin Camp & Associates; 218: Dan McCoy/Rainbow; 220, 225, 226, 227, 228, 232, 233, 237, 239: Robert J. Capece/McGraw-Hill; 241: Frank Whitney/The Image Bank; 243: Eric Kroll/Taurus Photos; 244: Dr. Francis C. Kenel/AAA; 245: Nancy Grimes/McGraw-Hill; 246: Sybil Shelton/Peter Arnold; 246, 249, 250, 252, 254: Robert J. Capece/McGraw-Hill; 248: Shostal Associates; 256: Peter Vadnai/McGraw-Hill; 258: Barbara Kirk/The Stock Market; 262, 264, 268: Robert J. Capece/McGraw-Hill; 265: Brett Froomer/The Image Bank; 270, 272, 275, 276, 278, 279, 280: Robert J. Capece/McGraw-Hill; 273: Barbara Burnes/Photo Researchers; 282: Peter J. Kaplan/The Stock Shop; 286: Gary Gladstone/The Image Bank; 288, 289, 290, 291, 292, 295, 297, 299: Robert J. Capece/McGraw-Hill; 293: Eric Carle/Shostal Associates; 301: Marvin Lyons/The Image Bank; 303: AAA map; 305: Philip Jon Baily/Stock, Boston; 306: Dennis Stock/Magnum Photos; 307: Nancy Grimes/McGraw-Hill; 311: Gary Gladstone/The Image Bank; 312: Robert J. Capece/McGraw-Hill; 313: Chuck Fishman/Woodfin Camp & Associates; 315: Peter J. Kaplan/The Stock Shop. Special thanks to P.S. Motors, Manhasset, NY.